Too Black to Be Here?

Too Black to Be Here? Exploring Racism in Norway through Four Critical Case Studies

BY

PAUL THOMAS

University of South-Eastern Norway, Norway

emerald
PUBLISHING

United Kingdom – North America – Japan – India – Malaysia – China

Emerald Publishing Limited
Emerald Publishing, Floor 5, Northspring, 21-23 Wellington Street, Leeds LS1 4DL

First edition 2025

British Library Cataloguing in Publication Data
A catalogue record for this book is available from the British Library

ISBN: 978-1-83662-165-2 (Print)
ISBN: 978-1-83662-162-1 (Online)
ISBN: 978-1-83662-164-5 (Epub)

INVESTOR IN PEOPLE

Contents

About the Author

Paul Thomas is a Professor of Pedagogy at the University of South-Eastern Norway specializing in Critical Pedagogy and Multicultural Education.

Introduction

> At the university, I read some appalling novels about Africa (including Joyce Cary's much-praised *Mister Johnson*) and decided that no one, no matter how gifted or well-intentioned, could tell the story we had to tell. (Achebe, 2016)

The citation above by Chinua Achebe, the renowned Nigerian novelist, poet, professor, and critic, echoes a profound truth that resonates deeply with the author as a Black-Norwegian academic. Achebe's assertion encapsulates a sentiment that has guided my own journey of reflection and analysis. Literature, media representations, and academic discourse perpetuating stereotypes and misrepresentations of people of color, including those of African descent, compelled me to confront the inadequacy of external narratives in capturing the complexity and richness of our lived experiences. Like Achebe, I came to the realization that outsiders, no matter how gifted or well-meaning, cannot authentically tell or understand the stories of marginalized communities.

This realization served as a catalyst for me to embark on a journey of "re-analysis," particularly in the context of the four cases examined in this book. Each case serves as a microcosm of the broader societal issues surrounding race, privilege, and identity in Norway. The aim was to scrutinize these narratives through a critical lens, informed by research and theory, to uncover the nuances and complexities often overlooked or misrepresented in mainstream discourse. Furthermore, Achebe's assertion underscores the importance of marginalized voices reclaiming their own narratives and asserting their agency in shaping representations of their communities. In a world where dominant narratives often perpetuate stereotypes and distortions, it is imperative for individuals from marginalized backgrounds to assert their own perspectives and truths.

In every utopia, including the societal model often admired in Norway, there exists a suppressed realm of shadows. This book ventures into the depths of these obscured realms, aiming to elucidate the experiences of the racialized amid the

Too Black to Be Here?, 1–5

doi:10.1108/978-1-83662-162-120251001

darkness of utopia. Through diligent inquiry and scholarly discourse, it endeavors to unveil the complexities and injustices that persist beneath the surface of Norway's purported "colorblindness." By incorporating marginalized voices and challenging prevailing narratives, it argues that we can work toward a more inclusive and equitable discourse that recognizes the complexity and diversity of human experiences. It is not merely the "brown" shift in demographics that presents challenges in Norway; rather, it is the unprecedented nature of this transition in a country historically characterized by homogeneity in terms of skin color, religion and other identity markers. Moreover, what complicates matters further is the failure of some "native" White Norwegians to recognize their own biases against non-White individuals. As an educator in Norway, the above presents serious challenges. I find inspiration in the warnings voiced by the Black educator Carter G. Woodson almost a century ago.

> As another has well said, to handicap a student by teaching him that his face is black is a curse and that his struggle to change his condition is hopeless is the worst sort of lynching. It kills one's aspirations and dooms him to vagabondage and crime. It is strange, then, that the friends of truth and the promoters of freedom have not risen up against the present propaganda in the schools and crushed it. This crusade is much more important than the anti-lynching movement, because there would be no lynching if it did not start in the schoolroom. (Woodson, 2023, p. 8)

This book is not merely a recounting of events but a critical exploration and analysis of the intricate web of racism in Norway through the lens of four contemporary and well-publicized cases. These cases serve as focal points for dissecting the systemic issues at play, unraveling the layers of prejudice, discrimination, and marginalization faced by people of color in Norway. Each case study is meticulously examined to understand its roots, manifestations, and repercussions. By delving into the specific details and contexts of these incidents, the book aims to provide an incisive exploration of how racism operates.

Furthermore, the book engages with Carter G. Woodson's powerful metaphor of mental "lynching" to underscore the gravity of the harm inflicted upon people of color when they are taught that their race determines their worth and potential. This metaphor serves as a lens through which to analyze the psychological and emotional toll of racism, highlighting how it undermines self-esteem, aspirations, and a sense of belonging. The convergence of a mixed-race teenager (Benjamin Hermansen), a Somali female poet and social critic (Sumaya Jirde Ali), and non-White-adopted individuals in Norway may initially appear disparate, with little in common except their shared pigmentation. However, their collective experiences serve to expose the insidious influence of White supremacist ideologies and seemingly innocuous "off-the-cuff" racist remarks as elucidated by Bonilla-Silva's concept of "racism without racists." These individuals, despite their diverse backgrounds and perspectives, are united by their encounters with systemic racism and discrimination.

Paradoxically, the racists failed to anticipate that their physical and verbal racialized violence would serve to unite disparate non-White groups that seemingly have nothing in common. What commonality could there possibly be between an adopted girl from South Korea or China and a Muslim woman wearing a hijab? Yet, it is the pervasive gaze of the White racist, such as White Islamophobe Anders Breivik, rooted in a socially constructed fantasy, that inadvertently creates a shared experience among individuals from diverse backgrounds. In Norway, this shared experience manifests in unexpected solidarity, as exemplified by a South Korean person and a Somali person standing together under a Black Lives Matter banner. Despite their contrasting backgrounds and motivations, these individuals find themselves compelled to confront and resist the systemic oppression they encounter.

Through their collective experiences of discrimination and marginalization, they are united in their resolve to challenge and dismantle the structures of racism within Norwegian society. In doing so, they inadvertently catalyze and organize anti-racist action among Norway's diverse non-White communities, forging bonds of solidarity that transcend their individual differences. The book invites readers to reflect on the broader implications of racism and consider their role in challenging and dismantling oppressive structures. The book urges educators, policymakers and advocates to join the fight against racism and work toward a future where all, irrespective of their race, ethnicity, sex, or religion, can thrive.

Frantz Fanon's assertion that the coexistence of White and Black races has birthed a profound psycho-existential complex underscores the urgent need for critical examination and deconstruction. "I believe that the fact of the juxtaposition of the White and Black races has created a massive psychoexistential complex. I hope by analyzing it to destroy it" (Fanon, 1986, p. 149). In alignment with Fanon's poignant sentiment, this book endeavors to serve as a potent instrument for dissecting the intricate workings of racism within the Norwegian context. Rather than merely recounting incidents of discrimination and prejudice, this book seeks to delve deep into the underlying mechanisms and ideologies that perpetuate racial inequalities in Norwegian society. By unraveling the complexities of systemic racism, it aims to illuminate the pervasive nature of racial biases and their detrimental effects on individuals and communities.

Despite being born into slavery, Fredrick Douglass (1818–1895) taught himself to read and write, defying laws that prohibited enslaved individuals from receiving an education. His intellect and eloquence propelled him to the forefront of the antislavery cause. In his memoir, *My Bondage and My Freedom*, Douglass describes a poignant exchange with his owner, Master Hugh, regarding the prohibition of his education. Master Hugh vehemently opposed Douglass's learning to read and write, expressing the belief that education would render an enslaved person unfit for servitude. He infamously declared "If you give a nigger an inch, he will take an ell. A nigger should know nothing but to obey his master – to do as he is told to do. Learning would spoil the best nigger in the world" (Douglass, 2014, pp. 117, 118). Master Hugh feared that education would empower Douglass to challenge his enslavement and ultimately seek freedom.

Much like Douglass's master, those invested in perpetuating systemic racism prefer people to remain unaware of racism's nuances.

This book seeks to modestly contribute to greater awareness of racism's language and structure, encouraging more individuals to familiarize themselves with the intricacies of racial injustice. Just as Master Hugh feared the empowerment that education would bring to Douglass, so too do proponents of the status quo fear an enlightened populace who may challenge prevailing systems of oppression. By illuminating the pervasive manifestations of racism in Norwegian society, I hope to evoke a sense of discontent and dissatisfaction with the prevailing state of affairs. Much like Douglass's quest for literacy threatened the foundations of slavery, the pursuit of racial literacy among Norwegians has the potential to unsettle entrenched power structures and catalyze meaningful social change. Just as Douglass's acquisition of literacy marked the first step toward his emancipation, so too can the acquisition of racial literacy serve as a catalyst for collective liberation and justice in Norway and beyond.

Each chapter offers a compelling narrative that not only sheds light on the persistent manifestations of racism and systemic oppression but also calls for critical reflection and collective action to dismantle structural inequalities. In terms of methodology, this research employed a systematic literature review where pertinent keywords were meticulously entered into the media archive *Retriever*. The process continued until a saturation point was achieved, ensuring a comprehensive scope of relevant articles. Subsequently, a meticulous selection process identified representative articles, which then underwent thorough content analysis. An interdisciplinary framework enriched the analysis of the resulting findings, drawing insights from critical race theory, whiteness studies, post-structural theory (exemplified by the work of Michel Foucault among others), and postcolonial theory. These theoretical lenses provided nuanced perspectives and facilitated a deeper understanding of the complex dynamics surrounding race, privilege and identity in Norwegian society. The author conducted all translations from Norwegian to English, ensuring maximum accuracy and fidelity to the original texts. Where doubt existed, several colleagues were consulted, and decisions based on interrater reliability. This meticulous approach aimed to uphold the integrity of the research and minimize the potential for misinterpretation or distortion of the data.

Chapter 1 introduces us to Benjamin Hermansen, whose tragic murder serves as a stark reminder of the deadly consequences of unchecked racism and White supremacy. Through his story, we are confronted with the urgent need for greater awareness and education surrounding issues of race and ethnicity. Benjamin's narrative compels us to engage in meaningful dialogue and advocacy for genuine inclusivity and social justice. Chapter 2 delves into the aftermath of Anders Breivik's ghastly attacks, highlighting the deeper societal issues rooted in White supremacy that fueled his actions. By examining Breivik's motivations and the societal conditions that enabled his radicalization, we gain insight into the enduring legacy of racism and the imperative to confront and dismantle systems of White supremacy. Chapter 3 brings to light Sumaya Ali Jirde's traumatic experience of racial abuse, underscoring the enduring silence and complicity that often accompany acts of injustice. Sumaya's ordeal serves as a stark reminder of the pervasive racism that continues to plague communities of color, demanding a shift in societal attitudes toward recognizing the humanity and equality of all individuals.

Finally, Chapter 4 explores the tragic case of Johanne Ihle-Hansen, shedding light on the pervasive nature of racism within Norwegian society and the transnational dimensions of structural racism inherent in adoption practices. Through Johanne's story, we confront the systemic failures within adoption oversight and regulation, emphasizing the need for ethical and equitable adoption practices grounded in principles of social justice and human rights. These chapters challenge us to confront uncomfortable truths, confront our own biases, and advocate for meaningful change. This book serves as a call to action, urging readers to engage in nonstop education, dialogue, and advocacy in the ongoing struggle for racial justice and equality. By embracing the responsibility to confront racism in all its forms, we can work toward fostering a more equitable and inclusive society for future generations.

Chapter 1

Black Skin, Targeted Hate: The Benjamin Hermansen Case

> He [Negro] is a social and not a personal or human problem; to think of him is to think of statistics, slums, rapes, injustices, remote violence... his continuing status among us were somehow analogous to disease – cancer perhaps, or tuberculosis – which must be checked, even though it cannot be cured... Our dehumanization of the Negro then is indivisible from our dehumanization of ourselves: the loss of our own identity is the price we pay for our annulment of his. (James Baldwin, *Notes of a Native Son*, 2017, p. 26)

On January 26, 2001, two young men and a young woman from a neo-Nazi milieu, the Boot Boys, intoxicated by White supremacist ideology, goaded each other on to physically assault random immigrants. They drove to Holmlia, a neighborhood in the southern part of Oslo, Norway's capital city, roughly 12 kilometers southeast of the city center. Benjamin Hermansen was a 15-year-old boy of mixed heritage – a White Norwegian mother and a Ghanian father – who passed away when Benjamin was just 4 years old. Benjamin was chatting with a friend when the neo-Nazi youth, easily distinguishable by their stereotypical appearance, pulled up in a car: shaved heads symbolizing rebellion against societal norms and concomitant dedication to perceived militant or authoritarian ideology, combat boots that reinforce an aura of strength and aggression, along with Nazi paraphernalia such as swastikas and other hate symbols, all with the aim of projecting an image of power and dominance and striking fear in the hearts of "non-Aryans," to borrow from their vocabulary. A 16-year-old friend of Benjamin, who also faced the predators but managed to escape, stated that the neo-Nazis were "on a manhunt" and "could have assaulted anyone with a different skin color" (Buggeland, VG, 2001). He goes on to state:

Too Black to Be Here?, 7–51

doi:10.1108/978-1-83662-162-120251002

I screamed "run" to Benjamin and took off running. However, the two almost got hold of him a couple of times and managed to block his way. They pushed the 15-year-old Norwegian-African into a corner near the Spar store, positioning his back against the fence at the food center's warehouse entrance. Stumbling and cornered, Benjamin had no choice but to leap over the fence. But he fell to his stomach and was motionless on the ground. Then one of the neo-Nazis sat on Benjamin and stabbed him several times, first in the side and then in the stomach and chest. Benjamin screamed, according to the 16-year-old. (Buggeland, VG, 2001)

Today, the name Benjamin Hermansen is one of the most recognizable in Norway. His murder enraged many in the country: the royal family, the Prime Minister and his cabinet, members of Parliament, and various figures from the world of sports, culture, and entertainment publicly denounced the perpetrators and called for the nation to unite against the forces of bigotry. The news garnered attention abroad. The BBC, for instance, reported: "Nearly 40,000 people, including politicians and royals, took to the streets to show their disgust for what had happened. Until then, most Norwegians never considered racism to be a serious problem in their largely White nation" (BBC, 2002). The demonstrations were the largest ever since World War II until then (Nrk, 2021). Much ink flowed from day one with regular secretions into the public domain, paying homage to the memory of Benjamin Hermansen. Typing the key words *Benjamin Hermansen* and *Holmlia-drapet* (Homlia murder) in *Retriever*, the leading company in media analysis and communication insight in the Nordics, turned up 2,802 hits. As indicated by the peaks in Fig. 1, interest in the case reached its highest points in 2011 and 2021, aligning with the 10th and 20th anniversaries of the murder.

As previously mentioned, Benjamin Hermansen is one of the most recognized names in Norway today. Every year, on the anniversary of his death, memorial events are held in various cities across Norway. Among others, candlelight vigils are held, speeches are made, and performances are enacted to honor his memory. The Benjamin Prize, established in 2002, is awarded annually to individuals or organizations that have made substantial contributions to advancing diversity, equality, and anti-racism in Norway. The prize serves as a tribute to Benjamin Hermansen's legacy and ideals. Schools utilize Benjamin's legacy as a cornerstone for anti-racist education, aiming to nurture empathy, tolerance, and comprehension of associated values within a country that has witnessed a steep rise in its Black and brown population.

Among the sensational headlines bidding to outdo each other in voicing outrage, the national newspaper Aftenposten (2001) carried the following headline: "They say it is the first time." The author, Inger Anne Olsen (2001), wrote:

The last week must have been a turning point for Norway. We presumably have lost our innocence. Neo-Nazis killed a boy last weekend, likely because he was black. But white Norwegians have killed, threatened, stabbed, set fire to, and beat up black people for many decades.

01.01.2001 - 02.04.2024

Søk: Benjamin Hermansen, Holmlia drapet

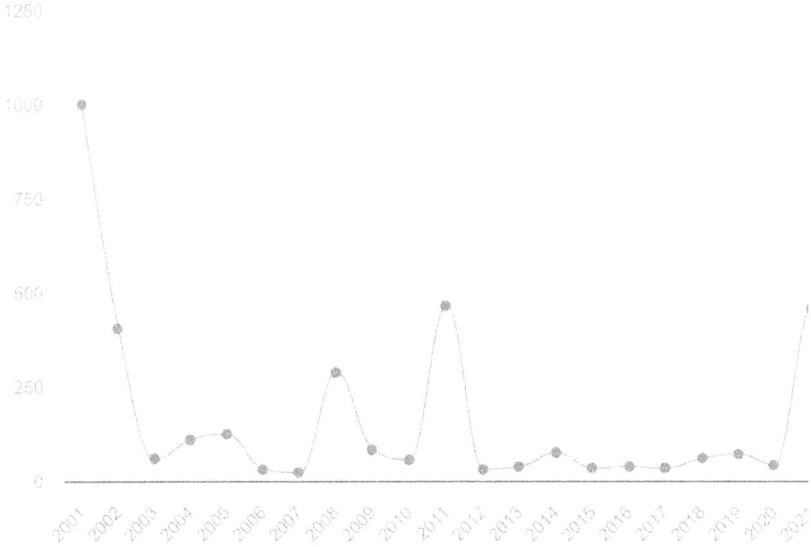

Fig. 1.   Media Coverage of the Benjamin Hermansen Murder Case 2001–2024. *Source:* Created by author based on publicly available data from Retriever.

Among others, Olsen draws up a litany of hate crimes directed against people of color. She reports over 30 incidents from 1959 to 2001, including the murder of Benjamin.

- In 1959, Mehdi Hemmat, a Persian merchant, embarked on the Norwegian vessel "Hamlet" docked in Abadan, in the Persian Gulf. Sadly, within hours, he succumbed to the actions of three inebriated Norwegians who cast him into the sea and drowned. The perpetrators received a mere 11-month prison sentence. "In January 2001, we spoke to a man who met the three released sailors in 1960, shortly after they had arrived back in Norway. He says that the three joked, laughed, and talked about how they had 'tricked the Arab'." Based on the three's self-expression, he was certain that this was a murder with a racist undertone.
- September 9, 1978: "Now you can lie down and die, you damn paki, because here there is no one who can help you." An 18-year-old Pakistani explained that he heard this parting remark after a youth gang picked on him. The

teenager had experienced assault, beatings, and kicks from Norwegian youth for the second time in five months. The police had no doubts about what it was all about: "The aim is to eliminate any potential for such racial animosity in the future," according to investigator Sten Grindhaug.

- April 30, 1988: While the owner was sleeping in the basement, a firebomb hurled through the window, completely destroying the shop "8–8" in Brumunddal. Racist slogans and smashed windows had plagued the shop for a long time. "This is not about organized racism. I would rather call it hooligan behavior" said the police inspector at Hamar police station.
- On April 26, 1999, 17-year-old Arve Beheim Karlsen, adopted from India and raised in Hafslo in Sogn, Norway, died in Sogndalselva. Boys yelling racial slurs pursued him, resulting in his drowning in the river. The prosecution initially charged two 17-year-olds with deliberate murder but dropped the charges due to lack of evidence. The prosecution later reduced the charges of violence and serious threats. Arve's mother demanded prosecution under the racism section, leading to a reconsideration of whether yelling racial slurs constituted a racist act. Arve was born in India and adopted as a child. He had previously experienced racially-motivated violence and bullying.
- On September 12, 1999, someone lobbed a Molotov cocktail at a fast-food outlet in Nordstrand, Oslo. Ten minutes later, someone threw another firebomb at a fast-food restaurant in Holmlia. Immigrants ran both establishments, and racist posters adorned their walls. The three perpetrators belonged to a far-right milieu.
- Stavanger, a city in southwest Norway, saw the stabbing of two ethnic Africans on March 4, 2000. According to the police, the attack was racially motivated.

Olsen (2001) concludes:

> This is far from an exhaustive list of violence and attacks against black people in Norway. It's just a tiny part – the most visible part – of some of the cases that have been in the public eye. Now, in February 2001, the police say there are 150 active neo-Nazis in Norway, right-wing extremists whom the police believe are capable of perpetrating violence. Could they have done all of this? Must they not have had help from someone? Perhaps from our parents, our children, siblings, friends, or neighbors? Perhaps even from you and me? (Olsen, 2001)

1. The Paradox of Black Visibility

Ralph Ellison's celebrated novel *Invisible Man* (1980) poignantly opens with the words, "I am an invisible man. No, I am not a spook like those who haunted Edgar Allen Poe, nor am I one of your Hollywood movie ectoplasms. I am invisible, understand, simply because people refuse to see me" (Ellison, 1980, p. 3). Herein lies the paradox of contemporary Black visibility: it appears that Black people, such as Benjamin Hermansen, are "invisible" in white societies until they become the locus of either a massive crisis or extraordinary achievements. Visibility for Black people often hinges on achieving remarkable feats, such as the spectacular sight of Usain Bolt's 9.58-second record in 2009 in the 100-meter sprint, or tragically, becoming a victim of extremist violence, as Benjamin did, or more recently, enduring the sight of a defenseless George Floyd uttering "I can't breathe, mama," pinned beneath the knee of police officer Derek Chauvin. Typical of Ellison's burlesque style of writing, replete with imagination and surrealistic distortion, the novel is haunted by his deceased grandfather's derisive curse, which he constantly returns to.

> That night I dreamed I was at a circus with him, and he refused to laugh at the clowns no matter what they did. Then later he told me to open the briefcase and read what was inside and I did, finding an official envelope stamped with the state seal; and inside the envelope I found another and another, endlessly, and I thought I would fall of weariness. "Them's years", he said. "Now open that one." And I did and in it I found an engraved document containing a short message in letters of gold. "Read it", grandfather said. "Out loud!" "To Whom It May Concern", I intoned. "Keep This Nigger-Boy Running." I awoke with the old man's laughter ringing in my ears. (Ellison, 1980, p. 33)

The cursory sight of neo-Nazis in Holmlia, paradoxically one of the most multicultural districts of Oslo, was an unmistakable signal for Benjamin and his non-White friends to take flight. Their deep-seated animosity was unmistakable, indicative of their immersion in a malicious doctrine of White supremacy.

> The non-hero is invisible because he has no identity; he does not know who he is. As he runs from situation to situation, forced on by authority, he finds that each new identity leads him back to confront once again the inscription, 'To Whom It May Concern, Keep This Nigger-Boy Running'. (Danielson, 1969)

How did Benjamin Hermansen, who was born and bred in Norway, a nation that has consistently topped the United Nations' Human Development Index since its inception in 1990, instinctively know when to run for his life? There is a language and semiotics that only Black and brown people, however young or old, are adept at deciphering. In this sense, immigrants are trilingual: they often learn the language of their parents, the language of their adopted country, and a unique dialect that Benjamin Hermansen fluently spoke: the intricate art of deciphering racism. The functions of this language – its syntax, semantics, pragmatics, morphology, phonology, and phonetics – elude those who are White. This language is not a "mother tongue" because people of color cannily imbibe it, much like the process of osmosis, way before Black mothers and fathers "have the talk" with their Black sons in particular.

This discourse, passed down through generations, is a visceral understanding of the social dynamics at play, an acute cognizance of the systemic biases ingrained in society, and an adroitness at decoding the subtle cues and overt manifestations of racial discrimination. For immigrants and people of color, fluency in this language is not simply a skill but a necessity for survival in a world where racial bias and discrimination persist. It is a tool for navigating societal structures, understanding power dynamics, and constructing resilience in the face of adversity. This language is the unwritten code of survival, resilience, and resistance, determining the lived experiences and collective consciousness of marginalized communities worldwide. Ta-Nehisi Coates (2015) referred to this language or education as the "philosophy of the disembodied." He sought to answer the question of how it feels to inhabit a Black body, presented in the form of a letter to his adolescent son in the book *Between the World and Me* (2015):

> And you know now, if you did not before, that the police departments of your country have been endowed with the authority to destroy your body. It does not matter if the destruction is the result of an unfortunate overreaction... Resent the people trying to entrap your body and it can be destroyed. Turn into a dark stairwell and your body can be destroyed. The destroyers will rarely be held accountable. Mostly they will receive pensions. (Coates, 2015, p. 9)

In the aftermath of Benjamin's murder, several media reports noted that he and some friends had an altercation with neo-Nazis on a trip to Denmark in connection with the Dana Cup, an international youth football tournament held in Hjørring, Denmark. The Dana Cup is Denmark's largest sports event and one of the top-ranked youth tournaments in the world. Under the headline "Fought against racism – became a victim himself," the national daily *Aftenposten* reported that neo-Nazis harassed Hermansen and the other players from Holmlia Sports Club during the Danish football tournament Dana Cup that summer. The episode inside the tournament's official disco led to "Hermansen appearing on TV to express his disgust against racism" (Aftenposten, 2001). Later, the paper states as follows:

> The boys reacted as they should have and left the disco immediately. After the episode, Benjamin appeared on *Dagsrevyen* [Norwegian TV news program] to share what had happened. Benjamin was the only one of the boys from the team who dared to come forward and talk about this on TV, says Ove Bevolden, chairman of Holmlia sports club and Hermansen's team manager for the last three years. The police do not rule out that there may be a connection between Hermansen's commitment to antiracism and his murder but have not yet been able to confirm this theory. (Aftenposten, 2001)

It is significant that Benjamin encountered neo-Nazis in Denmark, only to return home and fatally encounter Norwegian neo-Nazis who lived a mere 15 minutes away in Bogerud, Oslo. What must it have felt like for Benjamin to learn that his blackness evoked the same odious response in other Nordic countries, which appeared to also harbor neo-Nazis? Talking heads in the media can only conjecture at the sheer terror, pain, and sense of constant danger that is seemingly the burden of Black people. In the *Book of Genesis*, Cain killed his brother Abel in the first murder. Significantly, Cain did not offer a blood sacrifice to God while Abel did. Cain, blinded by murderous hatred after the deity rejected his sacrifice, committed fratricide. His punishment was as follows: "When thou tillest the ground, it shall not henceforth yield unto thee her strength; a fugitive and a vagabond shalt thou be on earth." And Cain said unto the Lord, "My punishment is greater than I can bear" (Genesis 4:12, 13; King James Version).

Several Christians seriously flirted with the possibility that Black skin was Cain's mark. Josiah Priest, in his book with the lengthy title *Slavery, as it Relates to the Negro, or African Race: Examined in the Light of Circumstances, History, and the Holy Scriptures; with an Account of the Origin of the Black Man's Color, Causes of His State of Servitude, and Traces of His Character as Well in Ancient as in Modern Times: with Strictures on Abolitionism* (1845), posed the following question: "Should we allow that Cain's mark, set upon him by the Divine power, was that of a black skin? This would not prove that it was derived from Adam's veins, but rather from a curse" (Priest, 1845, p. 134). Priest's writings, imbued with pseudoscientific rationale, were, among others, instrumental in laying the ideological groundwork for the *Trail of Tears* and the defense of slavery, contributing significantly to the underlying tensions that ignited the conflicts of the American Civil War. As Shakespeare noted in *The Merchant of Venice*, the devil can indeed cite Scripture for his purpose. In the US context, one could argue that dubious Christian hermeneutics found a convenient nexus between the mark of Cain and black skin color in order to provide a rationale for the transatlantic slave trade and the one drop of blood rule. The "one-drop rule" was a social and legal theory of racial sorting that was historically prominent in the United States. It stated that any individual with even one ancestor of African descent (however distant) is considered Black. This rule materialized in the 20th century and was a way of imposing a rigid binary classification of race, reinforcing the segregation and discrimination practices of the Jim Crow years. Unlike prior procedures that conceded multiracial lineage, the one-drop rule aimed to create a clear, intractable line between White and Black Americans, significantly affecting the social and legal status of individuals. And yet, despite Priest's drivel, the "mark or curse of Cain" ironically provides a heuristic framework elucidating what Benjamin and countless others knew all too well.

Balibar and Wallerstein (1991) explain white racists' elusive quest for the autochthons, the essence of "true nationals," which renders Black people nationless, rootless, and vagabonds much like the biblical Cain.

> T[he] racial-cultural identity of 'true nationals' remains invisible, but
> it can be inferred (and is ensured) a contrario by the alleged,

> quasi-hallucinatory visibility of the 'false nationals': the Jews, 'wogs',
> immigrants, 'Pakis', natives, Blacks... In other words, it constantly
> remains in doubt and in danger... racism thus inevitably becomes
> involved in the obsessional quest for a 'core' of authenticity that
> cannot be found. (Balibar & Wallerstein, 1991, p. 60)

One must keep in mind that Benjamin Hermansen was of mixed heritage: a White Norwegian mother and a Black Ghanaian father. Where should he be placed? In her compelling work *Mixed/Other*, Natalie Morris, born to a White English mother and a Black Jamaican British father, vividly articulates the vibrant mosaic of multifaceted identities clamoring for recognition.

> There is no singular story of mixedness, no one tidily explained
> experience that can convey the multiplicities of how we feel, how
> we see ourselves. The stories of my life as a black mixed woman in
> Britain – from my first carnival, to my first box braids, from being
> called "mongrel" by a black man, to being called "nigger" by a
> white man – are just a drop in the vast complexities of mixedness,
> the unique, varied, incomparable experiences that make us who we
> are. (Morris, 2021, p. xviii)

Neo-Nazis and other fascists champion a rigid, Manichean worldview that rejects such nuances of identity. To their minds, any notion of mixed identities, like the experiences Natalie Morris describes and those of Benjamin Hermansen, directly challenges their inflexible devotion to the illusion of pure, homogeneous Teutonic bloodlines, the kind once venerated by figures like Heinrich Himmler and Rudolf Hess. In fact, Norwegian media reported that the neo-Nazis were obsessed with enacting a march in honor of Rudolf Hess, Hitler's deputy leader of the party at the time. The rich tapestry of mixedness, with its myriad tones and textures, undermines the stark monochrome of fascist ideology. In the parlance of ancient Nordic myths – of Valhalla, Runes, and Ragnarök – there exists no tolerance for what they consider the adulteration of Aryan purity by those they debase as "Untermensch." This ideological purity, a cornerstone of fascist belief, categorically denies the intrinsic human complexity and the fluidity of identities that define our shared humanity. Morris's reflections underscore a basic truth: the reality of our identities is extensive and varied, a direct repudiation of the fascist's parochial and exclusionary vision of the world. Benjamin and other individuals of mixed racial heritage had no control over the bodies they inherited. With all due respect to Natalie Morris, the ideology of neo-Nazism and their acolytes permits the perception of only two colors: Nordic White or its absence, which is why most individuals of mixed racial heritage are aware that this problem – the problem of the colorline that W. E. B. Dubois famously identified as the problem of the 20th century – by default places mixed individuals squarely on the non-White side of the colorline. In Ralph Ellison's *Invisible Man*, the unnamed narrator, the "non-hero," appears to have stumbled upon an epiphanic sense of self-discovery as an invisible man retreating underground. "We first see him in this philosophical-spiritual state of invisibility." He finds himself in a cellar, sealed off from the rest of the building since the 19th century. His faith in reality shaken, he surrounds himself with 1,369 light bulbs to illuminate his reality and reassure himself of his existence (Danielson, 1969, p. 54). Benjamin Hermansen sought the comfort of "invisibility" among his own in Holmlia, many of whom were more dark-complexioned than he was. Tragically, fate would have it that the "invisibility" in his "hole in the basement," to borrow from Ellison, was no haven from the merchants of hatred.

Having clearly understood, as all people of color inevitably do in White societies, that his skin color was a liability in Denmark too, how could he become "invisible"? Like the captain of a ship sailing the high seas and set upon by pirates, Benjamin tried to escape in his "own" ship, his own familiar backyard, but there was no place else to go. One third of the demographic of Holmlia was non-White at the time, but that was of no consolation to the 15-year-old. Pirates understand that "invisibility" has its limitations due to the finite nature of the ship. Benjamin Hermansen's tragedy, among others, mocks those who criticize Black and brown minorities who voluntarily segregate themselves in ethnic enclaves in Oslo's east and south. For many, these enclaves are their "hole in the basement," the invisibility to which they must cling or risk epidermal betrayal. The skin can play the role of Judas – not a treacherous, premeditated deal with the Pharisees of racial bigotry, but one that ends in crucifixion nonetheless. "Yeah, my own familiar friend, in whom I trusted, who did eat of my bread, hath lifted up his heel against me" (Psalm 41:9, KJV).

The dilemma of the black body and its visibility is palpable captured succinctly in Frantz Fanon's incisive words:

> Look at the nigger!... Mama, a negro!... Hell, he's getting mad...
> Take no notice, sir, he does not know that you are as civilized as
> we are..." My body was given back to me sprawled out, distorted,
> recolored, clad in mourning in that white winter day. The negro is
> an animal, the Negro is bad, the Negro is mean, the Negro is ugly;
> look, a nigger, it's cold, the nigger is shivering, the nigger is
> shivering because he is cold, the little boy is trembling because
> he is afraid of the nigger... Mama, the nigger's going to eat me up.
> (Fanon, 1986, p. 114)

Black people are yet to "repossess" their bodies. Ever since the day the first African person was forcibly seized and commodified, relegated to a disposable cog in the machinery of predatory capitalism, the remnants of a bygone era where the term "proletariat" (even sub-proletariat is found wanting) mocked their plight, fear lingers. Some people may say that Black people have yet to take full possession of their bodies. Even after Lincoln, Wilberforce, and Jim Crow, Black people everywhere know that they dare not become comfortable in their black skins in the same way that White people do. The sugar plantocracy, the grotesque spectacle of lynching immortalized in Billie Holiday's mournful melodies, police brutality, and neo-Nazi murders collectively perpetuate a state of unease. The memory of figures like Benjamin Hermansen serves as a beacon of resistance, compelling us to remain vigilant against the systemic forces that deny Black people sovereignty.

2. White Privilege, Working-Class Unity: A Fatal Dilemma

In January 2018, Norway's flagship news broadcaster NrK (2018) ran a three-part podcast series entitled "Drapet på Benjamin Hermansen" [The Murder of Benjamin Hermansen]. In the first podcast, once the chants of "Sieg heil!" subside, a Norwegian neo-Nazi declares "We are Norwegian working-class youth. We want Norwegian power. We should have the freedom to express our support for Norway and Europe without facing accusations of racism (NrK, 2018). Joe Erling Jahr, who was sentenced for 18 years for the murder of Benjamin Hermansen in 2002, grew up in Bøler, Oslo, a suburb of Oslo built for the working class after World War II. In the podcast, Joe describes a turbulent childhood plagued by adversity. He shares how his mother's unemployment rendered her reliant on social welfare, amplifying the economic strain within their household. At the tender age of 14, a gang of Somali youths subjected Joe to bullying and physical assault within the underground railway system, a harrowing ordeal.

Joe recalls a sense of desertion in the aftermath of the incident, with no intervention even from law enforcement authorities. Gripped by anxiety regarding potential reprisals for disclosing the incident, Joe found solace and purported protection within the ranks of neo-Nazi groups, allegedly the only individuals offering refuge amidst his distressing circumstances. The year 2018 saw Joe's release, and he has since disassociated himself from his former Nazi affiliation. He has apologized to Benjamin's mother, Marit Hermansen, conceding that his apology cannot undo the untold suffering his action has caused. Furthermore, he expresses his newfound belief in tolerance and the importance of coexisting with individuals from diverse backgrounds. He attributes this shift in perspective to interactions with prison wardens during his incarceration, as well as dialogues with, among others, Albanian fellow-inmates, whose poignant narratives of Balkan war atrocities catalyzed his journey toward contrition and eventual reformation.

In the next part of my analysis, I'll look at the bigger, systemic aspect of the socioeconomic undercurrents. This will help me show how structural differences help people like Joe Erling Jahr come into the world and spread hateful ideas. I contend that, notwithstanding the purported egalitarian ethos in societies like Norway, these inequities harvest profound repercussions when marginalized White people fail to acknowledge their shared interests with minority ethnic groups, a significant portion of whom also belong to the working class. My argument aims to highlight how racial prejudices prevent White working-class individuals from recognizing common-class interests. The term misrecognition is commonly used in Marxist critical social theory to describe, among other things, the working class's failure to recognize their own class interests. *The Oxford Reference Online* (2024) defines misrecognition as follows:

> A process of self-identification in which a subject assumes an identity they mistake for their own. The concept derives from Jacques Lacan's account of the mirror stage of childhood development in which the young child (under 18 months) sees itself in the mirror and mistakes that image for itself. While the image in the mirror is obviously an image of them, it isn't actually them, but the child fails to make this distinction. Thus, the child's "I" is the product of its imaginary self and the result of an illusion.

Marxism has been critiqued for paying insufficient attention to the salience of racism in solely focusing on the machinations of economic exploitation and class struggle as the central dynamics of capitalist societies (Robinson, 1983). Noel Ignatiev (1940–2019) was a White American historian, author, and activist known for his work on race, racism, and whiteness studies. He was co-founder of the journal *Race Traitor*, which aimed to explore and contest the concept of whiteness as a social and political construct. In 1961, Ignatiev, working at a factory in Philadelphia, USA, expressed his desire to align with the revolutionary class of his era (Ignatiev, 2022, p. 16). Ignatiev noticed a disturbing pattern that affected him on a deeper level.

> Except for a couple of men who swept the floor, the workforce was all white. Did I take a job that might have gone to a black man (or woman)? I sure did, and so did every other worker in the place. One of my goals became to destroy that pattern, which a black comrade told me was typical of manufacturing plants in the city. (Ignatiev, 2022, p. 17)

It is interesting to contrast Ignatiev's (2022) candid early reflections with Joe Erling Jahr and his disaffected fellow-Nazis in the period before the murder. With all due respect to the memory of Benjamin and the bereaved, Joe and Benjamin Hermansen shared more similarities than differences: both were raised by single mothers, with Benjamin's mother being one of them (primary school teacher though); they both lived in what are called "drabantbyer" in Norwegian, which can be roughly be translated "satellite towns or suburbs."

According to one source:

> In urban planning, 'drabantby' means a bi-center with adjacent residential areas that are located in or outside the periphery of a larger city. A 'drabantby' must have good connection with the mother city's center and internal communication networks but should also offer local employment opportunities and have grocery stores, local businesses, schools, other community institutions, and more. (Lie, 2020)

Significantly, Norwegian politicians built these "new urban communities" because not only were the old villas and detached houses economically and spatially unfeasible but they were also undesirable as they were detrimental to social cohesion (Norgeshistorie, 2024). New urban communities began in places like Lambertseter (1951) and expanded to Manglerud, Oppsal/Skøyen, and Bøler in Østensjøbyen and Veitvet, Ammerud, Romsås and Stovner in Groruddalen during the 1950s and 1960s.

> Planners expected that housing shortages would lead applicants to come from all social strata. However, it was mostly young families and couples who were in the process of starting families who arrived. Socially, this new eastern side became an extension of the old one, although there was a larger presence of the lower middle class. (Norgeshistorie, 2024)

Rather than social cohesion, the high rises and subsequent stigmatization of "drabantbyer" sowed the seeds of racial tensions. These suburbs quickly faced negative perceptions as the construction of high-rises, the influx of immigrants, and the presence of the working class became equated. Some of the White residents began to scapegoat the "fremmedkulturelle" (those with alien cultures) and despised them. In the chapter with the title "White Blindspot," Ignatiev (2022) posits what he considers the greatest barrier to class consciousness encapsulated in "the original sweetheart agreement" – a 300-year-old capitalist deal between the US ruling class and White American workers:

> You white workers help us conquer the world and enslave the non-white majority of the earth's laboring force, and we will repay you with a monopoly of the skilled jobs, we will cushion you with health and education facilities superior to those of the non-white population, grant you the freedom to spend your money and leisure time as you wish without social restrictions, enable you on occasion to promote one of your number out of the ranks of the laboring class, and in general confer on you the material and spiritual privileges befitting your white skin. (Ignatiev, 2022, p. 47)

It is difficult to repudiate the notion that families comparable to that of Joe Erling Jahr may have harbored inclinations reminiscent of what can be termed a "sweetheart agreement" (Ignatiev, 2022, p. 247) despite their membership in the same socioeconomic milieu as Benjamin residing in nearby Holmlia. This sentiment becomes apparent in the earlier grievances articulated by the neo-Nazi speaker, who declared "We are Norwegian working-class youth. We want Norwegian power." Joe's family was on the lower end of the socioeconomic ladder, on par with many minority-background families who were now "swarming" these "drabantbyer." Obviously, this must have been a source of pain for Joe, who struggled in school and whose mother was on social benefits, as the narrator in the NrK (2018) podcast reveals. Writing about the halcyon days of Scandinavian social democracy, historian Stein Ringen (2023) writes in regard to Norway's Einar Gerhardsen ("Father of the Nation") and Gro Harlem Brundtland (Norway's first female prime minister) that the social democrats were "dominant in mid-twentieth century politics, but never hegemonic" and "sat on a foundation of class cohesion" (Ringen, 2023, p. 404). It is worth quoting Ringen at length to understand the ethos that inspired the ideal behind "drabantbyer":

> No feature has been more characteristic of the Scandinavian labor movements than their success in creating organizations governed by means of (in Lenin's language) democratic centralism.... They organized culturally beyond party and union activity to create "families" that looked after their flock from cradle to grave, establishing organizations in education, sports, song, theater, travel. They organized women, pensioners, housing tenants, Christian socialists. They celebrated feasts together, the 1st of May importantly but also others. They organized children and youth through the year and in summer and holiday camps. They embraced the cooperative movement, in everything from daily consumption via insurance and housing associations to funeral management. They had their own newspapers, magazines and publishing houses. Authors, artists, architects and academics flocked to the cause. (Ringen, 2023, pp. 403, 404)

The nation-building project of Scandinavian social democrats paradoxically was declining at a time in the 1970s that coincided with an influx of immigrants from the global south whose political interests aligned with the party program of the social democrats. Sadly, it appears that the "quasi-religious" nature of social democracy sketched by Ringen (2023) was not magnanimous enough to encompass dark-complexioned individuals who pledged allegiance to another Middle Eastern deity other than the one familiar to Norwegians. Women from Pakistan, wearing the traditional salwar kameez and dupatta, many of whom were stay-at-home moms, were not the kind of proletariat the labor unions were enthusiastic about. This new demographic celebrated feasts and holy months, such as Ramadan, buried its dead in separate cemeteries, and was skeptical of summer camps where youth imbibed alcohol, ate pork, and freely mingled with the opposite sex. Rather than broaden, adapt, and work harder to include this new demographic, the social democrats began to gradually compete with the anti-immigrant Progress Party whose leader, Carl I. Hagen, adeptly exploited the simmering tensions. Through its vote fishing in murky waters, with its general lack of respect towards stigmatized and disadvantaged groups, and through its play on Norwegians' anxiety and skepticism towards immigrants, the Progress Party helps to form and consolidate attitudes that may ultimately lead us to the murder of Holmlia. Under certain circumstances, even much, much longer (TvedtenBergen, 2001).

Scandinavian social democracy, then, was successful in so far as it relied on a relatively homogenous culture that was not "hamstrung" by diversity and multiculturalism. In fact, it was precisely the idyllic, grand ensemble of Scandinavian social harmony described by Ringen (2023) that the terrorist Anders Breivik sought to shatter when he killed 77 people in 2011. The island of Utøya, about 38 kilometers northwest of Oslo city center, was hosting a summer camp for the AUF, the youth division of the Norwegian Labor Party. Breivik claimed that his attacks were politically motivated, aimed at protesting against the "Islamization of Europe" and punishing the Labor Party for its policies on immigration and multiculturalism. To imply, as Breivik and certain followers contend, that the Labor Party deliberately orchestrated an influx of Muslims and other immigrants into Norway is a gross misrepresentation steeped in unfounded conspiracy theories. As I have argued, the reality is that the earlier symphony of class solidarity that characterized Scandinavian social democrats was hardly successful in incorporating the Black and brown working classes as effectively as they did the White working classes. Age-old divisions along racial, ethnic, and cultural lines, among others, impaired the narrative social democrats sought to weave about their tapestry of togetherness. Contrary to what some Norwegians think about the differences in race relations in the United States, there are several parallels, and one of them resonates with the sentiment below:

> The greatest ideological barrier to the achievement of proletarian class consciousness, solidarity, and political action is now, and has been historically, white chauvinism. White chauvinism is the ideological bulwark of the practice of white supremacy, the general oppression of blacks by whites. (Ignatiev, 2022, p. 47)

In his book *How the Irish Became White* (1995), Noel Ignatiev explores the historical process that assimilated Irish immigrants into whiteness in the United States. The Irish, who were formerly disparaged as Celts and Catholics, were "granted whiteness" if they acquiesced to the status quo of White supremacy and participated in the subjugation of African Americans and other non-White groups. In a reversal of fortunes, the Irish committed a form of "class suicide" by distancing themselves from their historically oppressed status at the hands of the Anglo-Saxons and assuming whiteness. Ignatiev's thesis challenges the notion of whiteness as an innate racial identity and instead frames it as a socially constructed category that bestows privilege and power, highlighting the machinations of race and racialization in American society. It is in the interstices of the above, I argue, that one can understand the phenomenon of extreme right-wing ideology, which, even as I write, is making a comeback in Norway. For instance, one newspaper carried the following headline recently: "PST warns of far-right minors in Norway: We are now experiencing that there are many. That is why we are concerned" (Kibar, 2024). PST (Politiets Sikkerhetstjeneste/Norwegian Police Security) is the agency in charge of maintaining Norway's homeland security.

We must not exaggerate the number of disaffected White youth who join extremist right-wing groups. Their numbers are minuscule relative to the general population. That is, nevertheless, little comfort to individuals such as Marit Hermansen who lost her son to racist violence. Before the murder of Benjamin Hermansen, Norway's history of racist violence was limited to the events of the World War II, when, in 1942, Norwegian police officers and taxi drivers, among others, apprehended 532 Jewish Norwegians and sent them to Oslo's port, Aker Brygge, where they were taken on board the *SS Donau* and sent to their deaths in Auschwitz. The Prime Minister Jens Stoltenberg (current NATO head) issued an apology only in 2012 (Thomas & Alhassan, 2022, p. 349). It is instructive, however, that the disgruntled working class who supported the Weimar Republic before its demise shifted support to the Nazi party of Hitler, given their dire circumstances. Contrary to the widely held view that the Nazi party was built on middle-class support, professor of modern German history Detlef Mühlberger argues that:

> In some parts of Germany, as far as we have detailed information, workers accounted for 40 percent or more of the Nazi membership by 1933. All the available evidence suggests that by January 1933 some 30–35 percent of the Nazi membership came from the working class… It should not really come as a surprise that a section of the German working class proved vulnerable to the Nazi appeal. (Mühlberger, 1980, p. 504)

We return, then, to Ignatiev's (2022) contention about White supremacy and privilege bedeviling class consciousness. It is important to keep in mind that the class divisions of bourgeois west Oslo and proletarian east Oslo predated the waves of immigration from the global south, beginning roughly in the 1960s. The newspaper *Dagsavisen*, catering to social democrats and the working class, stated in 2014 that Oslo has been a class-divided society since the 19th century. The river Akerselva has divided the city in two, with the working class populating the east and the more affluent in the west. According to Professor Thomas Hylland Eriksen, "The east side was east long before immigrants arrived" (Vetsreng, 2014). Nowadays, the class divide is particularly visible in the suburban areas of Groruddalen. However, the class division is no longer immigrants vs ethnic Norwegians. Today, it's not just White Norwegians moving out of Groruddalen. Second-generation immigrants are also relocating.

How does the above relate to the death of Benjamin Hermansen? As mentioned previously, Joe and Benjamin had more in common than divided them. W.E.B. Du Bois mourned the ignorance of closeness.

> All this goes to prove that human beings are, and must be, woefully ignorant of each other. It always startles us to find people thinking like ourselves. We do not really associate with each other, we associate with our ideas of each other, and few people have either the ability or courage to question their own ideas. (Du Bois, 2021, p. 86)

Social democrats failed to bridge the gap with neo-Nazis, who, entrenched in White supremacist ideology, rejected the notion of class solidarity with individuals of different racial backgrounds, such as Pakistanis, Somalis, Iraqis, and other brown and Black people. Ignatiev asserted that the primary barrier in the way to achieving class solidarity against predatory capitalism is White supremacy. Agonizing over their sense of loss and alienation, to borrow from Marx, the White working class, rather than close ranks with members of their own class, allowed race to trump class. In the excerpt below, Ignatiev forcefully rebuts any suggestion that White supremacy may be beneficial to White workers.

> White supremacy is the real secret of the rule of the bourgeoisie and the hidden cause behind the failure of the labor movement in this country. White-skin privileges serves only the bourgeoisie, and precisely for that reason they will not let us escape them, but instead pursue us with them through every hour of our life, no matter where we go. They are poison bait. To suggest that the acceptance of white-skin privilege is in the interests of white workers is equivalent to suggesting that swallowing the worm with the hook in it is in the interests of the fish. To argue that repudiating these privileges is a "sacrifice" is to argue that the fish is making a sacrifice when it leaps from the water, flips its tail, shakes it head furiously in every direction, and throws the barbed offering. (Ignatiev, 2022, p. 86)

The tragic murder of Benjamin Hermansen serves as a solemn reminder of the consequences of a discordant mentality within the marginalized working class. Rather than uniting against the predatory capitalist system, which remains largely untouched, the marginalized working class, ensnared in urban "trench warfare," akin to the phenomenon known as "Black on Black Crime" in inner US cities, turn their guns on each other. In their heyday in the aftermath of World War II, the Scandinavian labor movements blazed a glorious trail of solidarity and unity, but some argue that their success was largely due to a small, homogenous population. Through the creation of organizations governed by democratic centralism, they fostered a sense of community that extended beyond political and union affiliations. Today, sadly, the phenomenon of "white flight" from the "drabantbyer" continues unabated. The author has taught in high schools in east Oslo, where several classrooms had one or two White Norwegian students left. Despite its professed commitment to egalitarian principles, the realities on the ground in Norway tell a contrasting story. Du Bois (2021) could just as well have been describing Norway when he writes:

> So, too, it is those people who live in closest contact with black folk who have most unhesitatingly asserted the utter impossibility of living beside Negroes who are not industrial or political slaves or social pariahs. All this proves that none are so blind as those nearest the thing seen while on the other hand, the history of the

world is the history of the discovery of the common humanity of
human beings among steadily increasing circles of men. (Du Bois,
2021, p. 86)

Somehow, Norwegians will have to return to and reclaim the sense of hope and
vision – one that took care of its members from the cradle to the grave – that
informed and guided people such as Einar Gerhardsen, coupled with the understanding that Black and brown Norwegians must also be included in the new
Norwegian "we." Norway is currently awash with buzzwords such as "diversity"
and "inclusion." I contend that these slogans lack substance because they ignore
whiteness and its subtle permutations, hiding them behind platitudes such as
colorblindness. Occasionally, however, the veil of colorblindness unravels, much
like the deceptive facade of the wolf in the fable of Little Red Riding Hood,
revealing the ugliness of White supremacy. Sadly, the murderous, racially-rooted
hubris lurks in the shadows, waiting for an opportunity to strike. Only through
recognizing and challenging the inherent injustices perpetuated by White
supremacy can true class solidarity be achieved, enabling marginalized communities to unite in their struggle against predatory capitalism and systemic
exploitation.

The discussion thus far demonstrates the limitations of efforts toward social
justice buoyed by single-axis thinking, such as class alone. Kimberlé Williams
Crenshaw (1995) introduced the concept of intersectionality in the late 1980s to
explore the dynamics of difference and sameness with regard to social categori-
zations, such as race, gender, class, sexuality, ability, and other axes of identity, as
they relate to systems of oppression and discrimination.

> The problem with identity politics is not that it fails to transcend
> difference, as some critics charge, but rather the opposite – that it
> frequently conflates or ignores intragroup differences. This elision
> of difference in identity politics is problematic in the context of
> violence against women, fundamentally because other dimensions
> of their identities, such as race and class, often shape the violence
> many women experience. (Crenshaw, 1995, p. 357)

For the critical thinker, the paramount question is: what will it take for youth
who, like Joe Erling Jahr and Ole Nicolai Kvisler (his accomplice who was
sentenced to 15 years for the murder of Benjamin), misrecognized the commonality they shared with the racially otherized that they had been conditioned to
hate?

For instance, the first time Joe Erling Jahr realized that he was to be inter-
rogated by a person of color, he refused and invoked the n-word (NrK, 2018). In
reality, a person of color, in the main, would be better placed to empathize with
the socioeconomic deprivations and accompanying marginalization that were the
lot of Joe Erling Jahr. The concept of intersectionality recognizes that various
forms of oppression, discrimination, and privilege intersect and overlap, distilling
unique experiences for individuals who harbor a plethora of marginalized

identities. For instance, examining race and gender in a compartmentalized fashion fails to fully understand the different forms of discrimination a Black woman may face. Instead of including Jewish people in the concept of *Volksgemeinschaft* ("people's community"), a term that gained traction during WW1 and was deployed to unite individuals from all social classes in pursuit of common national objectives, the Nazis hijacked the term, expunged any class conflict and distinctions, and imbued *Volksgemeinschaft* with a racial (Aryan blood) element (Fischer, 2002).

It is a canard that the Nazis were socialists. While the Nazi Party started out as a socialist party, there was nothing socialist about it after 1934. In 1919, a Munich locksmith named Anton Drexler founded the Deutsche Arbeiterpartei (DAP; German Workers' Party) (Ray, 2019). Hitler and the Nazis were proficient at interpellating (Althusser, 2014) the working class into their hate ideology by exploiting their economic grievances and redirecting their frustrations toward the Jewish population. In later years, the siblings Otto and Gregor Strasser broadened the appeal of the party by coupling Hitler's racist nationalism with socialist rhetoric, resonating with the disenfranchised lower classes. This approach not only expanded the Nazi Party's appeal beyond its traditional Bavarian stronghold but also accelerated its growth. Once Otto Strasser realized that the Nazis eschewed socialist principles – among others, Hitler enlisted the backing of affluent industrialists who were anti-socialists – the Strasser's abandoned Hitler and the Nazis to set up the anti-capitalist Schwarze Front (Black Front). Gregor Strasser, who had participated in Hitler's Beer Hall Putsch in 1923 and headed the outlawed party during Hitler's imprisonment, was murdered on Hitler's orders during the Röhm purge of 1934 (Britannica, 2023). So much for class solidarity! Rather than a stark choice between Marx, Engels, and Lenin on the one hand or Adam Smith, Milton Friedman, and Friedrich Hayek on the other hand, some historians conclude that the Nazis offered a third path:

> The reader will discover that a large part of the Nazi Party's success at attracting skilled blue-collar workers, livestock farmers, and independent artisans and the party's failure to capture the allegiance of many semi- and unskilled laborers, female white-collar service employees, and grain-growing farmers can be attributed to the content of the Nazi Party's economic programs and the degree to which those economic programs corresponded to the material interests of the groups mentioned. As economic conditions deteriorated in Germany after 1925, many Germans would begin to look favorably at the Nazi Party economic orientation that represented for Germany a third path between Marxist centralized state planning and laissez-faire capitalism – an orientation that integrated elements of nationalist-etatist thinking and Keynesian economics. (Brustein, 1996, pp. 28, 29)

If history repeats itself, whatever the new permutations, it is clear that the grievances of the "wretched of the earth," to borrow from Fanon, must take seriously the elephant in the room: White supremacy and white-skin privilege. As far back as 1967, Ignatiev (2023) puts this stark choice succinctly when he states that White workers can either side with the boss or Black and brown workers: "abandonment of all claim to share in the shaping of our destiny, or repudiation of the white-skin privileges, for which we, in our very infancy, pawned our revolutionary souls" (Ignatiev, 2023, p. 58). Yanis Varoufakis warns about the pernicious way in which major tech firms, such as Meta, Amazon, Apple, etc., exert control over our attention and focus through monitoring our transactions. He argues in "Technofeudalism" (2023) that a new form of capitalism, something worse than Marx could foresee, has supplanted the economic order, which effectively transforms individuals into digital serfs addicted to posting, scrolling, and purchasing on their platforms. Instead of pursuing profits generated from labor, Varoufakis argues that these tech giants, whom he labels "cloudalists," profit by extracting "rents."

Clearly, the technofeudalists will create many new Joe Erling Jahrs and, tragically, Benjamin Hermansens, unless all stakeholders – parents, daycare centers, schools, sports organizations, politicians, and others – understand that identity formation must be reconceptualized in terms of intersectionality. Black and brown people cannot feel at "home" in the Labor Party and other left-leaning parties solely on the basis of being members of the "working class." How do the black and brown proletariat fit into this identity category, which, as Crenshaw (1995, p. 377) contends, "has been centered on the intersectional identities of a few"?

3. White Interpreters of Black Pain: Marit Hermansen's Observations

> And a lot of attention is paid to them [i.e. the neo-Nazi murderers]. I actually think it's almost worse than actually meeting them. They are asked if they can handle any more... "can you answer this? ... no, ugh... but you don't remember... Now you have to sit down... I think you should take a break". I get angry when I see how they cross-examined Hadi; he stood in the witness box for two days. He was a 16-year-old boy who had seen his friend killed and they peppered him with questions, and they doubted everything he said. "How could you know... you were so far away... it was dark?" and they kept doubting what he says, and he stands, and he stands, and he stands, and not a single person asks him if he is tired. But these two who have actually taken the life of another person – my child – they must be shown all possible care. "He had had such a difficult childhood, so it was no wonder that he went out and killed someone." I think, dear me, if everyone

who has had a difficult upbringing becomes a murderer, then there will be many murderers. (Transcription and translation of Marit Hermansen's interview in NrK podcast "Drapet på Benjamin Hermansen" [The murder of Benjamin Hermansen], 2018 part 3 of 3, 12:27–10:59)

In the same podcast, Marit, Benjamin's mother, alludes to the micro-aggressions her son faced growing up. He would tell her that, because she was White, she did not understand the racism he faced. She recounts an incident where she lost sight of Benjamin while boarding a train, only to discover the train conductor questioning him about his ticket. The conductor appeared suspicious of Benjamin's account that he was with his mother until she showed up, which significantly changed how the conductor acted toward them. Marit believes that situations like these point to racial profiling. However, proving this is challenging, potentially leading individuals to question their own cognitive assessments. Columbia psychologist Derald Wing Sue begins his article entitled "Micro-aggressions and 'Evidence': Empirical or Experiential Reality?" (2017), with the following citation to capture the elusive phenomenon of microaggression: "The true tale of the lion hunt will never be told as long as the hunter tells the story (African proverb)" (Sue, 2017, p. 170).

Microaggressions are about experiential reality and about listening to the voices of those most oppressed, ignored, and silenced. Those voices tell stories of the many hurts, humiliations, lost opportunities, need for change, and the often unintentional microaggressions endured as they struggle against an unwelcoming, invalidating and even hostile campus climate and society (Sue, 2013). People of color, for example, often have their lived racial realities about bias and discrimination met with disbelief by our society. They are often told that they are oversensitive, paranoid, and misreading the actions of others. They are asked, "Aren't you mind-reading? Aren't you distorting the truth?" (Sue, 2017, p. 171)

Once again, it is not the author's intention to desecrate the memory of the now deceased Marit Hermansen in light of the unspeakable suffering she had to endure. In examining the interview excerpt, my aim, notwithstanding the prima facie appearance of tactlessness, is to critically elucidate how Marit's experiences reveal the machinations of White bias and privilege subtly at work during the legal process involving the White youths in contrast to the handling of Hadi, Benjamin's best friend of Iranian ethnic background. Critical whiteness studies underpin this exploration, providing frameworks to comprehend the embedded racial hierarchies and privileges within societal structures, including the legal system. Critical whiteness studies expose the concealed operations of White privilege and bias, accentuating the importance of scrutinizing this case through its theoretical lens. This framework not only exposes the inconsistencies in treatment based on racial and ethnic backgrounds but also expands our understanding of how systemic racism and White normativity permeate legal and social institutions. Marit, in her dedicated pursuit of justice for her dark-complexioned son, would likely recognize the value of such an analysis. Marit had vowed she would ferociously pursue the truth and address the injustices faced by Benjamin. I argue that her quest would align with the insights provided by whiteness studies, emphasizing the significance of acknowledging and challenging the racial biases that influence legal proceedings and societal perceptions.

Let's once again introduce and name the elephant in the room. Marit Hermansen was White. It matters a lot. At the time when news of the murder just broke over the radio, the author was driving a taxi and dropping off a customer. I remember experiencing some apprehension, especially since I lived in Haugerud, not far from Holmlia. When I arrived home and tuned in to the news, I intuitively knew that this time it would be different because Benjamin's mother was White. A peculiar oxymoronic sensation washed over me as I felt both relieved and guilty simultaneously. The sense of relief stemmed from the awareness that neo-Nazis had been causing disruptions in our "drabantbyer" for many years. In this atmosphere, people of color – especially those employed as taxi drivers, bus drivers, or in food service, particularly the Black and brown proletariat with whom I frequently interacted – had long since given up on the expectation that law enforcement would take the threats posed by the extreme right seriously. Guilt crept in because it was perverse to refract a mother's infinite suffering through a lens of color, be it one of privilege or otherwise. Later, I will delve deeper into the complex emotions, but first, let's examine the list and criminal history of the three individuals sentenced for Benjamin's death:

> **Ole Nicoiai Kvister (21):** In 1999, Kvisler was sentenced to prison for a year and six months for aggravated robbery, bodily harm and bodily insult. The Oslo District Court considered the violence that Kvisler carried out to be serious "… since several of the violations occurred unprovoked and further resulted in mistreatment". He has also been apprehended after allegedly threatening a person with a firearm. 12 days before the murder of Benjamin Hermansen, Kvisler was arrested by the Swedish police for having disturbed public peace and order. Kvisler is also charged with having participated in the assault on a man of foreign origin at Storo on the night of 2 December last year. (VG, 2001)

> **Joe Erling Jahr (19):** was 14-years-old when he was arrested by the police for aggravated theft from a school in Oslo. He was 16 years old when he was arrested several times for taking part in illegal demonstrations. He is also registered for breaching the Weapons Act, several car thefts and theft. He is also charged with the assault in Storo [shopping mall] on the night of 2 December last year. (VG, 2001)

Veronica Andreassen (17): At the age of 13, the 17-year-old girl was caught by the police for stealing a bicycle. She has been arrested once for possession of a small quantity of drugs and arrested twice for damage to a car. Beyond that, she had a couple of other minor infractions. Now she is charged with premeditated murder. On New Year's Eve, she was thrown out of a window in a community center in Kristiansand because she came to the party dressed as a Nazi. (VG, 2001)

While he was checked out of the case early on, the newspaper headline focused on another neo-Nazi, Erik Lauritsen (20):

Since May last year, suspect Erik Lauritsen (20) has been waiting to serve a sentence of eight months in prison. He managed to be registered with 27 new incident reports in the police register, before he was arrested after the murder of Benjamin Hermansen. (VG, 2001)

In light of the above, the previously mentioned Black and brown proletariat could be forgiven for not only having lost faith in law enforcement's resolve to take the menace seriously but sensing that a White mother's agony and wrath would rattle the establishment, and they were not disappointed. Cheryl I. Harris (1995) operates with the term "whiteness as property" to refer to the tangible and economically valuable benefits that White identity bestows upon those who meet the criteria for whiteness in the United States. While the histories of Norway and the United States are different, Norwegian historians Brochmann and Kjeldstadli (2008) state that Norwegian concepts of racial hierarchy in the nation-building era (1814–1940) were influenced by Enlightenment ideals. They state that Norwegians, like many Westerners in the 19th century, entertained notions of racial superiority toward other peoples (Brochmann & Kjeldstadli, 2008, p. 94). Minorities in Norway faced substantial hardship due to a White racial framework founded upon the perceived superiority of the "Germanic," "Nordic," or "Norwegian race." The Sami people were characterized as "biologically degenerate" and doomed for failure in the face of civilization's progress while the Kven people were classified as Mongols, characterized by traits of "brutality" and "sentimentality." Additionally, plans were made for the dissolution of the Romani people as a distinct group (Brochmann & Kjeldstadli, 2008, p. 94). According to Andrew Hacker's (1992) study, "whiteness as property's" tangible economic value is evident in the US context:

The study asked a group of white students how much money they would seek if they were changed from white to black. "Most seemed to feel that it would not be out of place to ask for $50 million, or $1 million for each coming black year." (in Harris, 1995, p. 286)

One could add to the above that the Jewish community was devastated during World War II in Norway. Although occupied by the Nazis, several Norwegians cooperated in the Norwegian Holocaust. Way back in 1814, the "founding fathers" at Eidsvoll declared that Jewish people and Jesuits were prohibited from entering Norway under the Constitution. "Paragraph 2 is the religion section of the Constitution and established the Evangelical Lutheran religion as the state religion in Norway. In addition, in 1814, it denied Jesuits, monastic orders and Jewish people access to the kingdom." The last two sentences in the paragraph read: "Jesuits and Monk Orders must not be tolerated. Jews are still excluded from access to the Kingdom" (Ulvund, 2021). Note the use of "still": Jewish people were already prohibited from entering Norway; the "Jewish paragraph" confirmed the earlier ban and its perpetuation. In other words, a habitus of whiteness has always existed and thrived in Norway.

Therefore, Harris (1995) argued that considering whiteness as property was significant because it encapsulated all of an individual's legal entitlements. Referring to the perspective of the British philosopher Jeremy Bentham, Harris suggested that property is essentially the anticipated benefit one expects to derive from possession (Harris, 1995, p. 280). Clearly, a society that established whiteness as property elevated its owner to the pinnacle of the color hierarchy, bringing with it a corresponding set of expectations. Harris (1995) emphasizes how the law treated whiteness as a real and concrete entity despite its lack of inherent meaning or substance. It was this "whiteness as property" we intuitively sensed Marit Hermansen possessed that was the source of the previously mentioned "relief." If "whiteness became the quintessential property for personhood" (Harris, 1995, p. 281), then Marit was in this sense imbued with this full-fledged "personhood" that the Sami people, Jewish people, Romani people, Kven people, her own son of mixed heritage, and immigrants from the global south lacked. Marit Hermansen not only possessed whiteness as property, a potent asset in advocating for the rights of nonwhites, but also developed a "double consciousness" (Du Bois) through proximity to her son Benjamin. This closeness stemmed from her role as the White mother of a mixed-race son.

In *The Souls of Black Folk* (1903), Du Bois labeled the conflicted experience of African Americans who embodied two identities in one personhood as "double consciousness": one as an American and the other as a Black person. This twofold identity arises from the social construction of race and the historical experiences of African Americans living in a racially stratified society. The "double consciousness" signifies the inner turmoil and tension that African Americans face as they navigate between these two identities and the broader societal expectations and prejudices associated with them. In a sense, Marit transformed into an "honorary Black individual" as she witnessed what Black people had been experiencing for years, a reality that White people plagued by colorblindness could not comprehend. Unlike Benjamin's best friend, whose Middle Eastern origin denied him the benefits of whiteness as property, Marit witnessed the murderers' differential treatment. As Harris asserts, "Inherent in the concept of 'being white' was the right to own or hold whiteness to the exclusion and subordination of blacks" (Harris, 1995, p. 283). As a result of the opprobrium the court exchange provoked in her, she reacted more to this obsequious treatment of the murderers than to the physical encounter.

> And a lot of attention is paid to them [i.e. the neo-Nazi murderers]. I actually think it's almost worse than actually meeting them. They are asked if they can take handle any more... "can you answer this... no, ugh... but you don't remember... Now you have to sit down... I think you should take a break".

It is also conceptually fruitful to bring in critical race theory (CRT)'s tenets of interest convergence and counter or subversive storytelling (Delgado & Stefancic, 1998; Delgado & Stefancic, 2012). Marit's whiteness played a critical role in the massive attention the murder generated. Interest convergence, a concept within CRT, advances the notion that the interests of oppressed groups are only addressed when they align with the interests of the hegemonic White majority. In the words of Harvard legal scholar and "father" of CRT, the first tenured African American professor of law, Derrick Bell:

> The interest of blacks in achieving racial equality will be accommodated only when it converges with the interests of whites. However, the Fourteenth Amendment, standing alone, will not authorize a judicial remedy providing effective racial equality for blacks where the remedy sought threatens the superior societal status of middle- and upper-class whites. (Bell, 1995, p. 22)

Bell (1995) contended that White people accommodated the landmark *Brown v. Board of Education of Topeka* (1954) only because they discerned economic and political advances could be derived once the 50-year "separate but equal" policy of segregation was jettisoned. Bell (1995) cautioned that Black people were serving two masters, despite applauding Thurgood Marshal and his legal team for their role. Through legal action, Black people exerted a lot of effort in eradicating racism, such as the desegregation of schools. However, desegregating schools did not automatically translate into improved education for Black people. What is missing from the calculus is a focus on economic and political power to support Black education, irrespective of the racial composition of schools. Successful litigation on the part of Black people seemed to have become a goal in itself, Bell argued. Lawyers did not represent the parents, but rather a few elite, fee-paying Black parents with ambitions for their children. Who is the client? Bell asks.

> First the decision helped to provide immediate credibility to America's struggle with communist countries to win the hearts and minds of emerging third world people. At least this argument was advanced by lawyers for both the NAACP and the federal government. The point was not lost on the news media. *Time* magazine, for example, predicted that the international impact

of *Brown* would be scarcely less important than its effect on the education of black children. (Bell, 1995, p. 23)

This was in the heyday of the Cold War when Julius and Ethel Rosenberg were convicted of spying for the Soviet Union, sentenced to death in 1953, and countless numbers of American citizens, including Robert J. Oppenheimer of the Manhattan Project fame and civil rights leader Martin Luther King were accused of "un-American" activities by the omniscient and omnipotent surveillance reach of FBI Director J. Edgar Hoover, among others. The *Brown v. Board* ruling also coincided with the apogee of the Korean War and the witch hunts of McCarthyism, which peaked around 1950–1954, with hearings, investigations, and blacklisting of suspected communists or their sympathizers in various sectors of society. Hence, and commensurate with Bell's (1995) CRT tenet of interest convergence, the racist US authorities were not struck by a sudden epiphany of "love thy [Black] neighbor" but deemed the risk of Communist sympathies infiltrating disaffected Black people so great that they reluctantly acquiesced to the NAACP's (National Association for the Advancement of Colored People) demand for desegregation. As Bell notes:

> Second, Brown offered much-needed reassurance to American blacks that the precepts of equality and freedom so heralded during World War II might yet be given meaning at home. Returning black veterans faced not only continuing discrimination but also violent attacks in the South that rivaled those that took place at the conclusion of World War I. (Bell, 1995, p. 23)

In addition, and across the Atlantic, Ducey and Feagin (2021, pp. 34, 35) debunk the canard that British slavery was abolished because White British people experienced a moral transformation. Rather, and commensurate with the interest convergence tenet of CRT, the real reason was rooted in the fact that slavery was no longer as economically viable as it used to be. They conclude:

> This interpretation is in keeping with African American scholar Derrick Bell's description of the interest convergence that sometimes takes place between part of the white elite and dissenting people of color, as it did in the era of racial change that led to British slavery's abolition. (Ducey & Feagin, 2021, p. 35)

In the case of Benjamin Hermansen, the centering of a devastated White mother, Marit Hermansen, served as a compelling springboard for public attention and outrage. To borrow from a hackneyed stereotype in Norway and the West by extension, this was not a Black or brown woman wearing a headscarf, struggling to articulate herself in coherent Norwegian in the company of bearded male relatives chanting "inshallah." Marit's whiteness, education, and effortless articulation acted as a conduit that touched a nerve so that the broader society could empathize with and connect with the victim, thus marshaling support for justice. This convergence of interests around a White mother seeking justice for her son was bound to tip the scales of justice in favor of heightened attention and societal response: long prison sentences for the perpetrators, a 40,000-strong demonstration, and an annual Benjamin Award to the school that works most diligently against racism and discrimination.

The subtle racism that Marit Hermansen claims made her more outraged than physical proximity to the murderers is something people of color find refreshingly honest and validating. Validating because people of color have been voicing such complaints for years without being taken seriously. In 1970, the Black Harvard psychiatrist Chester M. Pierce (1970, 1974) coined the term "microaggression" describing it as a health issue and psychological disorder – a false belief in the superiority of White individuals over Black individuals, promoting actions and attitudes that reinforce this perceived superiority.

It is such thorny issues that Black psychologist Beverly Daniel Tatum explores in her book *Why Are All the Black Kids Sitting Together in the Cafeteria? And Other Conversations About Race* (1997). Omissions and a dearth of alternative perspectives reveal a significant blind spot regarding people of color's profound encounters with racism as articulated by Tatum. Tatum asserts that the primary obstacle to promoting meaningful dialogue across racial lines is the inclination for White Americans to largely engage in discussions with others of their own race. Subsequently, many White people lack the social context required to comprehend the realities experienced by people of color (Tatum, 1997, p. 45). This observation resonates with Bell's (1995) interest convergence theory, wherein the interests of dominant groups concur with the needs or experiences of marginalized groups. As African American abolitionist Frederick Douglass noted, the benevolence of White enslavers in the sugar plantocracy of the antebellum, USA, often appeared devoid of kin altruism.

> I say nothing of father, for he is shrouded in a mystery I have never been able to penetrate. Slavery does away with fathers, as it does away with families. Slavery has no use for either fathers or families, and its laws do not recognize their existence in the social arrangements of the plantation... The name of the child is not expected to be that of its father, and his condition does not necessarily affect that of the child. He may be the slave of Mr. Tilgman; and his child, when born, may be the slave of Mr. Gross. He may be a freeman; and yet his child may be a chattel. He may be white, glorying in the purity of Anglo-Saxon blood; and his child may be ranked with the blackest of slaves. Indeed, he may be, and often is, master and father to the same child... My father was a white man, or nearly white. It was sometimes whispered that my master was my father. (Douglass, 2014, p. 44)

Additionally, the concept of counter or subversive storytelling within CRT underscores the importance of narratives that destabilize dominant narratives and disrupt power structures. One must keep in mind that while the murders of ethnic minorities had occurred previously in Norway, they had often been downplayed or forgotten by the media and society at large. However, the involvement of Marit Hermansen and the ensuing media attention to Benjamin's case unsettled this pattern. By foregrounding the anguish and resolve of a White mother seeking justice for her son, the narrative shifted from one of "another victim of racial violence" to a broader indictment of societal injustice and the need for systemic change. This subversive storytelling approach successfully elevated the visibility of Benjamin's case and sensitized the public to the epidemic of extremist hate and violence, which, until Benjamin's murder, was considered a benign issue. The police even informed parents in one meeting that neo-Nazi youth were merely bored youth who posed no danger to wider society. Marit Hermansen's face, tears, words, and tenacious presence served as subversive storytelling.

Would the neo-Nazis have picked on Benjamin had they known that his mother was White like them, cut from the same cloth? Would they have run after him with murderous intent if they knew he was as Norwegian as they were, except for his skin color? Searching for answers to these questions is not an exercise in absolving guilt or assigning blame but rather an exploration of the complex interplay between racial identity, societal perceptions, and acts of violence. What triggered the unplanned stabbing frenzy? Was the lethal hatred targeted toward black skin color (or what his mother called "golden-brown"), or was Benjamin a synecdoche for the despised immigrants from the global south in the deep recesses of these extremists who resembled dystopian characters from the Mad Max films, embodying a grim vision of societal decay and ruthless violence in their pursuit of racial supremacy?

4. Skin Color Obsessions: Gjems-Onstad and Benjamin Hermansen

> Marit Hermansen, who lost her son Benjamin (15) in the Holmlia murder in 2001, tells TV2 News that she wants to report Gjems-Onstad for violating the racism clause. The reason is that Gjems-Onstad describes Benjamin's killer as "a giant". "He has been a giant in the fight against immigration, and he is, to use a military expression, 'wounded on the battlefield'", says former Supreme Court lawyer and war hero Erik Gjems-Onstad to TV 2 News. (Almendingen, Nettavisen, 2008)

Erik Gjems-Onstad (1922–2011) was a Norwegian lawyer, politician, and war hero. During World War II, he served in the Norwegian Independent Company, also known as Kompani Linge, and engaged in resistance and sabotage activities against the German occupation of Norway. Few war heroes have been as deco-rated as Gjems-Onstad for his wartime courage, including receiving the War Cross, Norway's highest military honor (Askheim, 2023). After the war, Gjems-Onstad built on this sterling wartime reputation and pursued a career in law. He became a prominent lawyer and later, a Supreme Court attorney. As he ventured into politics, his right-wing coloration began to manifest itself in representing the newly formed Anders Lange's Party (ALP) in the Norwegian Parliament (Stortinget) during the 1970s. Anders Lange, the founder of the party, cautioned against a "Jewish invasion" in Norway and endorsed South Africa's apartheid regime until he passed away in 1974 (Møllersen, 2017).

Over time, Gjems-Onstad's progression toward increasingly murky far-wing ideology and his advocacy for individuals linked to extremist and nationalist movements became increasingly conspicuous. Gjems-Onstad's views on immigration and race were highly controversial. He was obdurately anti-immigration and made belligerent statements about race, alleging the superiority of the White race. Despite his unvarnished racist views and actions, he maintained influence within certain political and legal circles, using his position to agitate for anti-immigrant policies and support far-right groups (SIAN, 2011). Gjems-Onstad often stole the limelight for the wrong reasons and remained a polarizing figure, feted by some for his wartime heroism and legal expertise while condemned by others for his racist views and alliances with extremist ideologies. Clearly, Gjems-Onstad does not exemplify racism in Norway nor is the decision to showcase his racist legacy meant to generalize one individual's actions at the expense of the broader population. His legacy reflects the complexities of Norwegian society and its ongoing struggles with issues of race, immigration, and social justice.

This is a book about racism and its myriad avatars, particularly as they have emerged over the past few decades in the context of Norway. The choice to contrast the racism of a highly decorated wartime hero and lawyer with that of neo-Nazi youths, frequently viewed as social outcasts, provides a compelling viewpoint. In 1979, it came to light that Gjems-Onstad had been acting as a mole for several years, providing information to the Rhodesian (now Zimbabwe) authorities about institutions and individuals in Norway, including the press. In response to an invitation from the Rhodesian Information Department, he visited the capital of Rhodesia, Salisbury, that same year. He cited Norway's stance on the African liberation movement as the basis for his active support of the Rhodesian regime. During his stay in the country, he held discussions with Prime Minister Ian Smith, Foreign Minister P. K. van der Byl, Army Commander General Peter Walls, and the Chief of Police. Gjems-Onstad referred to the Norwegian reactions to his activities as "hysterical and comical" (VG, 1979). In 2008, more shocking news emerged.

Erik Gjems Onstad received several medals during and after World War II as a resistance fighter against the Nazi regime. But after this, Melbye Pettersen believes that it is high time that these were withdrawn. When you help give money to Nazi organizations and people who have committed Nazi murders, Norway should not allow them to adorn themselves with medals for having fought against the Nazis during the war. People who are decorated are people we should be able to be proud of, and it is impossible to be proud of a person who actively "rewards" Nazi murders, he says (Nettavisen, 2008).

It is surprising that Gjems-Onstad, an erudite wartime hero against the Nazi occupation of Norway, was unable to extend the same passion and yearning for freedom and sovereignty to Black Africans solely on the basis of White supremacy. Whether they were colonial settlers or neo-Nazi murderers, the conviction that White people are right and must prevail at all costs guided Gjems-Onstad. When he describes Benjamin's killer as a "giant in the fight against immigration" and "wounded on the battlefield," scholars of race and whiteness studies do not consider such blatant racism an aberration. Individuals such as Gjemstad-Onstad are not outliers but part of an architecture of White hegemonic thinking that is capillary or matrix-like – what has been called the *Racial Contract* (Mills, 1997) or White racial frame (Feagin, 2013). Mills (1997, p. 11) describes the racial contract in the following manner:

> The Racial Contract is that set of formal and informal agreements or meta-agreements... between one subset of humans, henceforth designated... as "white"... to categorize the remaining subset of humans as "nonwhite" and of a different and inferior moral status, subpersons, so that they have a subordinate civil standing in the white or white-ruled polities... but in any case the general purpose of the Contract is always the differential privileging of the whites as a group, the exploitation of their bodies, land, and resources, and the denial of equal socioeconomic opportunities to them. All whites are *beneficiaries* of the Contract, though some whites are not *signatories* to it. (Mills, 1997, p. 11)

What unites a motley crew mix of individuals from across Africa and Norway, including a Norwegian war hero, Rhodesia's Ian Smith, and neo-Nazis? Mills' (1997) discussion of the Racial Contract sheds light on this seemingly incongruous alliance, emphasizing a shared foundational agreement based on racial ideologies. How can we fathom the fact that a Norwegian war hero failed to appreciate the universal desire for freedom from oppression, evident not only in Norway's struggle against Nazi occupation but correspondingly in the battles against apartheid in Rhodesia and South Africa? For those subjugated under the regimes of Rhodesia and South Africa, the diabolical chains of apartheid were as cruel and intolerable as the tyranny of Nazism was to the people of occupied Norway. For instance, Chris Hani (1942–1993), the prominent South African anti-apartheid activist and leader, said the following about the experiences that gave impetus to his ideology and activism:

> Now I had seen the lot of black workers, extreme forms of exploitation. Slave wages, no trade union rights... They get peanuts in order to survive and continue working for capitalists... I belonged to a world, in terms of my background, which suffered, I think, the worst extremes of apartheid. (Smith & Tromp, 2009, pp. 30–31)

Another key figure in the struggle against apartheid was Oliver Tambo (1917–1993), who served as President of the African National Congress (ANC) from 1967 to 1991. Tambo writes:

> The policy of uncompromising apartheid was carried out with vigor, violence, hate and haste… The country has been in a state of perpetual political crisis now since 1948. It has been the blackest period since the Boer invasions of the eighteenth and nineteenth centuries. In 15 short years, hundreds of innocent Africans have been wounded by police-gunfire during raids, while under arrest, and while in prison… millions of Africans have been convicted of petty offences, and the average number sentenced to death annually… has been higher than in any corresponding period since Jan van Riebeeck landed in the country in 1652. (Tambo, 2014, p. 59)

It is not difficult to empathize with a Steve Biko longing for justice when he declares:

> I am against the intellectual arrogance of white people that makes them believe that white leadership is a sine qua non in this country and that whites are divinely appointed pacesetters in progress. I am against the fact that a settler minority should impose an entire system of values on an indigenous people. (Biko, 2017, p. 26)

Erik Gjems-Onstad, a highly honored war hero, displays a perplexing utter indifference toward the well-documented atrocities suffered under the minority White settler regime. This indifference transmogrifies into perversion in Onstad's tribute to the racially motivated murder of Benjamin Hermansen. It raises questions as to why Onstad opposed the Nazis during Norway's occupation, given his apparent adherence to a similar strand of White supremacist ideology. Mills (1997, p. 16) fleshes out the *Racial Contract* and states that it "restricts the possession of this natural freedom and equality to White men." It imposes a "partitioned social ontology… between persons and racial subpersons, Unter-menschen, who may variously be black, red, brown, or yellow – slaves, aborigines, colonial populations – but who are collectively appropriately known as 'subject race'."

Perhaps in the twisted mind of Onstad, the Nazi's unforgivable error was to "violate" the *Racial Contract* by attacking and subjugating fellow Anglo-Saxons. Hitler, Josef Terboven (Reichskommissar for Norway during the German occupation), and Quisling's grave error was to invalidate the *Racial Contract* in that all Norwegians were members of the *Herrenvolk*. In militarily occupying and humiliating fellow *Herrenvolk*, there was a loss of the psychic and material payoffs – what W.E.B. Du Bois called "the wages of whiteness" – that come with being members of the master race. "As European, as white, one knew oneself to be a member of the superior race, one's skin being one's passport" (Mills, 1997, pp. 29–30).

The above demonstrates that Benjamin Hermansen was not White for the ilk of Onstad and, hence, part of the "subject races." "And these subpersons – niggers, injuns, chinks, wogs, greasers, blackfellows, kaffirs, coolies, abos, dinks, googoos, and gooks – are biologically destined never to penetrate the normative rights ceiling established for them below white persons" (Mills, 1997, p. 179). In this tragic tale, the lethal ideology championed by Onstad, the orchestrators of apartheid in South Africa and Rhodesia, and the Norwegian neo-Nazi perpetrators who preyed upon Benjamin in "ideological unanimity." In such a warped racial Ragnarokk worldview, Marit Hermansen's "grave sin" was her audacity to conceive a child with Black heritage, for in this unbending crusade envisioned by the extreme far-right, the one-drop rule remains unassailable. Miscegenation is a cardinal sin. All White women received a warning: the seed of "subpersons" must never "colonize" the White womb (Mills, 1997). In the ominous narrative of racial supremacy, the warriors, exemplified by figures like Onstad, aspire to Åsgard, the hall of the Norse gods such as Odin, and Valhalla, reserved for the fallen brave warriors called Einherjar, chosen by Odin's Valkyries. Thus, Onstad elevates Joe Erling Jahr to the status of Einherjar, calling him a "giant" who suffered "wounded on the battlefield" in the fight against immigration (Almendingen, Nettavisen, 2008).

For multiracial individuals like Benjamin, there is a sense in which their "mixedness" or "inbetweennes" (Morris, 2021) relegates them to just that: a world between a White one and a Black one – a twilight zone akin to a scene from the film *Terminal* (2004). Tom Hanks portrays Viktor Navorski in the film, trapped at a New York airport by political unrest in his home country. Viktor, denied entry into the United States and the chance to return home, finds himself compelled to inhabit the confines of the airport terminal. As he navigates life in this transitory space, he forms connections with airport staff and other travelers, finding both challenges and unexpected friends.

Multiracial individuals may resonate with the feeling of being "stranded" or caught between multiple cultural identities, much like Viktor is physically suspended between the stifling narrow world lived between the departure and arrival gates. They may struggle to fully belong to any single racial or cultural group, feeling disconnected or misunderstood by both. The ambiguity and sense of dislocation experienced by Viktor in the film may mirror the complex emotions and identity struggles faced by multiracial individuals as they navigate their sense of self and belonging in a world that often valorizes predetermined racial categories. In her book, *Mixed/Other* (2021), Natalie Morris mentions Joseph who grew up in Hull, East Yorkshire, in the 1960s. Joseph's father was Nigerian and mother White English. Joseph tells Natalie as follows:

> When I was growing up, you were just "half caste" ... You were this kind of mongrel child, loved by neither one nor the other...
> Later at university, Joseph had bricks painted with Nazi swastikas thrown through his window. He says these experiences informed

his opinions on mixedness, but also told him so much about white people's attitudes towards race... We were told – you're not black, you're not white, you're this abnormal person in the middle. (Morris, 2021, pp. 19–20)

No doubt Benjamin Hermansen precociously received an early education in the machinations of this liminal realm of "inbetweennes." Morris (2021, p. 20) writes that "Joseph identifies as Black. He has never thought of himself as mixed... He also takes issue with the term mixed race'; like me, he doesn't like the implication that we are some kind of hybrid of two or more pure states." It would be futile for multiracial individuals to reside in a sea of whiteness, assuming that White people see the whiteness "inside" their golden-brown exteriors. To many White minds, unless intimately acquainted with mixed individuals, the exterior determines the interior, hence the bricks with swastika through Joseph's window and the murder of Benjamin. It is perhaps for the same reason – the fact of blackness, to borrow from Frantz Fanon – that Marit Hermansen settled in Holmlia, one of the most multicultural neighborhoods of Oslo. We are born into skin colors with prepackaged meanings and spend a lifetime discovering and adapting to that meaning as James Baldwin astutely observed:

> Likewise, innumerable people have helped me in many ways; but finally, I suppose, the most difficult (and most rewarding) thing in my life has been the fact that I was born a Negro and was forced, therefore, to effect some kind of truce with this reality. (Truce, by the way, is the best one can hope for). (Baldwin, 2017, p. 5)

In *We Were Eight Years in Power* (2017), Ta-Nehisi Coates refers to the cabal of conspiracy theorists who coerced President Obama to share his birth certificate. Donald Trump, not satisfied with this, demanded disclosure of Obama's college grades, promising $5 million in reward money. He insisted that Obama was not intelligent enough to attend an Ivy League university and that a White man, Bill Ayers, had ghostwritten his acclaimed memoir *Dreams from My Father* (Coates, 2017, p. 342). President Obama's ordeal serves as a stark illustration of the ruthless scrutiny and suspicion aimed at individuals from mixed racial back- grounds. Despite Obama's successes and achievements, he faced unfounded allegations and demands to validate his qualifications and legitimacy. This relentless questioning of his intelligence, education, and even authorship of his memoir reflects a broader societal reluctance to fully accept individuals of mixed race as legitimate members of the White community. Just as Benjamin Her- mansen and Joseph (Morris, 2021) experienced the torment of being trapped in a state of "inbetweennes," Obama's ordeal underscores the ongoing struggle faced by mixed-race individuals to be recognized and accepted as equals in a society still wrestling with deeply entrenched racial biases. Despite progress in civil rights and increasing awareness of racial diversity, the hate that murdered Benjamin persists transcending borders.

It would be comforting to assert that the brand of racial hatred perpetuated by the likes of Erik Gjems-Onstad is limited to a few "nutcases." Sadly, in the US context, "Trump received about 74 million votes in the 2020 presidential election, according to the Federal Election Commission. That's almost 47% of the popular vote" (Mulroy, USA Today, 2020). This is not to suggest that all these voters subscribed to Trump's blatant racism, but that the majority (if not all) knew that whiteness is neither notional nor symbolic in Trump's ideological universe, "but is the very core of his power" (Coates, 2017, p. 343). Coates states that "whereas his forbears carried whiteness like an ancestral talisman, Trump cracked the glowing amulet open, releasing its eldritch energies" (Coates, 2017, p. 343).

> Trump truly is something new – the first president whose entire political existence hinges on the fact of a black president. And so it will not suffice to say Trump is a white man like all the others who rose to become president. He must be called by his correct name and honorific – America's first white president. (Coates, 2017, p. 344)

The broad appeal of Trumpism is an excellent rationale, if we ever needed one, to dissect and study the imbrications of the hate ideology that murdered Benjamin. Much like Antonio's introspection in *The Merchant of Venice*, there should be an insatiable yearning to unravel the roots and intricacies of this antiblack ideology although this pursuit is fraught with innumerable complexities and frustrations, particularly in light of the unparalleled erosion of human rights, dignity, democracy, and civil discourse witnessed within the supposed bastion of Western democracy in recent times.

> What stuff 'tis made of, whereof it is born,
>
> I am to learn;
>
> And such a want-wit sadness makes of me,
>
> That I have much ado to know myself.
>
>   (Antonio, *The Merchant of Venice*, Shakespeare, Act I, Scene I)

There are White people who are exasperated at what they perceive to be the relentless obsession of Black and brown people with race issues. To their minds, "the lady [Black and brown people] doth protest too much, methinks." Perhaps a fitting analogy to counter this line of reasoning could compare the racial concerns of Black and brown people to symptoms of an illness while also acknowledging that White people invented and perpetuated the illness itself. In such an analogy, White individuals act as both the creators of the illness and the ones who hold the power to diagnose it. Black and brown individuals are then expected to accept this diagnosis and act accordingly. "White civilization and European culture have forced an existential deviation on the Negro. I shall demonstrate elsewhere that what is often called the Black soul is a white man's artefact" (Fanon, 1986, p. 16). As James Baldwin observes:

> It is part of the price the Negro pays for his position in this society
> that, as Richard Wright points out, he is almost always acting. A
> Negro learns to gauge precisely what reaction the alien person
> facing him desires, and he produces it with disarming artlessness.
> (Baldwin, 2017, p. 70)

The Black and brown people of Holmlia were not exaggerating their fears of
becoming the latest victims of an age-old revulsion toward their pigmentation.
What good is it if Black people are aware of and have even internalized what
Fanon (1986, p. 13) called the "epidermalization of inferiority" and have, with
Fanon's help, benefited from what he called "the liberation of the man of color
from himself"? (Fanon, 1986, p. 10). Nevertheless, we must persevere as long as
this pernicious anti-Black sentiment and ideology persist, and, like Fanon,
continue to seek a cure.

> I believe that the fact of the juxtaposition of the white and black
> races has created a massive psychoexistential complex. I hope by
> analyzing it to destroy it. Many Negroes will not find themselves in
> what follows. This is equally true of many whites. But the fact that
> I feel a foreigner in the worlds of the schizophrenic or the sexual
> cripple in no way diminishes their reality. The attitudes that I
> propose to describe are real. I have encountered them
> innumerable times. (Fanon, 1986, p. 14)

5. Whose Statue Must Fall? Defacing Benjamin's Memorial

> The memorial to Benjamin Hermansen has been defaced with the text
> "Breivik was right." The Oslo police believe it is serious that this is
> happening 10 years after the events on Utøya [where the Norwegian
> anti-immigrant terrorist Anders Breivik murdered 69 people] ...
> Prime Minister Erna Solberg (Conservative) says it is terrible to see
> that the memorial has been defaced just before 22 July [anniversary of
> the Utøya murders]. It saddens and upsets me, and this shows how
> important it is that we stand up against racism and hate speech every
> single day, she tweets. (NrK, 2021)

Benjamin Hermansen's friends demonstrated their deep affection and respect
for him by taking the initiative to construct a memorial to commemorate his short
life. This act mirrors the strong bond and sense of community among his friends
as they collectively honored his memory. The unveiling of the memorial on
November 1, 2002, marked a significant date for both Benjamin's friends and his
loved ones, representing a moment of tribute and reflection. Moreover, the
establishment of a website in Benjamin's honor signified a commitment to

safeguard his memory and legacy in the digital realm, guaranteeing a broader audience's continued remembrance and appreciation of his story and impact. This digital monument serves as a platform for sharing stories, memories, and condolences, allowing friends, family, and even strangers to pay their respects and keep Benjamin's spirit alive in cyberspace.

Sadly, the memorial was defaced just a few months shy of its 20th anniversary with the words, "Breivik was right." The coordinated bombing in Oslo's government district, followed by the mass shooting at a youth camp on the island of Utøya, resulted in the loss of 77 lives and left many others injured and scarred for life. This tragic event shocked the nation and had profound and lasting impacts on Norwegian society, making it one of the most significant acts of terrorism in the country's modern history. Anders Behring Breivik carried out the attacks on July 22, 2011, guided by his extremist ideology, as detailed in his manifesto, "2083: A European Declaration of Independence." Motivated by far-right, anti-Muslim, and anti-immigrant beliefs, Breivik perceived a threat to European culture and civilization and sought to ferment a nationalist revolution through acts of terrorism.

Why would racists wish to deface or desecrate the memorial of Benjamin Hermansen, an innocent 15-year-old whose only crime in the eyes of hate mongers was his skin color? The key lies precisely in his skin color. To the perverse mind of a racist, it is not enough that the blackness of Benjamin's body was eradicated; the black bust of Benjamin, 20 years later, is still unacceptable. The memorial, a bust erected in memory of Benjamin Hermansen, is mounted on a granite pedestal with the words "Forget not" inscribed on it. This pedestal furnishes a stable and dignified platform for the bust, elevating it both physically and symbolically. The use of granite, a durable and enduring material, emphasizes the lasting impact of Benjamin's life, as well as the significance of the memorial in preserving his memory and inviting contemplation from visitors. Overall, the bust and its granite pedestal combine to create a somber and dignified tribute to Benjamin Hermansen, guaranteeing the reverence and respect of his memory for future generations.

In this sense, Benjamin's memory has been "sacralized" or consecrated in the memorial. Statues of Black people in White Norway are as common as a polar bear wearing sunglasses and sipping a piña colada on a sandy beach. The Black face of Benjamin had to be defaced, with the words "Forget not" replaced by "Breivik was right." This should come as no surprise. The annals of White history have frequently been inscribed in the language of "blood and iron," borrowing from Otto von Bismarck's lexicon. However, this historical narrative has also shown a remarkable proclivity for whitewashing the mayhem that often follows such policies, analogous to the desires of White supremacists who seek to vandalize and topple statues like Benjamin's, echoing a scene reminiscent of the memory-erasing agents in *Men in Black*.

While Benjamin's friends, who were behind the memorial project, wanted everyone to "forget not" what had happened to Benjamin, the defacement by hateful White supremacists is evidence of racism's perpetual quest to erase the memory of its crimes against people of color. In the *Men in Black* film series, the agents use a small, handheld device known as the "Neuralyzer" to make people forget what they saw. This contraption emits a bright flash of light when activated, which deletes the memories of anyone looking directly at it. The agents can control the Neuralyzer to determine how far back in time the memory erasure goes, allowing them to delete specific memories while leaving others intact. After using the Neuralyzer, the agents typically provide those affected with a credible cover story to fill the gaps left by the erased memories, ensuring that the individuals carry on without suspicion or trauma related to their encounter with extraterrestrial activities. This apparatus is one of the hallmarks of the *Men in Black* organization, allowing them to maintain secrecy and conceal alien activities on Earth.

The *Rhodes Must Fall* movement highlights an intriguing paradox. The *Rhodes Must Fall* movement materialized as a student-led protest movement primarily in South Africa, initially taking aim at the statue of British colonialist Cecil Rhodes at the University of Cape Town in 2015. The movement demanded the removal of symbols linked with colonialism, racism, and White supremacy from academic institutions, contending that they perpetuated systemic inequalities and marginalized non-White voices. The movement ignited broader discussions about decolonizing education and addressing historical injustices, leading to protests and debates at universities worldwide. While the removal of statues was a crucial point, the movement also sought institutional reforms to promote inclusivity and diversity within higher education. The *Rhodes Must Fall* movement accordingly became emblematic of broader struggles for social justice and equity in post-colonial societies.

When the statue of Cecil Rhodes was erected in 1911 at Oriel College, Oxford, it was at Rhodes's behest, and he signed away a considerable part of his fortune to Oriel's endowment. This signifies the social and capital accumulation that made the statue possible. It is important to note that there are two notable statues of Rhodes relevant to the Rhodes Must Fall movement: the one erected in the United Kingdom in 1911 at Oxford and another in Cape Town, which was erected in 1934. Both statues have been focal points in discussions around colonial legacy and racism. When the statue was erected in 1911, it was at Rhodes behest, and he signed away a considerable part of his fortune to Oriel's [Oxford] endowment, in other words, the social and capital accumulation that made the statue possible. When the statue of Cecil Rhodes was erected in 1911 at Oriel College, Oxford, it was at Rhodes's behest, and he signed away a considerable part of his fortune to Oriel's endowment. This signifies the social and capital accumulation that made the statue possible. It's important to note that there are two notable statues of Rhodes relevant to the Rhodes Must Fall movement: the one erected in the United Kingdom in 1911 at Oxford and another in Cape Town, which was erected in 1934. Both statues have been focal points in discussions around colonial legacy and racism (Gebrial, 2018, pp. 26, 27). Ludvig Holberg, a Danish-Norwegian writer and playwright who lived from 1684 to 1754, was not directly involved in the slave trade himself. However, he did have ties to it through his investments. Holberg was a shareholder in the Danish-Norwegian trading company Det Vestindisk-guineiske Kompagni (The Danish West India

Company), which had a monopoly on the slave trade in the Danish-Norwegian realm during the 18th century and transported roughly 120,000 enslaved people from Africa to the Caribbean (Thomas & von Hof, 2024). While Holberg's precise involvement and culpability regarding the company's role in trading enslaved people remain debated among historians, his financial ties to the company suggest some degree of secondary involvement with the slave trade. Therefore, some contemporary detractors argue that paying tribute to Holberg through statues or awards without recognizing this dimension of his legacy perpetuates an incomplete or whitewashed narrative.

> In Norway, the debate about decolonization has had a lower temperature than in many other countries, but recently both politicians and campaigners have advocated for removing statues and paintings and changing district names. In Oslo, a signature campaign is approaching 5,000 signatures. The campaign's list of what are referred to as "racist statues" includes, among others, Ludvig Holberg, the Danish-Norwegian poet who has given his name to one of the world's most prestigious academic awards. (Svendsen, Khrono, 2020)

It was this conflicted legacy of Ludvig Holberg that the Black British race scholar, Paul Gilroy, was asked to reflect on as a recipient of the prestigious Holberg Prize in 2019 in Norway. Gilroy (2019) took a nuanced view on the removal of statues, particularly referencing the anti-racist demonstration in Bristol where a statue of enslaver Edward Colston was thrown into the river. While Gilroy generally opposed the concept of decolonization, he admitted to deriving some satisfaction from the act. He welcomed the hunger for knowledge and the passion for justice and redress, driving movements to remove statues of controversial figures, which he saw as inspirational. Gilroy underlined the importance of contextualizing historical figures like Ludvig Holberg, acknowledging their shortcomings while also recognizing their positive contributions. He supported the debate surrounding the removal of statues but suggested that it should not serve as an alternative for broader efforts to oppose institutionalized racism and rethink historical narratives. Furthermore, with respect to the controversy revolving around Winston Churchill statues, Gilroy concedes the vital role he played in World War II as well as his problematic views on race. Ultimately, Gilroy's stance reflects a call for nuanced dialogue and critical engagement with historical symbols rather than a straightforward endorsement or condemnation of their removal.

In light of the broader context of the *Rhodes Must Fall* movement and the debate surrounding the legacy of Ludvig Holberg, the vandalism of Benjamin Hermansen's memorial reinforces the persistent theme of the whitewashing of racist crimes against Black individuals in historical narratives. The movement, which was born out of a desire to interrogate and subvert symbols of colonialism and White supremacy, challenges institutions to acknowledge the exploitative origins of their wealth and the systemic injustices perpetuated by such symbols.

Similarly, Holberg's ties to the slave trade highlight the complexity of venerating historical figures without addressing their involvement in oppressive systems. Paul Gilroy's nuanced perspective on the removal of statues emphasizes the need for contextualization and critical engagement with historical symbols, advocating for a broader effort to oppose institutionalized racism and reshape historical narratives. In this light, the defacement of Hermansen's memorial serves as a reminder of the ongoing struggle to confront and dismantle the whitewashed narratives that perpetuate racial inequalities. The statues become the ground zero of the tug of war between White supremacists and anti-racists – between invisibility and hypervisibility. Anti-racists fight to make visible ("forget not") what racists wish to deface and erase from memory in Benjamin's memorial while racists in other contexts (e.g., Colston's statue) fought to retain memorials of enslavers and colonialists.

> However, in order for the statue to stand above the glowing inscription "by means of the generous munificence of Cecil Rhodes", the heart of what Rhodes represented – settler colonialism and the blueprint of South African apartheid – must be forgotten. The sterile language with which he is spoken of – as a "benefactor" and "businessman" – actively erases the history of violence that enabled his "generous munificence". (Gebrial, 2018, p. 27)

Former Prime Minister Boris Johnson lashed out at demonstrators in Bristol, United Kingdom, after they dismantled, rolled, and dumped the statue of Edward Colston into the city harbor, accusing them of usurping and "subverting" the movement (Ducey & Feagin, 2021, p. 31). Edward Colston was a disreputable and prosperous enslaver whose fortune was amassed through the abuse and suffering of approximately 80,000 men, women, and children forcibly transported from Africa to the Americas between 1672 and 1689. Despite the incontestable brutality inherent in Colston's deeds, his memory has been revered in Bristol for centuries, with several buildings, streets, and institutions bearing his name. His charitable endeavors, which included generous donations and endowments, were praised, overriding his involvement in the cruel slave trade. Colston's statue in the city center remained untarnished, its inscription exalting him as an honorable and wise son of Bristol.

However, recent efforts to confront Bristol's collusion in the slave trade have challenged the veneration of figures like Colston. Activists, such as those in the Countering Colston campaign, have pushed for a more honest acknowledgment of the city's history, backing permanent public artworks memorializing the victims of slavery and exhibitions detailing the city's participation in the transatlantic slave trade. While some resist such changes, arguing against what they perceive as erasing history, others recognize the need for a more honest approach to commemorating individuals like Colston, acknowledging both their contributions and their grim legacies. The debate surrounding Colston's memory reflects broader discussions occurring in cities worldwide as communities grapple with how to remember history without beatifying its sinister chapters. Ducey and Feagin (2021, p. 31) counter former Prime Minister Johnson's condemnation of the protestors who tore down Colston's statue by drawing attention to Johnson's scapegoating of people of color.

> In 2016, he [Boris Johnson] questioned why US President Barack Obama had removed a bust of the openly racist Winston Churchill from his presidential office, writing, "Some said it was a snub to Britain. Some said it was a symbol of the part-Kenyan President's *ancestral dislike* of the British empire – of which Churchill had been such a fervent defender… [I]f that's why Churchill was banished from the Oval Office, they could not have been more wrong". (Ducey & Feagin, 2021, p. 31)

Race scholar Joe R. Feagin (2013, p. 10) employs the term White racial frame to explain the overarching and destructive worldview created by White people in North America and elsewhere – a worldview that extends across class, gender, and age. He traces its contours to the 17th century and argues for its centrality and dominance as a racialized lens through which White people in North America and much of the Western world perceive, reference, and act. The White racial frame is broad and complex, with several components. There is a belief aspect distilled in racial stereotypes and ideologies. In addition, there are cognitive elements evidenced in racial interpretations and narratives. Racialized images and language accents, among others, comprise visual and auditory elements followed by a "feelings" aspect such as racialized emotions and a proclivity to action as in the tendency to discriminate. Feagin (2013) argues that the White racial frame is ill-disposed toward nonwhites who are oppressed and exploited while it encompasses a strong positive orientation toward White people and whiteness.

> []… early in this country's history this overarching racist framing includes a central subframe that assertively accents a positive view of white superiority, virtue, moral goodness, and action. For centuries the white racial framing of ingroup superiority and outgroup inferiority has been, to use Antonio Gramsci's term, hegemonic. It has been part of a distinctive way of life that dominates major aspects of society. For most whites, thus, the white racial frame is more than just one significant frame among many; it is one that provides the language and interpretations that help structure, normalize and make sense of society. (Feagin, 2013, p. 11)

The elements of the White racial frame were clearly evident in the defacement of Benjamin's memorial by White supremacists. First, the belief aspect manifested in racial stereotypes and ideologies was apparent in the veneration of White superiority and the denigration of non-White individuals like Benjamin. This belief system fueled the perpetrators' actions, reinforcing their sense of entitlement and superiority. Such a belief system refuses to countenance the erecting of statues of Black individuals on (White), Norwegian soil. Second, cognitive elements were manifested in the racial interpretations and narratives surrounding the memorial. White supremacists viewed Benjamin's memorial through the lens of their racist worldview, interpreting it as a threat to their perceived dominance and supremacy. "Breivik was right" was deliberately invoked and imposed on Benjamin's memorial. Breivik was marshaled as the White crusader, the Teutonic knight who hunted down and killed those in power who opened the doors of Norway to nonwhites. Racialized images and language were used to justify their vandalism, portraying Benjamin and his legacy in a negative light. Additionally, the feelings aspect of the White racial frame was apparent in the racialized emotions of antipathy, resentment, and intimidation directed toward the broader Black, brown, and White community in Holmlia, for whom the defacement was tantamount to sacrilege. These emotions fueled the perpetrators' inclination to action, leading them to deface the memorial as a form of racial animus and proclamation of White dominance. Overall, the defacement of Benjamin's memorial exemplifies how the White racial frame perpetuates discrimination against nonwhites while reinforcing a positive orientation toward White people and whiteness.

The revulsion expressed by White supremacists toward the defaced memorial dedicated to Benjamin Hermansen stands as a stark witness to their irritation with confronting the reality of racist violence. Hermansen's memorial, operating as a grave reminder of a life unfairly taken due to racial hatred, presents a direct challenge to their worldview built on delusions of White superiority. In contrast, their approval and even delight at blackface performances in entertainment reveal a worrying double standard. Blackface, originating from nineteenth-century theater and radio, has long been used as a tool for White actors to render exaggerated and dehumanizing caricatures of Black people. These performances perpetuated harmful stereotypes, portraying Black individuals as lazy, sexually aggressive, and intellectually deficient (Brand, 2023). The act of defacing Benjamin's memorial by some White supremacists draws comparisons with the provocative Dutch Christmas tradition of Black Pete, portrayed by a White individual in blackface as Santa's "helper."

Black Pete, Santa Claus's associate, is conventionally described in Dutch folklore as being black-faced because he descends chimneys, leaving children mystified about his curly hair, bright red lips, and immaculately clean clothing, features not typically associated with the aftermath of a chimney sweep. Some scholars hypothesize that Black Pete could be influenced by Germanic mythology or European customs where blackening one's face was meant to induce alarming, supernatural figures. In addition, there's discussion about whether Black Pete's imagery could be related to the representation of enslaved individuals, drawing parallels with historical art showing Black children in similar costumes or roles as servants. Despite this, a substantial section of the Dutch population today denies the notion that the character perpetuates racism (Mesman et al., 2016). This stance has significantly divided opinions within Dutch society, elevating the controversy to a level that demands attention. The debate intensifies annually, marked by protests, legal disputes, and heated media discussions.

Children's understanding of Black Pete also underscores the problematic aspects of his portrayal; they recognize him as subordinate to Sinterklaas, often referring to him as a "helper" or "servant," and sometimes even as a "slave," indicating an understanding of an oppressive relationship based on servitude. Black Pete is depicted performing menial tasks under Santa Claus's command. The controversy over maintaining Black Pete in blackface has propelled calls for change, highlighting a resistance among adults to alter a tradition that many see as archaic and racially insensitive. This clash between preserving tradition and addressing contemporary concerns about racism and equality reflects broader societal challenges in resolving historical practices with modern values.

Despite its deeply racist pedigree, blackface has persisted in various forms, evolving alongside changing cultural norms. While some argue that certain instances of blackface may seek to challenge racial boundaries, the majority remain embedded in the legacy of minstrelsy, reinforcing harmful stereotypes and sustaining existing power structures. In essence, the juxtaposition of White supremacists' aversion to Hermansen's memorial and their acceptance of black-face highlights a broader pattern of racial hypocrisy. They reject the visibility of Black suffering and resistance while simultaneously embracing caricatures that degrade and dehumanize Black individuals. By interrogating the legacy of blackface and its continued presence in popular culture, we can gain insight into race's enduring power dynamics and the ongoing struggle for racial justice and equality.

Someone quickly discovered the defacement of Benjamin's memorial. Hundreds, if not thousands, of individuals pass this memorial every day. Even when out of sight, it served as a panopticon (Foucault, 1977) – one that reminded the residents of Holmlia of the homicide of Benjamin. DiAngelo's (2021) distinction between shame and guilt in relation to the White racial frame is relevant. At the risk of being reductionist, shame is a temporary and, ironically, benign, transient, and socially acceptable emotion as opposed to guilt, which demands penance and action (e.g., reparations).

> For white progressives, shame is seen as socially legitimate (or we wouldn't express it), a sign that we care and that we feel empathy. This may be why we express shame so much more readily than guilt. Guilt means we are responsible for something; shame relieves us of responsibility. If I focus on what I did, I must take responsibility for repair. If I focus on who I am, it is impossible to change, and I am relieved of responsibility. (DiAngelo, 2021, p. 123)

It is argued, commensurate with DiAngelo (2021), that Norwegian media-scape's coverage of the history of the Benjamin racist murder is characterized more by guilt than shame. However, a critical exception exists: the blame is specifically directed at neo-Nazis, effectively isolating them as the sole culprits, while mainstream society is exempted from introspection. This narrative deflects from the necessary, albeit uneasy, conversations about how various segments of society – including politicians, journalists, taxi drivers, teachers, and pensioners –

are implicated in creating an environment that fueled the hatred leading to Benjamin's murder. The broader examination of society's role in perpetuating such hatred is conspicuously absent, sparing the collective conscience from a deeper, more uncomfortable scrutiny.

> Guilt is generally understood as based on something bad we have actually done and for which we are responsible, and shame refers to something we believe we inherently are and cannot change. Put simply, guilt is a feeling we have about doing bad, and shame is a feeling we have about being bad. I have observed that white progressives will readily express feelings of shame about racism but hesitate to express guilt. (DiAngelo, 2021, p. 121)

DiAngelo emphasizes that expressing shame is socially acceptable and even welcomed as it triggers a flood of comfort and reassurance from others, thereby confirming our inherent goodness (DiAngelo, 2021). This process, while it may offer immediate solace, perhaps does little to challenge or demolish the deeper, structural facets of racism. For the White Norwegian audience, a shift in media focus from stimulating shame to triggering a sense of guilt could promote a more profound engagement with the issues at hand. Guilt, unlike shame, can drive individuals to recognize their roles and responsibilities in perpetuating racism, thus making it a more potent catalyst for change. The surge in White anti-racist political action in Norway in the aftermath of the George Floyd murder is commendable, yet as DiAngelo (2021) advocates, there is an urgent need to navigate beyond the crude binary of shame and guilt that Smooth (2014) dubbed the "rhetorical Bermuda Triangle." These emotions, if leveraged considerately, have the potential to challenge the deep-seated structural and systemic racism that persists unaddressed.

The question of how race is performed in "White spaces" in homes, offices, schools, cafés, etc. is of the essence. Bonilla-Silva (2022) argues that we are all implicated in secreting racist values into the juggernaut that becomes systemic racism. The unsettling realization emerges that such hostile "White spaces" may correspond to an unspoken or explicit "code of honor," committed to preserving these very spaces. When a significant number of individuals across diverse official institutions embrace this "code of honor," we are faced with systemic and structural racism. Bonilla-Silva elaborates on this in *What Makes Systemic Racism Systemic?* (2022), arguing that the pervasive nature of racism involves the collusion of White individuals across the political continuum, from conservatives to progressives. He articulates, "Racism becomes systemic because it engages whites from diverse ideological backgrounds in its maintenance" (Bonilla-Silva, 2022, p. 837). This concept is reminiscent of Foucault's (1977) critique of examining power solely as a top-down process, analogous to the Marxist critique. Instead, Foucault (1977) proposed a vision of power as a network or web where individuals labeled as "powerless" actively contribute to the maintenance of power structures through the internalization and propagation of dominant discourses. In this framework, power is seen as "productive" as it manifests and is exercised in varied and nuanced ways across society.

In scrutinizing the heart-rending demise of Benjamin Hermansen, one discerns a dominant narrative that conveniently positions atavistic neo-Nazis as the solitary culprits of this atrocious act, ostensibly exonerating the broader societal structures from any form of liability. DiAngelo (2021) outlines this perspective, suggesting that Norwegian authorities and media quickly seized the opportunity to assign all the blame to a marginalized and demonized subgroup of the population. Primarily branded as working-class, unemployed youths, many of whom had not completed their schooling and immersed in a subculture that celebrated narcotics, alcohol abuse, and violence, Norwegian authorities and media summarily labeled these individuals as the pariahs of society. This storyline positions them as the incarnation of societal degeneration, thereby absolving the remainder of Norwegian society from any responsibility or need for introspection.

The framing of these criminals as the classic "other" – alienated from mainstream values and societal norms – operates within a convenient dichotomy that polarizes "decent" society from its presumed outliers. However, this dualistic generalization overlooks the sophisticated socioeconomic and cultural dynamics that foster environments conducive to such radical ideologies. It disregards the examination of systemic failures, including the education system's incapacity to retain these individuals, the economic structures that fail to employ them, and the social welfare systems that fail to rehabilitate or integrate them back into society. Not least, this narrative fails to address the quiescent biases and tacit validations of racial superiority that may permeate "decent" society, implicitly fueling the ideologies that embolden such hate groups. The problem is attributed to the actions of a few, allowing the majority to exonerate themselves from any responsibility for the systemic and cultural conditions that facilitate racism.

In addition to parodying the complex roots of racial violence, this eclectic allocation of blame and the accompanying moral distancing by Norwegian authorities and media and the broader public sphere also impede the comprehensive societal reflection and reform required to address these issues at their core. The singular focus on the most extreme and visible manifestations of racism, represented by the neo-Nazi groups, diverts attention from the more subtle, pervasive forms of racism and structural inequalities that persist within a broader society. In this context, the tragedy of Benjamin Hermansen becomes a missed opportunity for profound societal self-examination and transformation, reducing it to a superficial condemnation of an easily identifiable enemy rather than a catalyst for addressing the deeper, systemic issues of racism and exclusion.

> People who live in the neighborhood quickly took action and removed the graffiti. Kristina Lie-Hagen was sitting at home in her living room in Holmlia when she saw a picture of the vandalism in a local Facebook group. Then I got very angry and uttered some nasty words. She went down to her shed and found white-spirit and some old rags. She thought the vandalism had to go away as soon as possible. A caretaker with a grinding wheel helped her. They ground away most of it, then had to wash away the remaining

residue. So now there's an ugly stain on Benjamin. Although it
bothers us, the written words are no longer visible. (NrK, 2021)

Reflecting on the memorial dedicated to Benjamin Hermansen offers a glimmer of
hope amid the gloom of racism in Norway. In a promising display of solidarity,
residents of Holmlia, both White and non-White, took instant action against the hate
speech defacing Benjamin's memorial, bonding to erase the dreadful declaration that
"Breivik was right." Their communal efforts to purge the graffiti, although leaving
behind a lingering stain, denote the memorial's broader significance as a reflection of
racial dynamics within the country. This undertaking sums up the community's
refusal to let hate speech stain the memory of Benjamin and their shared spaces.
Norway's encounter with racism, particularly against Black and brown individuals
(besides the historical racism against the Sami people, Jewish people, etc.), is a
relatively recent phenomenon, tracing back to the influx of immigrants in the 1960s.
The abrupt demographic shifts presented unique challenges to the predominantly
White Norwegian society, unaccustomed to the diversity of their new neighbors.
Historically, the presence of Black individuals in Norway was so rare that their
encounters were predominantly through foreign travel, television, or stereotypical
portrayals on commercial products, such as the controversially named "Black Boy"
spice brand. A notable reflection of this naiveté came in 1985 when the acclaimed
poet and troubadour, Ole Paus, remarked on the absence of black individuals in
Elverum, highlighting the rarity of such encounters outside Norway's major cities.
"Neger" was not considered offensive at the time.

> Journalist: You grew up in Oslo and in Elverum?
> Ole Paus: Since I was physically behind my peers, I got used to
> living in a kind of inner exile relatively early on. I heard by the way
> little Richard at Elverum.
> Journalist: Live?
> Ole Paus: No, they haven't seen a negro [neger] in Elverum yet
> (Thomas, 2016, p. 241)

However, the landscape of Norwegian society is evolving. The naming of Oslo
streets after individuals of Pakistani origin, like Rubina Rana, marks a meaningful shift toward recognizing and esteeming the contributions of non-Western
immigrants to Norwegian society. Rubina Rana's story, from her migration from
Pakistan to her pivotal role in Oslo's local politics and her historic leadership in
the Norwegian Constitution Day celebration, illustrates the gradual but meaningful integration of immigrants into the fabric of Norwegian life. Her legacy,
cemented by the naming of a street in her honor in Grønland, Oslo, represents a
beacon of change, exemplifying the slow but steady progress toward a more
inclusive Norway. These changes, from the communal defense of Benjamin's
memorial to the recognition of immigrant contributions, signal a broader societal
shift. While challenges remain and the stain on Benjamin's memorial serves as a
somber reminder of the work still to be done, these acts of solidarity and

recognition offer hope for a more inclusive and understanding Norwegian society, one that embraces its diversity as a strength rather than a source of division.

In conclusion, the disfigurement of Benjamin Hermansen's memorial, vandalized by the inscription "Breivik was right," underscores a troubling trend in contemporary society where symbols of racial equality and commemoration become objects of hatred and bigotry. Prime Minister Erna Solberg's condemnation of this act emphasizes the severity of the situation, accentuating the imperative to combat racism and hate speech on a daily basis. However, the defacement of the memorial raises deeper questions about the pervasive presence of racism and its many avatars in society. Benjamin Hermansen's memorial, erected by his friends to honor his life, symbolizes a joint effort to preserve his memory and legacy. The unveiling of the memorial and the creation of a dedicated website serve as tributes to Hermansen's impact and solicit contemplation and introspection from visitors, ensuring that his spirit lives on beyond his tragic death. Yet, the defacement of the memorial with a perverted message indicates an obstinate negation of Hermansen's humanity and the systemic racism that augmented his untimely demise.

We must understand the defacement of Hermansen's memorial within the broader context of racial inequality and historical whitewashing. The act of "deleting" Benjamin's blackness from the memorial finds its counterpart in other racialized customs, such as the Dutch tradition of Black Pete, wherein a White individual dons blackface to depict Santa's black "slave." Both instances reveal a disturbing pattern of expunging the humanity of Black individuals and reveling in harmful stereotypes. Furthermore, the defacement of memorials like Hermansen's is symptomatic of a broader struggle to confront and dismantle racist narratives in society. Just as the *Rhodes Must Fall* movement challenges the veneration of colonial figures like Cecil Rhodes, the defacement of Hermansen's memorial underscores the need to re-examine the deification of historical figures with ties to racism and oppression. The debate surrounding Ludvig Holberg's legacy exemplifies this tension as efforts to remove statues and rechristen streets compel society to confront unpleasant truths about its past.

In essence, the defacement of Benjamin Hermansen's memorial reflects the ongoing battle between those who seek to uphold White supremacy and those who strive for racial justice and equality. It serves as a poignant reminder of the enduring legacy of racism and the urgent need for collective action to dismantle systemic inequalities and confront historical injustices.

Chapter 2

Anders Breivik and the Crusade for "White Emancipation"

The following essay includes an assessment and conclusions around the anti-European or "anti-White" racist aspects of multiculturalism. Initially, I was hesitant to incorporate any references to race, whiteness, or ethnicity, primarily due to my innate aversion to writing about such topics. My upbringing involved indoctrination in a multiculturalist system for 30 years, to be more precise. Partly, I also convinced myself originally that I was first and foremost against Islam, and that writing about skin color (or multiculturalism, for that matter) would only complicate this fight... But above all, if you believe that non-White racism exists, it is actually immoral not to deal with the problem and its victims. I am convinced that not just non-White, but especially anti-White racism is real and a very underestimated phenomenon. (Anders Breivik, *2083: A European Declaration of Independence, 2011*, pages not numbered)

Breivik executed two attacks on July 22, 2011, resulting in 77 deaths and several injuries. He first detonated a car bomb near government buildings in Oslo, killing eight people. He then traveled to the island of Utøya, 38 km (24 miles) northwest of Oslo city center, where he shot and killed 69 participants, mostly teenagers, at a Workers' Youth League (AUF) camp. Anders Breivik's voluminous 1,518-page Manifesto (2011) is replete with profound apprehensions for the continued hegemony of European whiteness, so much so that the over 200 fevered references to White people (especially males) give the impression of an unparalleled existential peril looming over the construct of whiteness. A decade after the murder of Benjamin Hermansen, another White Norwegian, ensnared within a realm of fantasy that descended into toxicity and violence, unleashed a cataclysm of terror

Too Black to Be Here?, 53–99

doi:10.1108/978-1-83662-162-120251003

and death that shattered the collective psyche of the nation, ripping up old wounds that may remain unhealed for generations. A search in the internet media archive service Retriever turned up 19,496 (key words: Anders Behring Breivik, 22. juli, Utøya, 2083 manifest…).

Much ink has flowed in the last decade seeking to understand Breivik's killing spree through the lens of far-right ideology, the "lone-wolf" phenomenon, Islamophobia, and issues of belonging, to name a few (Bangstad, 2013, 2014; Seierstad, 2016; Skoglund, 2013). In this chapter, I delve more deeply into the Breivik case, employing the lens of critical whiteness studies, which is particularly pertinent given Breivik's pronounced fixation on whiteness. I argue that very few analysts have broached the subject, leveraging a critical race/whiteness framework. The lion's share of analyses has adhered to the conventional trope of the White male "loser" whose grievances stem from personal failures in career and relationships, and seeks retribution or vindication through an act of catastrophic terrorism. While Skoglund (2013) does not overtly concentrate on or apply conceptual analytical frameworks from critical race and whiteness studies, she recognizes the salience of incorporating whiteness into any scrutiny of figures like Timothy McVeigh and Anders Breivik. The excerpt below from her book with the telling title *Angry White Men* (2013) captures the importance of this perspective:

> The white man's right to rule unrestrictedly recurs in the motivational sphere of lone terrorists. Whether he kills abortion doctors, immigrants, feminists, government employees, or Sikhs, he stands as a defender of the right he perceives himself to have as a white man, in a historical context where rights have gradually been taken from him. He often refers to a glorified past when things were in order, and everyone recognized this undeniable right. He feels entitled to a position he believes others have stolen from him. And by acting on behalf of his gender and his race, he can once again become the hero he – due to his particular personality construction, but also based on cultural beliefs – feels destined to be. (Skoglund, 2013, p. 159)

President Franklin D. Roosevelt famously used the phrase "a day that will live in infamy" in a speech to the United States Congress on December 8, 1941, the day after the Japanese attack on Pearl Harbor. July 22, 2011, is Norway's day that will live in infamy. The main difference, however, is that while the US's day of infamy was the denouement of a vicious surprise attack by Japan, Norway's day of infamy was inflicted by one of its own sons. In Norwegian history, there is another historical precedent for a betrayal of monumental proportions. Vidkun Quisling's actions were so egregious that his name has since transcended national boundaries, becoming synonymous with treason. Notably, the English lexicon has assimilated the name "Quisling" as a noun, denoting "a person who helps an enemy that has taken control of his or her country" (Oxford Learner's Dictionaries, 2024). While Quisling is not the subject of this chapter, it is significant to note the fact that both of these extremists were in thrall to White supremacist ideas.

By 2014, Breivik's extremist ideology had evolved away from Christianity toward Nazism, and a particular devotion to Vidkun Quisling. "After being refused his application to visit Quisling's grave, Anders Behring Breivik (35) is said to have sworn allegiance to the traitor Vidkun Quisling with his right hand raised" (Karlsen, ABC Nyheter, 2014). In due course, psychiatric experts concluded that Breivik exhibited signs of psychosis and severe mental impairment, rendering him unable to be held legally accountable for his actions in a court of law. Consequently, they advised mandatory psychiatric treatment for him. Among others, the psychiatrists Torgeir Husby and Synne Sørheim based their assessment on the following claims made by Breivik (Dagbladet, 2011).

- He serves as the ideological leader of the Knights Templar, a secret organization that draws inspiration from them. He has the authority to decide who will live and who must die.
- He becomes regent in Norway after a coup d'état.
- He will become regent Sigurd the Crusader II.
- He is tasked with deporting Muslims to African ports.
- He faces the risk of death.
- His actions are going to set off a nuclear war.
- There is a civil war in Norway.
- 2020 will see a revolution that deposes the Royal House.
- Everyone must be DNA-tested. He asserts that the discovery of the remains of Harald Hardrada, Olav's half-brother Hardrada, or Olav the saint must precede the appointment of a new regent.
- Next, we will conduct DNA tests on the Norwegian population to identify the most closely related individual. This person can become the new regent in Norway.

Members of the public, as well as Breivik himself, protested the suggestion that he was deranged and not mentally responsible for the terror attacks. Contrary to the expert committee's recommendation, the court concluded that Breivik was mentally competent to stand trial for his actions. This decision was commensurate with the view of one of Norway's most distinguished psychiatrists, Randi Rosenqvist, who has examined Breivik on seven occasions in total and maintained from the beginning that he was not mentally ill. Rosenqvist argued that killing sprees do not, in and of themselves, constitute evidence of insanity. Rosenqvist refuted the notion that Breivik was psychotic due to his advocacy for the deportation of all Muslims, asserting that many Norwegians share this sentiment, which does not imply insanity. Almost a year into meeting and assessing Breivik, one news outlet reported: "In her first report from August 2011, Rosenqvist writes that Breivik has good impulse control and that he has a very good ability to 'do double bookkeeping', which has enabled him to carry out the attack on July 22" (NrK, 2012). The court finally concluded:

> Arntzen [the judge] says the court believes it is difficult to see
> Breivik's actions in light of a paranoid schizophrenic diagnosis.
> Breivik had the stamina and impulse control to carry out the
> actions he wanted to take. The court believes that this cannot be
> seen in the context of a paranoid schizophrenia diagnosis. He was
> well-dressed and well-groomed, and he paid his mother's rent. He
> has also run stock trading and became a member of the Masonic
> Lodge. In 2007–2008, he resumed some contact with friends. The
> judges believe that none of the friends have pointed out anything
> unusual about him. (NrK (b), 2012)

Breivik knew from the start that the authorities would do their utmost to declare him insane, and he was equally determined for this not to occur. His prediction came true. How do we account for this? Respecting the memory of the victims, we might best analyze the conundrum under the following thesis: Breivik put whiteness itself on trial. If one were to hold the notion that Breivik was indeed of sound mind and cogent in his actions, a rattling revelation presents itself, one that demands a profound examination of the Norwegian public's collective consciousness. Breivik, who comes from a middle-class background and is the son of a diplomat, personifies an archetype in Norwegian society. His actions, largely drawn from established Western literature, not only implicate him but also serve as a mirror reflecting the darker aspects of Norwegian society. From this perspective, I cautiously suggest that some segments of White Norwegian society, especially those who firmly believed in Breivik's insanity, might have fallen victim to their own self-deception. In this regard, Breivik was not the solitary inhabitant of a perilous realm of self-delusion.

As previously mentioned in Chapter 1, the philosopher Charles Mills' *Racial Contract* (Mills, 1997) is a conceptual framework that explores the tacit agreement among members of society, particularly those who identify as White, to uphold and perpetuate racial hierarchy and privilege. This contract, often unrecognized by its beneficiaries, shapes social, political, and economic institutions to sustain the dominance of White people over other people. It operates through systems of oppression, exploitation, and exclusion, thereby maintaining the status quo of racial injustice. Mills (1997, p. 17) examines the moral and empirical epistemology associated with the norms and procedures for establishing criteria for the world's moral and factual knowledge. Mills weaves through the Western contours of contractarianism based on natural law, distilling our contemporary notions of morality, whether Locke's divine version or a revised version of Hobbes' Leviathan. He concludes that what appears "natural" or "objective" in everyday cognition to all people is deliberately distorted or misinterpreted in the execution of official policy by White epistemic authority in order to maintain the Racial Contract.

> Thus, in effect, on matters related to race, the Racial Contract
> prescribes for its signatories an inverted epistemology, an
> epistemology of ignorance, a particular pattern of localized and

global cognitive dysfunctions (which are psychologically and socially functional), producing the ironic outcome that whites will in general be unable to understand the world they themselves have made. (Mills, 1997, p. 18)

Following Mills, we ought to ask: What is the world that White people in Norway have created and misrecognized in relation to Breivik's actions? Following the killing spree, several commentators candidly vented their frustrations in a manner that few would volunteer for today. The Spanish paper *El Mundo* published the views of one such commentator, Petter Nome, a Norwegian television personality and journalist, in English. He wrote in his opinion piece with the title *To You Who Nurtured a Murderer*: "His 'philosophy' is obviously extreme and pervaded with hate, but many of his main views and arguments are not obscure nonsense in the mind of a freak. They are all too well present in everyday conversations in the streets and pubs—and in mainstream politics. First of all, his generalizing anti-Muslim gospel and fear of 'multiculturalization'" [*sic*] (Nome, 2011; Dagsavisen). Indeed, the painful truth surfaces: Breivik's monstrous deeds are not merely an isolated anomaly but rather an indication of latent attitudes that pervade the fabric of Norwegian society. The upsetting realization dawns that Breivik's actions, propelled by a warped ideology and an equally fiendish sense of righteousness, could be perceived as an extension of part of the collective consciousness of his countrymen. He becomes, in a sense, a grim prototype of the potential suppressed within any Norwegian citizen – a disquieting reminder of what lurks beneath the mask of societal norms and gentility.

Like Pontius Pilate, part of the White public superficially "cross-examined" Anders Breivik but had already determined what the outcome should be. On Pilate's part, it was acquittal, and the same went for many among the Norwegian public, but the latter was with a twist: they summarily concluded that Breivik was "insane" because "insane" was synonymous with "White innocence." It was crucial that they visibly "washed their collective" hands under the vigilant gaze of an international media spotlight. The implication was that such behavior was incompatible with the perceived attributes of whiteness, particularly as under-stood within the Norwegian context. Confronted with such a traumatic revela-tion, the urge to distance oneself from Breivik's carnage becomes palpable. The impulse to label him as mentally deranged and, in so doing, exonerate White society of any complicity or reflection becomes an irresistible proposition. It serves as a tantalizing diversion from the unsettling reality of Breivik's actions which while extreme in their manifestation, are embedded in a broader social context – a reality that strikes at the very core of the Norwegian conscience.

Ultimately, akin to Pontius Pilate's initial decision being reversed, the initial ruling of insanity was overturned. Whiteness as a hegemonic adverse force has historically survived and thrived because of the power of the machinations of this misrecognition of this faulty moral compass. "To a significant extent, then, white signatories will live in an invented delusional world, a racial fantasyland, a 'consensual hallucination', to quote William Gibson's famous characterization of cyberspace, though this particular hallucination is located in real space" (Mills, 1997, p. 18).

It is this creation of a "racial fantasyland," the one that Petter Nome argues is responsible for creating Breivik, which Mills (1997) would simultaneously nuance and add has been misrecognized by its creators, not only in Norway but also going back to the founding fathers of Western moral theory. Mills co-implicates Immanuel Kant in this misrecognition of a racial fantasy. Kant infamously stated in *Observations on the Feeling of the Beautiful and Sublime* that,

> So fundamental is the difference between [the black and white] races of man... it appears to be as great in regard to mental capacities as in color... A clear proof that what a [Negro] said was stupid was that this fellow was quite black from head to foot (Mills, 1997, p. 70)

Furthermore, Kant argued that "the black person, for example, can accordingly be denied full humanity since full and 'true' humanity accrues only to the White European" (Mills, 1997, p. 71). Put differently, contemporary versions of misrecognizing a world spawned by White supremacy have long rested upon the cornerstone of the Racial Contract, which privileges whiteness and disadvantages all others.

> But the embarrassing fact for the white West (which doubtless explains its concealment) is that their most important moral theorist of the past three hundred years is also the foundational theorist in the modern period of the division between Herrenvolk and Untermenschen, persons and subpersons, upon which Nazi theory would later draw. Modern moral theory and modern racial theory have the same father. (Mills, 1997, p. 72)

Following the Brevik attacks, the public discourse failed to address this issue of "White" racism. Myrdahl (2014) calls Anders Breivik a White supremacist and argues that Norway failed to seize the opportunity following the terrorist attacks to confront this scourge. Myrdahl contends that Breivik's supremacist ideologies have filtered through mainstream discourse, overshadowing genuine efforts to challenge and undo the underlying White supremacist views lodged in the concept of "Norwegianness." Instead of engaging in meaningful dialogue to confront these supremacist views, post-attack rhetoric has often resorted to shallow expressions of "tolerance" and "inclusion." Furthermore, Myrdahl's observation that Breivik's supremacist views have become mainstream highlights the insidious nature of the Racial Contract.

Of course, one must hedge talk about Breivik's views becoming "mainstream," but the author assumes Myrdahl is alluding to the numerous instances in Norwegian media where the Labor Party has faced accusations of "exploiting" the tragedy for political purposes, among other things. While the ugly incident about the defacement of Benjamin Hermansen's memorial with the words "Breivik was right" may be dismissed as the work of a "lone wolf," many in Norway have been taken aback by the intermittent support and defense of Breivik in some circles.

One primary school teacher posted the following on his Facebook page: "I hope AP [the Labor Party] will again deploy AUP [the youth division of the Norwegian Labour Party] on Utøya in the coming year, and that the year offers another great hunting season out there" (Nilssen, VG, 2012). The teacher, who faced termination for his posts and violent video content, expressed his agreement with Breivik's perspective on integration policy. "On Breivik's terms, I can understand how he saw the world and why he did what he did. But that doesn't mean I think the actions are right, he explains" (Nilssen, VG, 2012). Despite the violent nature of Breivik's actions, the normalization of his ideology suggests a broader societal acceptance of White supremacist notions, perpetuated through discourses and institutions. Myrdahl concludes:

> Breivik wanted his actions to lead to a revolution and a new Norway defined by explicit white supremacist policies. The dominant Norwegian response to the experience of white supremacist terrorism failed to interrogate some of the core assumptions that the majority culture shares with the terrorists. Thus, despite the initial disruption of national belonging constructions, the nation's whiteness quickly regained its status as the invisible norm. (Myrdahl, 2014, p. 497)

Myrdahl's (2014) contention is a testament to the tenacity of the Racial Contract. Her critique of the post-attack rhetoric, illustrated by the platitudes of "tolerance" and "inclusion," also resonates with the Racial Contract framework. Such rhetoric may serve to maintain the status quo of racial hierarchy by masking meaningful conversations about systemic racism and White privilege. Myrdahl's assessment, when viewed through the prism of the Racial Contract, stresses the urgent need for Norwegian society to confront and dismantle the structures of White supremacy embedded within its institutions and discourses. Failure to do so further reinforces systems of racial injustice and inequality, cementing the cycle of oppression outlined in the Racial Contract. This was not the first time, nor will it be the last, that whiteness was on trial. Breivik's name and mission have become synonymous with conspiracy and disinformation that Joseph Goebbels would have been proud of. In this contemporary era, when, to paraphrase Churchill, an iron curtain of fake news and propaganda is descending across the West, epitomized in Trumpism and Putinism, there is the need to acknowledge and expose the Racial Contract which, I argue, is Europe's "original sin" in the sense that the misrecognition of the world it has created or distorted in its own image boomerangs back to cause untold suffering and damage.

> One could say then, as a general rule, that *white misunderstanding, misrepresentation, evasion, and self-deception on matters related to race* are among the most pervasive mental phenomenon of the past few hundred years, a cognitive and moral economy psychically required for conquest, colonization, and enslavement. And these phenomena are in no way a*ccidental,* but *prescribed* by the terms of

> the Racial Contract, which requires structured blindness and
> opacities in order to establish and maintain the white polity.
> (Mills, 1997, p. 19)

Christ returns to earth in Fyodor Dostoevsky's "The Grand Inquisitor" from *The Brothers Karamazov* (2007), only to face rejection and exclusion from the very priests tasked with spreading his teachings. In a lengthy monologue, the Grand Inquisitor lectures Jesus, who appeared in Seville during the Inquisition's pinnacle. The Grand Inquisitor expounds on several touchy issues: he avows that only the principles of the devil can reconcile humanity; that by providing bread, governing consciousness, and leading the masses, one can dominate the world; that whereas Jesus chose to minister to only a select few, the Catholic Church has built on his teachings to reach everyone; that the Church governs vicariously in God's name but employs the tactics of the devil; and that Jesus was misguided in his high regard for human nature. Jesus remains silent throughout this harangue. White Norwegian society, much like the Orthodox clergy in Dostoevsky's rendition, is unable to fathom its own distortions and misappropriations of foundational principles, not unlike heresies of religious dogma. This is precisely how scholars such as Myrdahl and others, who understand, in the words of Audre Lorde (2003), that the master's tools will never dismantle the master's house, feel:

> Thus, not only is whiteness invisible, but the tools with which it
> might be brought to light and disassembled are rejected. In
> Norway, in the late summer and autumn of 2011, this meant
> that the analyses of and solutions to the questions of national
> belonging raised by the 22 July bombing and massacre were
> severely hampered by an impoverished conceptual framework,
> unable to understand or critically examine the exclusionary
> terms of the national community or consider how to change
> these terms. (Myrdahl, 2014, p. 495)

Charles Mills' concept of the Racial Contract, in a similar vein, advances the idea that Western societies privilege White people, thereby normalizing and making invisible a system of oppression. Not only is this contract a sociopolitical agreement, but it also encompasses an epistemological aspect that whitewashes the very understanding of knowledge and truth. This skewing does not simply advantage one group over another; it constructs a thorough worldview that rationalizes White supremacy and dominance through purportedly "natural" hierarchies. As Myrdahl (2014) argues, the discourse in the aftermath of the Breivik attacks was a squandered opportunity. Alexander Pushkin's play *Boris Godunov* (1824) ends with the famous lines:

(The People are silent with horror.)

Why are ye silent? Cry, Long live the tsar Dimitry Ivanovich!

(The People are speechless.)

In a poignant inversion, the Norwegian people were silent with horror and speechless when news of Breivik's killing spree first filtered through. They were silent with horror and speechlessness because, for a fleeting moment, it appeared that the culprit, White supremacy, had finally materialized in plain sight – all could see the illegitimacy of Boris's usurpation of the throne, to borrow from Pushkin. Unfortunately, however, with the passage of time, it became unmistakable that the Racial Contract, temporarily impaired and seemingly on life support, recovered its strength and resumed its usual operations. This echoes the distortion within societies that consider themselves paragons of virtue and worthy of emulation while engaging in practices that undermine these very ideals. We can excuse the populace in Pushkin's *Boris Godunov*, primarily composed of illiterate and superstitious peasants, for being oblivious to the intrigues of the triumvirate of the Tsar, the boyars, and the Orthodox clergy (resurrected today in Vladimir Putin, his oligarchs, and the Russian Orthodox clergy). The affluent, well-educated, and widely traveled Norwegian populace does not share the same ignorance.

Perhaps some "confessional" reflexivity would not be out of place at this juncture. At the time of the bomb detonation near the government buildings, my 15-year-old daughter, whose mother is White, was in the vicinity. For a terrifying few moments, the possibility of her becoming a victim haunted us. Thankfully, she responded to our calls sometime later, rattled but unharmed. Therefore, for various reasons, I do not approach the Breivik attacks from a secluded and detached perspective. Throughout my 35-year stay in Norway, I have encountered what DiAngelo refers to as "Nice Racism" (2021) in her book of the same name, as well as the direct, confrontational form of racism, particularly in my younger days as a cab driver in Oslo, where potential customers would open the door at night and remark, "We don't sit with niggers!"

The protagonist or nonperson in Ralph Ellison's *Invisible Man* reminds us of the author's "Black" perspective. Whether it was the Arve Beheim Karlsen case, the Benjamin Hermansen case, the Eugene Obiora case, the Ali Farah case, or the topic of this chapter, Anders Breivik, I, like many other individuals with whom the only commonality I share is the same skin color, have time and again felt like the *Invisible Man* in Ralph Ellison's novel who finds his grandfather's derisive words come back to haunt him: "To Whom It May Concern... Keep This Nigger-Boy Running" (Ellison, 1980, p. 33). Like the protagonist, we have held onto the optimism that this time will be different – Norway, heralded as one of the most enlightened countries in the world, will "smell the coffee," wake up to the issues rooted in the construct of whiteness, and undertake a genuine introspection. Alas, the resolve of whiteness continues to fuel a mistaken optimism that real change is just around the corner.

1. White Supremacy's Existential Anxiety: The Ascendancy of the "Other"

We have only a few decades to consolidate a sufficient level of resistance before our major cities are completely demographically overwhelmed by Muslims... As the social revolutionaries readily proclaim, their purpose is to destroy the hegemony of white males. To accomplish this, all barriers to the introduction of more women and minorities throughout the "power structure" are to be brought down by all means available. Laws and lawsuits, intimidation, and demonizing of white males as racists and sexists are pursued through the mass media and the universities... To achieve this, the Critical Theorists of the Frankfurt School recognized that traditional beliefs and the existing social structure would have to be destroyed and then replaced. The patriarchal social structure would be replaced with matriarchy; the belief that men and women are different and properly have different roles would be replaced with androgyny; and the belief that heterosexuality is normal would be replaced with the belief that homosexuality is equally "normal." (Breivik, 2083: A European Declaration of Independence)

The poet, playwright, and journalist Johann Dietrich Eckart (1868–1923) was one of the first ideological influences on Adolf Hitler. Hitler paid tribute to Eckart, the spiritual co-founder of Nazism, and described him as "a guiding light of the early National Socialist movement" (Volker, 2017). Together with Gottfried Feder (1883–1941) and Alfred Rosenberg (1893–1946), he edited a journal titled *Auf gut Deutsch* (In good German) while being a member of the German Workers' Party (DAP), founded by Anton Drexler (1884–1942) in 1919. Eckart later edited the Nazi official newspaper, *Völkischer Beobachter* (People's Observer), and is credited with writing the lyrics for the song "Germany Awake." Like many others who later became prominent figures in the Nazi party, such as the pilot ace and WWI hero, Hermann Göring, Eckart held contempt for the Treaty of Versailles, the formation of the despised Weimar Republic, and the rise of Marxism-Bolshevism. Alongside Hitler, Eckart took part in the disastrous Beer Hall Putsch of November 1923, resulting in imprisonment at Landsberg Fortress. However, his ill health led to his release in 1923, and he passed away shortly thereafter.

The rambling and nervous diatribes in Breivik's *Manifesto* echo a modern attempt to mimic Hitler's *Mein Kampf*, paralleling Johann Dietrich Eckart's tirades against Jesuits, Jewish people, and a distorted version of Christianity as Germany's adversaries – this echoes through Breivik's call to action: "Norway awake." The *Secret Conversations of Hitler*, also known as *Hitler's Table Talk*, is an assortment of unofficial conversations Adolf Hitler had with his inner circle from 1941 to 1944, revealing his thoughts on topics like religion, race, and politics. Members of his entourage, primarily Heinrich Heim, Martin Bormann, and Henry Picker, noted these talks, intended to remain private, providing insights into his personal beliefs and plans for Germany. However, inconsistencies between the original German texts and their translations have led to debates about the authenticity and truthfulness of these records.

The final entry of the *Secret Conversations*, dated November 29–30, 1944, marks a significant convergence of Judaism, Christianity, and Communism.

Hitler opens the conversation with a provocative statement: "Jesus was most certainly not a Jew." He elaborates on his theory, supported by alleged scholars, that Jesus was of Aryan ancestry, attributing his birth to Roman legionaries in Galilee. Hitler argues that Jesus condemned the materialism and greed of his time, thereby positioning him as a rabble-rouser against the Jewish establishment. Hitler further asserts that St. Paul engineered Christianity, which he likens to modern-day Communism, as a tool for challenging Jewish authority. Martin Bormann interjects with a condemnation of Jewish people as historical agitators, asserting the innate anti-Jewish stance of National Socialism. Hitler concludes with a reflection on the entangled relationship between Communism and Christianity, accenting their perceived threat to the Nazi regime.

> If the Society of Jesus was founded by a Jew and the rules of Society were based on "Jewish thinking" then it was a small mental leap for the Nazis to argue that Christianity, like Bolshevism, was a Jewish attempt to undermine the non-Jewish world, promote chaos and disorder, and seize control... By linking Jesuits, Jews, Catholics, and Bolsheviks together, Hitler attempted to forge one existential enemy for the German nation to fight. (Griech-Polelle, 2018, p. 53)

In the Breivik Manifesto, Muslims supplant the historical role of Jewish people as Europe's "favorite" scapegoats, yet we should not be beguiled by this temporary vicariousness. It is no different from offering a mere ceasefire or truce in the perpetual war of White supremacist ideology against its traditional targets. Breivik's progression into a self-styled Nazi figure, complete with the requisite salute and homage to Vidkun Quisling, reinforces this unnerving continuity with extremist ideologies of the past. What common thread held together figures like Hitler, a failed artist rejected by Vienna's Academy of Fine Arts; Joseph Goebbels, a PhD holder resentful of Jewish influence on his writing career; Heinrich Himmler, captivated by occultism and besotted with Norway for its apparent Aryan heritage; and Hermann Göring, a decorated (Blue Max/Pour le Mérite) World War I pilot and symbol of upper-class heroism? Beyond their unrelated backgrounds, their concord lay in the scapegoating of Jewish people, Marxists, and even followers of traditional Christianity. Similarly, Breivik and White supremacy are only as influential as their capacity to knit together a disparate array of "enemies" perceived as existential threats to the structure and dominance of whiteness.

We can usefully explore Breivik's narrative construction through Ernesto Laclau's (Laclau, 2005) chain of equivalence. Like a skilled weaver, Breivik stitches together a compelling quilt of disparate enemies – Muslims, feminists, cultural Marxists, and liberals – into a cohesive fabric of alleged threats to White supremacy. Laclau's theory illustrates how Breivik integrates these seemingly disparate elements into a chain of equivalence, where the shared element of posing a threat to the perceived hegemony of whiteness links each adversary. By framing these diverse adversaries as part of a unified front against traditional values and societal order, Breivik's narrative gains potency and resonance among those receptive to White supremacist ideologies.

> But the logic of that division is dictated, as we know, by the creation of an equivalential chain between a series of social demands in which the equivalential moment prevails over the differential nature of the demands. Finally, the equivalential chain cannot be the result of a purely fortuitous coincidence but has to be consolidated through the emergence of an element which gives coherence to the chain by signifying it as a totality. This element is what we have called empty signifier. (Laclau, 2005, pp. 43, 44)

Individuals such as Breivik and his White acolytes have been embittered by what is perceived as a deep humiliation or loss. They have all experienced their "Treaty of Versailles," so to speak: an abiding loss of face and honor with an accompanying thirst for revenge. For Hitler's inner cabal, it was the sight of French and Belgian troops marching into Germany and, most painfully, the demilitarization and loss of the Rhineland, perhaps the most iconic emblem of Germany's cultural, economic, and strategic sovereignty. On one occasion, Hermann Göring experienced physical assault, a fact he never forgot and actively sought redress for. Hell has no fury like whiteness scorned. Why do some White people, especially Anglo-Saxons, use their skin color as a weapon whenever they perceive a real or imagined loss of power and prestige? Let us not forget that during WWI, the Central Powers lost to the allies, who were all White except Japan. Just as the pigs in Orwell's *Animal Farm* declared they were more equal than other animals, Aryan whiteness claims undisputed preeminent whiteness among all White people. In some ways, Hitler's blitzkrieg was just that: a painful reminder to his fellow White people that Aryan whiteness is whiter than all others. Two years later, while German troops were advancing deep into the Soviet Union, Hitler would proclaim that the border between Europe and Asia ran between the Germanic and Slavic peoples. The issue was to "place it where we wish."

> He and Goebbels routinely referred to Russians as "beasts" and "animals". The Germans also drew upon tradition. Images of inferior and hostile Slavs – above all Russians and Poles – had been nurtured in certain quarters for centuries and served as justification for aggressive designs upon the East.... Max Weber had argued that only a "systematic colonization of German peasants on German soil" could hold back the "Slavic flood". (Connelly, 1999, pp. 14, 23)

For Breivik and his ilk, White Europe has been so infected by what they perceive as the "mongrelizing" impact of the virus of the secular left, that mainstream whiteness no longer has the wherewithal to jettison and repel the "chain of equivalences" of Muslims, feminists, gays, and cultural Marxists. It is for this reason that Breivik concocted the ultimate, White "Messianic" figure of the crusading Teutonic knights and held so religiously to a contemporary existence of this order that he held obstinately to the claim that he was a member of the knights Templar and even claimed to attend their meeting in London in 2002. There are 46 references in his *Manifesto* to Charles Martel, whom he credits with halting the advance of Muslims into Europe at the Battle of Tours (732 AD). Breivik's admiration for Charles Martel is so great that he proposes using Norway's oil fund to establish a fund honoring his memory and those he perceives as anti-Muslim crusaders.

> This fund could be called the Theo van Gogh Memorial Fund, the Asma bint Marwan Memorial Fund after the poetess who was killed by Muhammad's followers 1400 years ago for mocking Islam, or perhaps the Charles Martel Foundation for Intercultural Understanding. (Breivik, Manifesto, 2011)

Hitler's distortion of Judaism, Christianity, and Communism as intertwined threats resonates with Breivik's demonization of Islam in his *Manifesto*. Both Hitler and Breivik concoct narratives that misrepresent these religions or ideologies as existential dangers to their respective notions of a White utopian society. Hitler's rhetoric against Jewish people as agitators and fomenters of rebellion finds a modern-day equivalent in Breivik's portrayal of Muslims as intruders and cultural usurpers. While Hitler's exchanges principally focus on religious and political ideologies, his misogynistic opinions are evident in his broader worldview, which delegates women to a subservient role. Similarly, Breivik's manifesto contains misogynistic sentiments, viewing feminism as a threat to conventional gender roles and societal stability. Both Hitler and Breivik perceive the empowerment of women as a destabilizing force, undermining their visions of hierarchical order. Consider the following excerpt:

> Most Europeans look back on the 1950s as a good time. Our homes were safe, to the point where many people did not bother to lock their doors. Public schools were generally excellent, and their problems were things like talking in class and running in the halls. Most men treated women like ladies, and most ladies devoted their time and effort to making good homes, rearing their children well and helping their communities through volunteer work. Children grew up in two-parent households, and the mother was there to meet the child when he came home from school. Entertainment was something the whole family could enjoy. (Breivik, Manifesto, 2011)

This rose-tinted view of Breivik disregards not only the suffering and trauma inflicted by Breivik's violence but also is a perverse attempt at sanitizing the past of a pervasive racism in Norway under which the Sami people, Jewish people, Romani people, and Tartar (Tatar) people, among others, suffered. As previously mentioned in Chapter 1, the Norwegian historians Brochmann and Kjeldstadli (2008, p. 94) state that Norwegians, much like many Westerners in the 19th century, held beliefs in racial superiority toward other ethnic groups. This racism, based on notions of classical biological hierarchies, rooted in notions of the superiority of the "Germanic," "Nordic," or "Norwegian race," subjected minorities in Norway to considerable hardships. The Sami people were disparaged as "biologically degenerate" and judged incapable of advancement in the face of civilization, while the Kven people were derogatorily classified as Mongols, stamped with traits of "brutality" and "sentimentality." Furthermore, there were intensive efforts to assimilate or dissolve the Romani people as a distinct ethnic group (Brochmann & Kjeldstadli, 2008, p. 94).

In Breivik's excerpt, there are echoes of Donald Trump's "Make America Great Again" slogan (The Hill, 2024), predating Trump's rise and decision to run for president in the United States in 2015. Once again, the attempt to evoke nostalgia for a past era of American greatness, portrayed as a time of economic prosperity and social stability, is a chimera. This narrative conveniently sidesteps the systemic racism and discrimination that non-White communities (and many White people), particularly African Americans, faced during that period – a time when Black people could not vote, and Jim Crow laws consigned them to separate Negro establishments – and highlights the stark contrast between the embellished image of the past and the exacting realities experienced by marginalized groups. For White supremacists, though, unencumbered by the truth, the aphorism "never let the truth get in the way of a good story" is pertinent.

Although not overtly addressed in Hitler's "Secret Conversations," his regime's harassment and persecution of LGBTQ+ individuals reflect a broader bigotry toward sexual and gender diversity. Breivik's manifesto contains homophobic language, portraying LGBTQ+ rights as part of a wider cultural Marxist program with a view toward undermining traditional values. Both Hitler and Breivik view LGBTQ+ individuals as menaces to their respective visions of social order and purity. In *Mein Kampf*, Hitler, in his typically rambling fashion, reviews the outcome of WWI, the Battle of Jutland, or Skagerrak, the role of General Ludendorff, and pays tribute to the German army for, among other things, countering the spread of effeminacy among young men.

> The army trained what at that time was most surely needed: namely, real men. In a period when men were falling a prey to effeminacy and laxity, 350,000 vigorously trained young men went from the ranks of the army each year to mingle with their fellowmen. In the course of their two years' training, they had lost the softness of their young days and had developed bodies as tough as steel. The young man who had been taught obedience for two years was now fitted to command. The trained soldier could be recognized already by his walk. (Hitler, 1939, p. 219)

According to scholars, the Nazi regime's persecution of gay men resulted in approximately 100,000 arrests under Paragraph 175, of which approximately

53,400 led to convictions (United States Holocaust Memorial Museum, 2023). Between 1937 and 1938, the SS began a process of marking prisoners in concentration camps, using color-coded badges sewn onto uniforms to detect the reason for an individual's imprisonment. A chart of prisoner markings from Dachau concentration camp explains this system. The concentration camps incarcerated a subset of prisoners, totaling between 5,000 and 15,000, as "homosexual" offenders. In order to delineate this group's particular "offence," not just gay men, but any man who had engaged in sexual relations with another man, was required to wear a pink triangle on their uniforms – the pink was intended to visualize their "perversion" and justify their separation within the camp system. Survivor accounts indicate that pink triangle prisoners faced severe abuse, both physical and sexual, from camp guards and fellow inmates. Pink triangle prisoners often received the most severe labor tasks and underwent inhumane medical experiments, including forced castration. Buchenwald concentration camp, for example, was infamous for subjecting pink triangle prisoners to such atrocities.

As previously alluded to, White supremacy brooks no opposition to such forces deemed subversive to its unchallenged reign. In his book *Here Comes Everybody: The Power of Organizing with Organizations* (2008), Clay Shirky writes about the revolutionary impact the internet is having on social relations and the empowerment of traditionally marginalized groups. In 2005, an individual named Galen McAllister from Ireland set out to explore the influence of online communities. He anonymously placed an ad on Craigslist, offering free moving services. His alleged motive? Having recently come out as gay, he aimed to convey gratitude to the LGBTQ+ community for their backing. Remarkably, within mere hours, his inbox flooded with responses from individuals keen to lend a hand – strangers united solely by their desire to aid a fellow community member. While the internet has also been implicated in the loss of individual freedom, undermining democracy, exacerbating wealth inequality, undermining attention span, and other serious issues, it has also served to burst the banks of aspects of traditional White male supremacy. It is fruitful to analyze Breivik and other White supremacists in light of the internet-induced shrinking of White space. Rather than share [cyber] space with the "everybody" Shirky (2008) writes about, White supremacists like Breivik in time-honored fashion would prefer to monopolize space, be it physical or digital. We see this "digital lebensraum" in the meticulous planning executed by Breivik wherein he planted not a material bomb outside the government offices, but a "digital" one, in the form of the 1,518-page Manifesto, written in the foremost language of the internet, English. For days on end, national and international media anxiously logged on in search of the Manifesto of Hatred.

Theodor W. Adorno and Max Horkheimer, who are mentioned with some venom 20 times and 9 times, respectively, in Brevik's (2011) *Manifesto* as examples of "subversive" cultural Marxists, write in their *Elements of Anti-Semitism*:

> The portrait of the Jews that the nationalists offer to the world is in fact their own self-portrait. They long for total possession and unlimited power, at any price. They transfer their guilt for this to

the Jews, whom, as masters, they despise and crucify, repeating ad infinitum a sacrifice which they cannot believe to be effective. (Adorno & Horkheimer, 2022, p. 370)

This, in a nutshell, is the essence of White supremacy. Elijah Anderson (2022, p. 320) writes about the "White space" as one where "Black people are either absent, not expected, or marginalized when present." Anderson specifically observes that changes in demographics affect public spaces, influencing not only the occupants and conception of the space but also its occupation (Anderson, 2022, p. 320).

It is precisely the changing demographics in traditional bastions of White spaces, such as Norway's capital city Oslo, that upsets White supremacists. Breivik's whiteness has not consented to this "browning" and "blackening" of White space. Hijabs, beards, and mosques, which epitomize Black and brown bodies as the architecture of Islam, represent an affront to the White line of vision – a blemish that requires eradication. We must also view populist politicians' attacks on halal branding in this context. The former leader of the right-wing Progress Party, Siv Jensen, famously constructed the neologism *snikislamisering* [covert Islamization] (Thomas & Selimovic, 2015) to refer to what she perceived as a conspiracy to smuggle in Islam and subvert traditional Norwegian values. Halal branding is one such cog in the machine of "covert Islamization," according to populists (with a good deal of support from many in the mainstream). In 2009, Siv Jensen's first deployment of the neologism caused such a furor that even the flagship Scandinavian airlines (SAS) had to assure the public that they were not serving halal food for everyone. "SAS refutes the notion of substituting meatballs, ham, and liver paste with halal food on its flights. SAS reflects the Scandinavian, also in the food," states the company (NrK, 2010). The hysteria surrounding the invented and exaggerated "menus" spread to Denmark too where the Prime Minister Thorning-Schmidt lent some gravitas to the "war against the terror of halal food":

> The Prime Minister, Helle Thorning-Schmidt joins the so-called "frikadelle-war" and says resolutely no to removing pork meat from the menu in public institutions. "One should not slowly sneak them (bacon roast and frikadeller) out of our public institutions because one should accommodate another culture"... "Frikadeller" are flat, pan-fried Danish meatballs made out of minced pork meat. (Thomas & Selimovic, 2015)

Whiteness cannot tolerate the sight of "brown food," "brown clothes" and a "brown way of life" that appear to threaten to encroach and sully the very "throne," the inner sanctum of whiteness – places like the flagship airline carrier SAS. Whiteness can create a storm in a teacup because, to their minds, and reminiscent of the butterfly or chaos effect where a butterfly flapping its wings could potentially cause a typhoon, halal food, hijabs, and gender-segregated swimming pools have the potential to create the "Norwegian Caliphate" in the not-too-distant future. The only Black and brown people palatable to whiteness are those who repeatedly distance themselves from their blackness and brownness and pay homage to the values embodied in Nordic exceptionalism.

It is difficult not to read the zeitgeist inherent in the writings of White supremacists as nothing but the loss of White power and prestige (Versailles Treaty syndrome) in a society becoming more globalized. Breivik strives to preserve what remains viable. To his mind, the cultural Marxists, who never cease to fight the "good old" fascists, have weakened and diluted the "Aryan, Martian spirit." Friedrich Nietzsche's criticism of Christianity's effect on Germany emanates from his belief that it expounded a "slave morality" characterized by docility and self-abnegation, which, in his view, weakened the spirit and morale of the German people. Nietzsche compared this with his concept of "master morality," which lionized strength, assertiveness, and individual excellence. He contended that Christianity's emphasis on otherworldly salvation and moral codes was a derivative of Judeo-Christian traditions, muted the natural instincts and drives of individuals, hindering their "will to power" – the inborn desire to assert oneself and seize power. Nietzsche envisioned the "Übermensch" or "overman" as the romanticized individual who surpasses conventional morality to generate their own values and live authentically according to their inner drives and instincts.

> Slave morality, for him, is the morality for the weak. It is a place of solace for the lazy ones. In slave morality, silly ideas like equality and generosity are promulgated. This form of morality urges "virtues" like humility and pity. By so doing, it encourages people to live inauthentic life and deny obvious facts of nature. It makes a virtue out of weakness and cowardice. Thus, it prevents the strong-willed from reaching their full potentialities. Other qualities valued in slave morality include kindness, love and generosity. Nietzsche championed as master morality, the morality of the strong-willed. For the strong willed, anything considered noble, strong or powerful is good. The essence of master morality is nobility. (Ezema et al., 2017)

Ultimately, whiteness finds itself gravitating toward "master morality," its kindred ideology. One could argue that since its inception, or self-consciousness, whiteness has never really implemented the teachings of Christ as described by Nietzsche. When did White Christianity turn the other cheek, or truly love its enemy? Even in more recent times, "Martin Luther King described 11 o'clock on Sunday morning as 'one of the most segregated hours. . . in Christian America'" (Kuruvilla, 2021). It is because the White supremacist ideology of the ilk of Breivik felt a sense of perceived "powerlessness" at the proliferation of Islam in Norway and Europe that it initially recruited a syncretic blend of forces from Europe's past and sought to deploy these forces as a talisman to ward off the "old" foe Islam. The syncretic blend included elements such as medieval knights, European nationalism, cultural conservatism, Eurabia theory, anti-Marxism, anti-Globalism, and Christianity.

The syncretic brew did not last long, however, and Breivik overtly embraced Nazi ideology. "If you look at Breivik's development, you can see that he had already moved in the direction of Nazism during the trial in 2012" (NrK, 2015). The report goes on to state:

> In a four-page letter from November 2014, Breivik announced that he had converted to National Socialism on Quisling's birthday. In the letter, he praises Quisling, and believes he is a role model who loved us all. He also writes that fascism will prevail in Northern Europe, and that all previous statements he has made, which are not in line with the National Socialist doctrine, are no longer valid. (NrK, 2015)

I argue that this so-called "conversion" reveals the superficial and contrived nature of the beliefs held by Breivik and other disaffected White men. As they struggle to navigate in a diversifying, "browning" Europe, they attempt to revitalize bygone specters to combat what they see as Europe's new existential threat, Islam, following the historical denigration of Jewish people. A slew of enemies, "Trojan horses," are identified as the cause of the West's perceived impotence against the proliferation of Islam. For instance, Breivik mentions the Eurabia theory 171 times in his manifesto. The Eurabia theory has become a notorious conspiracy theory that claims Europe is being intentionally transformed into a territory called "Eurabia," where Islamic adherents and culture will ultimately dominate. Disseminated by British author Bat Ye'or in her 2005 book "Eurabia: The Euro-Arab Axis," the theory suggests that European policies favoring immigration and multiculturalism, combined with high birth rates among Muslim immigrants and purported secret pacts with Arab nations, are enabling this transformation. Critics dismiss the theory as Islamophobic and xenophobic, devoid of empirical support, and argue that it oversimplifies complex sociopolitical issues, stoking anti-Muslim and anti-immigrant sentiments across the continent.

Given the complexity of this "witches brew" of disparate ideologies and conspiracy theories, it is not surprising that only a few fringe elements on the right joined Breivik's cause, much to his dismay. Norway and the Nordic countries are predominantly secular, so an appeal to Christianity is as effective as navigating a maze with a blindfold. Breivik personifies a new wave of young, White males of European lineage, including "Caucasians" in the United States, who find themselves at a loss as they witness a regression in the privileges accruing from their whiteness. In response, they delve into history to salvage and wield a narrative that matches the faith and ardor they perceive in a new generation of Muslims. They perceive these Muslims as steadily overtaking Europe due to their higher birth rates, generous welfare benefits, and what they perceive as subversive values propagated by the left. However, the turn toward pure Nazism ultimately exposes the emptiness of the earlier "witches brew," highlighting its inherent flaws.

2. "Invisible Knapsack": White Privilege's Deadly Legacy

> In PST [Norwegian Police Security], work is now being done to find out how he [Breivik] could slip "under the radar", as it is expressed... PST is prepared that questions will be asked about this and that criticism may come, but will not say anything for the time being... Breivik posted 75 posts on the website document.no in which he expressed strong nationalist, far-right, and anti-Muslim attitudes. Gro Harlem Brundtland [former Prime Minister, Labor Party] is referred to, among other things, as "landsmo(r)der" [not "mother of the nation" but "murderer of the nation"]. (VG, 2011)

PST (Politiets Sikkerhetstjeneste/Norwegian Police Security) is the agency in charge of maintaining Norway's homeland security. Incredibly, neither PST nor any other government agency monitoring activities considered detrimental to national security picked up Breivik on their radars. In the aftermath of the killing spree, another media broadcaster expressed incredulity at the fact that Breivik meticulously planned and executed his heinous crime for 9 years. "Anders Behring Breivik (32) has been preparing the mass murders in Oslo and on Utøya for over nine years, according to the *Manifesto* he has posted on the Internet" (NrK, 2011). For about 11 months, Breivik had been renting a farm in Åsta near Rena in Åmot, believed to be the site where he constructed the bomb later detonated in Oslo. Despite neighbors' increasing suspicions, including peculiar conduct and unfamiliarity with farming chores, such as mowing grass, Breivik remained hidden. Even encounters with locals, in which he covered windows and locked doors, failed to raise alarms. Svein Meldieseth, one of Breivik's neighbors, considered warning the authorities due to the peculiarities he observed, such as Breivik's displeasure when the neighbor made a call on him unannounced.

In addition, the farm's previous owner, Per Rønningen, also registered uncharacteristic activity, including someone removing advertising from a van on the property. I will argue that these incidents – Breivik's clandestine preparations, secret demeanor, and unfamiliarity with farming practices, all while evading suspicion – are telling of the advantages conferred by White privilege. This phenomenon allows individuals like Breivik to operate unnoticed, benefiting from societal assumptions that provide a buffer from scrutiny. In light of Peggy McIntosh's "invisible knapsack" hypothesis, the incidents revolving around Breivik's actions on the farm, as well as Per Rønningen's observations, emphasize the concept of White privilege. Breivik's ability to engage in covert preparations for 9 years, maintain a guarded demeanor, and display unfamiliarity with farming practices without provoking suspicion aligns with the notion of White privilege as an invisible advantage. Just as McIntosh describes White privilege as an "invisible knapsack" of undeserved advantages that White individuals carry by virtue of being White, Breivik's actions illustrate how societal assumptions provide a defensive shield, allowing him to operate without facing the same level of scrutiny or suspicion as individuals from minoritized groups. McIntosh defines the term as follows:

> I have come to see white privilege as an invisible package of unearned assets that I can count on cashing in each day, but about which I was "meant" to remain oblivious. White privilege is like an invisible, weightless knapsack of special provisions, maps, passports, codebooks, visas, clothes, tools, and blank checks. (McIntosh, 1989)

Consider some of the items in McIntosh's (1989) knapsack that are relevant to what we have read about Breivik's ability to rent the farm and his interactions with his neighbors on the farm:

- If I should need to move, I can be pretty sure of renting or purchasing housing in an area that I can afford and in which I would want to live.
- I can be pretty sure that my neighbors in such a location will be neutral or pleasant to me.
- I can swear, or dress in second-hand clothes, or not answer letters, without having people attribute these choices to the bad morals, the poverty, or the illiteracy of my race.

Breivik's purchase of approximately 500 kilograms of fertilizer for the bomb that detonated in the government headquarters adds to the previously mentioned list of unusual actions. When queried about Breivik's ability to get away with ordering such a large amount, one retailer stated that purchasing 200–300-kilogram sacks from *Felleskjøpet* is normal (Aftenposten, 2011). Felleskjøpet is a cooperative organization in Norway that provides agricultural supplies and services to farmers. Moreover, it emerged that Breivik established a company named Geofram 3 years earlier, intending to grow vegetables, roots, and tuber crops. Svein Meldieseth, the previously mentioned neighbor, confirms on record that he observed Breivik leaving much of his fertilizers unused. McIntosh (1989), in her reflexive soul-searching account, confesses to seeing the contours of a pattern emerging through the matrix of White privilege, a pattern that she, as a White person, has inherited.

> There was one main piece of cultural turf; it was my own turf, and I was among those who could control the turf. My skin color was an asset for any move I was educated to want to make. I could think of myself as belonging in major ways and of making social systems work for me. (McIntosh, 1989)

It is important to mitigate the above with the counterargument that the Nordic countries are characterized by some of the highest levels of trust in government. For instance, an OECD study places Norway (63.6%) as the country with the fifth highest levels of trust in its government, beaten only by Sweden (68.8%), Finland (77.5%), Luxembourg (78%), and Switzerland (83.8%), respectively (OECD, 2021). There is also the caveat that these figures for Norway may have undergone some strain in the last couple of years, given the steady stream of high-profile resignations of cabinet ministers for various kinds of infractions. According to the above, some would argue that Breivik was able to go under the radar precisely because of this culture of trust. I argue, commensurate with Stanfield (1985, p. 3), that what would be missing in such an assertion, championed by the White majority, is the failure to examine the "least understood inequality in social science issues... the production of racial inequality in the social scientific method." One would make the same blunder as the otherwise brilliant Alexis de Tocqueville, of whom Magubane (2022) writes:

> The formulation Tocqueville came up with in 1835, which allowed him to celebrate American democracy in the midst of American slavery, still holds conceptual, if not political, weight. Tocqueville described the Negro as "collaterally connected with my subject without forming a part of it". The segregation of race as a "topic" within sociology leaves little room for discussion of how race has structured and continues to structure the sociological enterprise. (Magubane, 2022, p. 100)

To circumvent the issue of White privilege concerning Breivik's ability to operate undetected for 9 years would be to omit a crucial aspect of the case from sociological, legal, and ethical perspectives. I argue that White privilege, a systemic advantage conferred upon White individuals due to their race, played a role in Breivik's actions and the response to them. From a sociological standpoint, White privilege perpetuates societal norms and assumptions that allow White individuals greater trust and independence, allowing Breivik to duck suspicion and scrutiny despite his worrying behavior. Social structures and biases deeply embed this phenomenon, affecting interactions and perceptions in subtle yet substantial ways. Consider the immediate attacks on several Black and brown individuals following the Breivik attacks. Their only crime was the color of their skin.

> On the online community Twitter, there have been many reports tonight that Muslims are being harassed on the open street in Oslo. Norwegian-Somali Kadra Yusuf writes, among other things, that a Pakistani boy is said to have been dragged out of a bus, and then beaten up. (Zondag, NrK, 2011)

Several such stories flooded the media before Breivik's blond-haired image silenced an entire nation. The author knows an Iranian cab driver who had to flee for his life after parking his cab and seeing a group of Norwegian youth mentioning the terror attacks and running toward him while hurling racial abuse. Black and brown individuals who have resided in majority White societies for any significant period profoundly feel the direct connection between skin color, bias, and perceived levels of danger at any given moment. Instances like the Breivik attacks underscore the gravity of this reality, which can mean the difference between life and death. Conversely, the benefits of their pigmentation often go unspoken for White individuals, a privilege they enjoy almost guiltily and discreetly, but never openly acknowledge or, worse, verbalize. From a legal standpoint, the consequences of White privilege in Breivik's case raise questions about equality before the law and the fairness of legal systems. In his travels in Europe, James Baldwin touches upon the reason why Europeans appear to be oblivious to the "burning question" of the humanity of Black people while the Americans have been unable to avoid it.

> This argument is the source of the venomous epithet Nigger! It is an argument which Europe has never had, and hence Europe quite sincerely fails to understand how or why the argument arose in the first place, why its effects are so frequently disastrous and always so unpredictable, and why it refuses until today to be entirely settled. Europe's black possessions remained – and still do remain – in Europe's colonies, at which point they represented no threat whatsoever to European identity. (Baldwin, 2017, p. 174)

Europe's "Niggers," to borrow from Baldwin, were in the main in the colonies and hence out of sight. News about European dealings with the "natives" in the heyday of empire was filtered through the lens of White colonial interests, one which molded a docile, "happy," and civilized "Nigger" thanks to the European civilizing mission in Kipling's *The White Man's Burden*. The "Niggers" were not on European soil, as they were in the United States, and hence "invisible." If a case can be made for the physical presence of Black people on *terra Europaea* sensitizing Europeans to the machinations of whiteness, then it would follow that Europe is barely literate in this increasingly crucial education. For instance, the British historian David Olusoga catalogs this history of how Britain neglected the presence, albeit few, and contribution of Black people while exaggerating fears of being "swamped" by Black and brown people who came with the *HMS Empire Windrush* ship and colonies in India and Africa, among others after the Second World War.

Once the *HMS Empire Windrush*, carrying West Indian immigrants to the United Kingdom, reached Tilbury, London, 11 Labour MPs penned a letter to the Prime Minister Clement Attlee (1945–1951) stating: "An influx of colored people domiciled here is likely to impair the harmony, strength, and cohesion of our people and social life and cause discord and unhappiness among all concerned" (Olusoga, 2021, p. 495). Winston Churchill is a venerated figure in Norway. Among others, he provided military support, diplomatic backing, and assistance to the Norwegian government-in-exile during World War II, strengthening Norwegian resistance efforts against the Nazi occupation. His leadership contributed to the subsequent liberation of Norway from German control in 1945. Churchill's magnanimity, however, did not extend to people of color.

In 1954, during lunch at Chequers with the governor of Jamaica, Sir Hugh Foot, Churchill expressed his concern that if West Indian migration continued, "we would have a magpie society: that would never do". A year later, Harold Macmillan reported in his diary, with some incredulity, that Churchill thought "Keep Britain White" might make an appropriate slogan with which to fight the upcoming election. (Olusoga, 2021, p. 499)

Anders Breivik's case highlights how his whiteness and the lack of critical inquiry into White identity and privilege in Norwegian society may have been instrumental to his ability to go undetected for years before his attacks. Breivik, being White, may have been able to manipulate societal blind spots regarding White fanaticism and violence, profiting from the prevalent notion that White individuals are less likely to commit acts of terrorism or violence. White individuals like Breivik, able to operate without exposure or interference, highlight discrepancies in the administration of justice and underscore the need for a more impartial legal framework.

Furthermore, studying Breivik's case through the prism of White privilege triggers critical reflection on the intersection of race, power, and accountability within legal institutions. Ethically, the implications of White privilege in Breivik's case induce us to confront issues of responsibility, accountability, and social justice. White privilege not only spared Breivik from suspicion but also abetted his actions to escalate unbridled, resulting in devastating consequences. In this context, addressing White privilege necessitates a dedication to scrutinizing and eliminating systemic inequalities, while striving for a more inclusive and just society that holds all individuals, irrespective of race, accountable for their actions. Ultimately, acknowledging and addressing White privilege in Breivik's case is essential for fostering greater awareness, accountability, and social change. While one cannot state categorically with iron-clad certainty that every instance of oversight in regard to Breivik's meticulous planning and execution of the devastating attacks can be pinned down to White privilege, and this is not the argument I am making, one cannot entirely dismiss a series of clear-cut incidents and observed behaviors which should have raised the alarm without also considering the role of White privilege. Breivik parked a huge white van a few meters outside the government building entrance. This was the very same van that a neighbor spotted Breivik scraping the advertisement from. Upon arriving at Utøya, Breivik was transported across the water in the Labor Party youth's own ferry. Despite Breivik donning a false police uniform and acquiring a forged ID, concerns arise regarding the lack of thoroughgoing investigation, especially considering the news of the Oslo bombing, which Breivik himself mentioned prior to being ferried.

At 17.17, Anders Behring Breivik disembarks on Utøya. After detonating a bomb in the center of Oslo, he has driven to Tyrifjorden. There he gets a ride on AUF's own ferry MS Thorbjørn to Utøya. Breivik says that he is from the Police

Security Service (PST), and that he will carry out a routine security check on the island after the explosion in Oslo. He is dressed in a fake police uniform, and around his neck he has a fake service certificate which he shows to the guard. (Faktisk, 2021)

The advantage of whiteness transmogrified into a liability in the case of Breivik on the July 22, 2011. With all due respect to the memories of the victims and bereaved, the explosion, killings, and "shock and awe" that followed could also be read as a call to "see" and interrogate whiteness' potential to provide a camouflage conducive to nefarious purposes. Progeny cannot afford to continue with the current discourse about the ilk of Timothy McVeigh, Anders Breivik, Philip Manshaus, and Brenton Tarrant, among others, being "lone wolves" – young men who were unsuccessful and harbored grievances against society. Centuries of secreting values of innocence, purity, goodness, and trustworthiness into white pigmentation failed to detect the murderous designs of Breivik as his "White Norwegianness," reinforced by a police uniform, elevated his whiteness credentials to the level of infallibility. Like a Pope, he could now act and speak ex cathedra.

I would argue that every person of color who witnessed the events of July 22, 2011 in Norway is tacitly aware and has reflected on the relevance of whiteness to the trauma that unfolded. In his autobiography *Familiar Stranger: A life Between Two Islands* (2017), Stuart Hall, the influential cultural theorist and sociologist, writes that it was in Britain that he became Jamaican. "England seemed simultaneously familiar and strange, homely and unhomely, domesticated but at the same time a thoroughly dangerous place for the likes of me. I knew a lot about it; and yet I didn't really know it" (Hall, 2017a, 2017b, p. 204). Hall captures the precarious sense of belonging inherent in Norway's ontology of existing as a visible minority. What use is the possession of an immaculate cultural habitus and skills of integration, to borrow from Pierre Bourdieu, when one's skin color is all it takes for one murderous Joe Erling Jahr or a Philip Manshaus to kill us? People of color implicitly understand, whatever else well-meaning mainstream society tells them, that the comfort and assurance that comes from whiteness will never be ours. Hall (2017b) captures this self-confidence well:

"Being English" had everything to do with this deep structure of national cultural identity, and "imagined community", in Benedict Anderson's phrase; based not only on a set of institutions, but on a "lived imaginary relation to its real conditions of existence", as Althusser has it: a fantasy of the nation, as well a gift of the gods, a state of grace. (p. 206)

The "imagined community" of Benedict Anderson, "the gift of the gods," and the "state of grace" are sadly imagined in terms of whiteness alone in Norway. These terms sound exciting and tantalizing to the Black and brown ear starved off belonging to the "imagined community," but they are, sadly, a chimera. There are hints of change on the horizon, but it will be some time before a paradigm shift occurs, before there is some "Black in the Norwegian Flag [Union Jack]" to "Norwegianize" *Paul Gilroy's book There Ain't No Black in the Union Jack* (2013). We must emphasize that whiteness is not a fixed phenomenon. Socialization imbibed the characteristics associated with whiteness, not inscribed in one's skin at birth. White supremacist convictions, like race, are floating signifiers (Hall, 2017a, 2017b). The reason we must analyze whiteness is because, by so doing, we hope to confront and dismantle it. Depicting whiteness as embodying esoteric or otherworldly attributes and placing it outside the province of understanding is counterproductive. This only serves to compound and elevate the phenomenon to an "untouchable" status, fostering an inert and fatalistic mindset suggestive of the rigid caste system described in the Code of Manu. As Linda Alcoff notes in her book *The Future of Whiteness* (2015):

> As a social category of identity, then, whiteness continues to have explanatory value, to inform our hermeneutic horizons and ways of being in the world, and to be a part of our collective material culture. Eliminating the term, or even the self-ascription, does not eliminate the thing, no matter how complex and changeable that thing is. (Alcoff, 2015, p. 145)

The reality, however unpalatable for some White people, is that we are, for the first time in centuries, witnessing the rise of the "rest," i.e., the non-White peoples of the world, in a way not seen before. Small Nordic countries have witnessed a "browning" of cultural imports branded "made in America" with a corollary of changes in the Norwegian cultural landscape: hip-hop and rap music; Black culture piggybacking on basketball; Hollywood movies with an array of Black stars, for example, Marvel's *Black Panther*; and perhaps the most unprecedented of all, the election of the first Black US president, Barack Obama. In a survey that questioned a total of about 7,500 people in Britain, Germany, France, Denmark, Sweden, Finland, and Norway in 2012, "more than 90% would have voted for President Barack Obama if they were able to cast ballots in the United States' election" (Schwartzstein, 2012). While Obama received the Nobel Peace Prize in Oslo with much aplomb, Breivik nursed his hatred of the multiculturalism Obama represented and worked away stealthily on his bomb and meticulous killing spree. Breivik was watching these events with disdain. Consider two references to Obama in Breivik's (2011) manifesto:

> Barak Obama received the Nobel Peace Prize for exactly the same reason Al Gore did.

> The prize is given by Thorbjørn Jagland, Chair of the Nobel Committee, who was also the Vice President of Socialist International. One can think they are pushing a global agenda of Enviro-Communism or Eco-Marxism that will force Europe and the US to cater for the global Eco-Marxist agenda. Their end

goal is to "punish" European countries (US included) for capitalism and success.

Less than eight years after the Jihadist attacks on the USA, a President raised as a Muslim with the middle name "Hussein" hails Islam's great contributions to American and Western culture. The USA currently looks more like a defeated nation than the world's sole remaining superpower. It's the only nation in history where the majority of the population has elected a member of an organization known for hating the majority population of that country.

The reason I labor the need to broach the Breivik phenomenon through the lens of whiteness, however uncomfortable and taboo (especially in Norway) it may be, is because with the "rise of the rest," whiteness will come under more scrutiny and struggle with its hitherto taken-for-granted position at the apex of a White-imposed hierarchy. As the British journalist and author Yasmin Alibhai-Brown argues, "The good news is that we may be coming to the end of this long period of settled racial omnipotence. The bad news is that a cataclysmic culture war has only just begun" (Bhopal, 2018a, 2018b, p. xiv). As educators dedicated to speaking truth to power and inspired by Paulo Freire's pedagogy of love, hope, and empowerment – both for the oppressor and oppressed – it is our responsibility to engage fervently and midwife a transition truly resonating with Dr. King's dream where no one will be judged by the color of their skin but by the content of their character. Left unchecked and permitted to "roam freely" as Breivik's whiteness did, White supremacist leanings can warp into something even more sinister. Consider the following:

He says that Breivik's previous explanation about exactly this came as a surprise to him. Pracon then tells how he perceived the defendant's words in court: That he looked right-wing – and not like a Marxist – and that Breivik recognized himself in the 21-year-old standing out in the water. "I will not allow it to affect me that he sees something so cruel in me, I don't want to even touch that. That is something I do not stand for", says Pracon. (Abcnyheter, 2012)

Breivik spared the life of Adrian Pracon because he stated that Pracon looked "right-wing." Drunk on its own omnipotent and omniscient ability to arbitrate on the right or wrong "ideological look," whiteness transmogrifies into an increasingly capricious and unpredictable beast. Whiteness alone is no longer sufficient; only "right-wing" whiteness can truly exist and flourish. The eminent scholar of racism, George M. Fredrickson (2002), stated that "racism exists when one ethnic group or historical collectivity dominates, excludes, or seeks to eliminate another on the basis of differences that it believes are hereditary and unalterable" (Fredrickson, 2002, p. 170). Breivik divided White people into two irreconcilable camps: those who looked Marxist and those who looked right-wing. Apparently, only Breivik was able to adjudicate on the difference as the judge, jury, and executioner. Breivik believed that it was necessary to intimidate liberal White people into remembering the supremacy of whiteness. It was these "silly," "bohemian" White people who were a "mortal danger" to whiteness to his mind, and as the self-appointed custodian of the "correct hue of whiteness," he deemed only right-wing White people deserving of life. Clearly, there comes a point when whiteness must go to war against its own kind, its own kith and kin, in order to ensure its viability and continuity. For Breivik and many of his fellow-ideologues worldwide, the cut-off point is when other White people are willing to "die to whiteness" or "commit treason against whiteness," in the words of Noel Ignatiev (Ignatiev, 2022). This is the unpardonable sin of White supremacists. Harris's (1995) "whiteness as property" and Andrew Hacker's (2010) study serve as reminders:

> The study asked a group of white students how much money they would seek if they changed from white to black. Most seemed to feel that it would not be out of place to ask for $50 million, or $1 million for each coming black year. (in Harris, 1995, p. 286)

Indeed, history has shown that beleaguered whiteness is extremely volatile. Yasmin Alibhai-Brown puts the zeitgeist of fear in stark perspective:

> White people, from the most to the least powerful, feel beleaguered. The ground beneath their feet trembles. India and China are becoming stupendously productive and assertive... Within Western nations, indigenous citizens feel demographically endangered as their numbers fall while immigrants with high birth rates "take over". These are primeval fears of survival, not in the usual sense of life over death, but the hitherto unconquerable might and right of whiteness. That currency is now devalued and causing much disorientation. (Bhopal, 2018, p. xiv)

For Breivik, whiteness cannot be monetized nor can be it distributed or apportioned to nonwhites, making him neither a capitalist not a socialist in this sense. Whiteness is sacrosanct as the preeminent boundary marker of White identity of which Breivik was the avenging angel. Breivik's claim of acting out of love for his people is undermined by the atrocious nature of his deeds, revealing a perverted reading of racial fidelity. This paradox exposes the hollow rhetoric often employed by extremists to justify their repulsive actions under the guise of racial preservation. In the antebellum South, Yankees were viewed as a stain on whiteness, while Hitler believed the rest of the West failed to comprehend the perceived danger posed by Jewish people, Bolsheviks, and other adversaries to Aryan whiteness. It is such perversions that led whiteness scholar David R. Roediger to claim that whiteness is a "nothing but oppressive and false" and that whiteness is a destructive ideology" (Roediger, 1994, pp. 13, 3).

3. Breivik's Islamophobia: Whiteness Reimagined

> The NCAAP and CORE have a right to do what they think, but I'm
> not going to be killed trying to force myself on people who don't want
> me. I like my life. Integration is wrong. The black man that's trying to
> integrate, he's getting beat up and bombed and shot. But the black
> man that says he don't want to integrate, he gets called a "hate
> teacher". Chubby Checker is catching hell with a white woman.
> And I'm catching hell for not wanting a white woman. People are
> always telling me what a good example I could set for my people if I
> just wasn't a Muslim. I've heard over and over, how come I couldn't
> be like Joe Louis and Sugar Ray. Well, they're gone now, and the
> black man's condition is just the same, ain't it? We're still catching
> hell. (Muhammad Ali in Hauser, 1991, p. 103)

In the biblical narrative in the Book of Genesis, Adam, as the head of the human
family, is authorized to have dominion over all the animals. One way in which
Adam exercised this "dominion" is through the act of naming all the animals. In
this way the "namer" exercises dominion over the "named." "And out of the
ground the LORD God formed every beast of the field, and every fowl of the air;
and brought them unto Adam to see what he would call them: and whatsoever
Adam called every living creature, that was the name thereof" (Genesis 2:19; King
James Version). It appears that part of White supremacy's vitriol, such as Breivik's, can be traced to this erosion of the power to name all they survey. For
instance, Bombay was officially renamed Mumbai on March 6, 1996. The Vic-
toria Terminus, the main railway station in Mumbai, was renamed Chhatrapati
Shivaji Maharaj Terminus (CSMT) in 1996, in honor of the Maratha warrior
king, Chhatrapati Shivaji Maharaj. Hamid Dabashi is an Iranian-American
scholar, cultural critic, and author. He is a Professor of Iranian Studies and
Comparative Literature at Columbia University in New York City. In his book
Can Non-Europeans Think? (2015), Dabashi articulates whiteness' rage at its
power to name the world:

> When their anthropologists and area specialists read the world for
> them, they assimilate this reading into what they already know;
> and what they know is to rule, how to own, how to possess, and
> how to map the world in defiance of its inhabitants' will, wishes,
> and resistance against their will to know. This will to know has
> made them the knowing subject since the pages of Immanuel Kant;
> the very same pages that state that we colored folks cannot think
> because we are colored, and consequently we are part of the
> knowable world. Another map more familiar to others will drive
> them mad, so they consider those who have created those maps
> and who live by them to be mad. (Dabashi, 2015, p. 28)

Breivik's *Manifesto* seethes with a zeal reminiscent of Hitler's frenzied tirades, but it targets Muslims instead of Jewish people. From Russia to the Western seaboard of the United States, Islamophobia disperses like a dense fog, clouding minds and shrouding understanding. Why are White supremacists increasingly obsessed with Islam in recent years? The obsession with Islam cannot stem from its Middle Eastern origins, as Breivik's initial professed Christianity also originates from the Middle East, despite its frequent portrayal of a Jesus that caters to the White aesthetic preferences of groups such as the Ku Klux Klan. The plain truth, as succinctly articulated by the outspoken Muhammad Ali, is that it could be said some Muslims, keenly aware of the denigration endured by Black Americans and other marginalized groups, are unwilling to submit and hence consistently resist integration into a racialized pecking order where White people reign supreme. The truth is, commensurate with Dabashi's (2015) contention, the likes of Breivik are mad because some Muslims may resist and frustrate Western attempts at a Kantian epistemological incarceration.

For Breivik and his acolytes, Islam not only dismisses Western claims to prominence with insouciance but also has the "gall" to claim that God's most beloved human being was an Arab. They demand Western converts bow down to Allah facing a shrine in Arabia, learn Arabic in order to understand God's revelations, and preferably discard the suit and tie in favor of the *thobe* (long robe), *ghutra* (headdress), and *bisht* (cloak), and forsake the practice of keeping dogs as pets following the Sunnah of the prophet. To their minds, this is nothing short of cultural totalitarianism. In one conversation with a White Norwegian years ago, this interlocutor, incensed with Islam, reminded me that Europeans never demanded converts to Christianity bow down to London or other centers of the West, forgetting that Christianity did not originate in the West. This demonstrates the hypocrisy of the West, which conveniently forgets its own history of Christian missionizing and proselytizing during colonization. Breivik and his followers criticize Islam for its cultural demands, yet they overlook the Christian missionary efforts imposed upon colonized peoples. They denounce Islam for dismissing Western claims to prominence, yet conveniently overlook Christianity's own non-Western origins.

This is not to exonerate a slew of evils also committed in the name of Islam (and of most religions): slavery, colonization, dhimmitude, gender inequality (women could only drive cars in 2018 in Saudi Arabia), and terrorism, among others. Tariq Ali's *Clash of Fundamentalisms: Crusades, Jihads, and Modernity* (2002) is a book that explores the geopolitical landscape in the wake of the September 11, 2001, attacks and examines the conflicts between several fundamentalist ideologies, particularly those of Islam and Western capitalism. Ali argues that understanding the events of 9/11 necessitates considering the broader historical context of Western intervention in the Middle East and the emergence of political Islam as a reaction to colonialism, imperialism, and economic exploitation. He explores how the clash between these two fundamentalisms – Islamic fundamentalism and the capitalist fundamentalism of the West – has influenced global politics and unleashed violence and conflict in the modern world. In regard to Islam, he asked, "Why has it not undergone a reformation?"

How did it become so petrified? Should Koranic interpretations be the exclusive prerogative of religious scholars? And what do Islamist politics represent today?" (Ali, 2002, p. 4).

Tariq Ramadan, the grandson of Hassan al-Banna, the founder of the Muslim Brotherhood, emerges as a major figure in the field of Islamic reform, advocating for a contemporary understanding of the faith that finds common ground with Western sensibilities. His commitment to fostering dialogue and inclusivity bridges cultural gaps, promoting an Islam that embraces diversity and upholds principles of tolerance. Through his emphasis on critical thinking and social justice within Islamic tradition (ijtihad), Ramadan presents a vision of Islam that not only remains true to its roots but also resonates positively with Western ideals, making significant strides toward fostering mutual understanding and cooperation.

However, Ramadan must be critiqued for failing to appreciate the Muslim's acute awareness of the West's White supremacist convictions that ultimately lie at the core of its call for integration. Ramadan dismisses some Muslims' preoccupation with what he considers superficial and even distortionist renderings of Islam in the halal market.

> Coke dominates the soft drink market, so a line of products labeled as "Cola" emerges (Mecca Cola, Zem Zem Cola, Medina Cola) to recall the "taste" of the parent company's product while they are alleged to resist the actions of the foreign company or constitute an alternative! There is no resistance in this, no alternative though, and indeed no originality...as is shown by Fulla the hijab clad-doll, an Islamized duplicate of the Barbie doll complete with a line of accessories that, like it, is made in China. (Ramadan, 2009, pp. 249, 250)

While it is easy to concur with Ramadan's critique of some Muslims' preoccupation with resisting Western brands while turning a blind eye to capitalist exploitation, the "Islamization" of Western products by Muslims represents a form of resistance against colonization fought on the turf of nomenclature, not unlike Muhammad Ali jettisoning the name given to his enslaved ancestors in an act of self-emancipation. Muslims wish to "Islamize" product names and hence destabilize what Harris has called "whiteness as property." Let us not forget that the West has been doing this for centuries. How many students in the West are aware that our decimal number system is also known as the Hindu-Arabic numerals? Rare is the moment when one of my postgraduate students answers this question correctly (often in classes numbering ca. 50 students). Coming of age during the 1970s and 1980s, my British education emphatically asserted that William Harvey (1578–1657) was the recognized discoverer of blood circulation. Ibn al-Nafis (1213–1288) received little attention. Yet, even now, this "clash of civilizations" persists on the battleground of epistemological supremacy. The reluctance to acknowledge Arab/Islamic contributions is evident in *Wikipedia's* confused entrances:

He [Ibn Nafis] is known for being the first to describe the pulmonary circulation of the blood. The work of Ibn al-Nafis regarding the right sided (pulmonary) circulation pre-dates the later work (1628) of William Harvey's *De motu cordis*. Both theories attempt to explain circulation. 2nd century Greek physician Galen's theory about the physiology of the circulatory system remained unchallenged until the works of Ibn al-Nafis, for which he has been described as "the father of circulatory physiology". (Wikipedia (a), 2024)

William Harvey (1578–1657) was an English physician who made influential contributions in anatomy and physiology. He was the first known physician to describe completely, and in detail, the systemic circulation and properties of blood being pumped to the brain and the rest of the body by the heart, though earlier writers, such as Realdo Colombo, Michael Servetus, and Jacques Dubois, had provided precursors of the theory. (Wikipedia (b), 2024)

Initially, *Wikipedia* completely overlooked Ibn-Nafis. William Harvey maintained his status as the foremost describer of blood circulation even after the creation of a page recognizing his discovery. Despite the evident contradiction, *Wikipedia's* anonymous contributors attempted to reconcile this incongruity by adding this qualifier to Harvey: "He was the first known physician to describe completely, and in detail, the systemic circulation and properties of blood." (Wikipedia (b), 2024). The absurdity of this situation becomes apparent when compared to another invention: the wheel. Would it then make sense to argue that, even though the Sumerians invented the wheel first, the West deserves credit for its more effective application, as demonstrated by Karl Benz's automobile millennia later?

I stress the foregoing points to contend that Breivik's perspectives on Islam are not original. He is the crystallization of a civilization and outlook that refuses to acknowledge the contributions of non-White peoples, as doing so would jeopardize White supremacy. In his book *Can Non-Europeans Think?* Hamid Dabashi (2015) points to the Kantian cul-de-sac as "the European knowing subject" that designates the "rest of the world" as their "knowing subject" (Dabashi, 2015, p. 23). Whiteness loathes and fears what it cannot fathom through the Kantian lens, and, conversely, those (like the ever-resistant Arabs/Muslims) who do not have the "common sense" to make themselves conformable to this Kantian cul-de-sac. Indeed, in line with Foucault's (1977) perspective, knowledge and power invariably intertwine. The intersection of Foucault's knowledge-power nexus and the undercurrents of whiteness in relation to Islam offers a nuanced understanding of the machinations through which power functions in shaping views and manipulating social dynamics. Whiteness, a hegemonic construct originating from colonial history, exhibits a tendency to uphold dominance and control over other racial and cultural groups. Foucault's theoretical framework articulates the intertwining of this hegemonic stimulus with the production, dissemination, and implementation of knowledge.

> But we should add that the exercise of power itself creates and causes to emerge new objects of knowledge and accumulates new bodies of information... The exercise of power perpetually creates knowledge and, conversely, knowledge constantly induces effects of power... It is not possible for power to be exercised without knowledge, it is impossible for knowledge not to engender power. (Foucault, 1980, pp. 51, 52)

According to Foucault, knowledge is not simply an unbiased reflection of reality but rather a product of power relations, informed by societal structures and institutions. Power dynamics closely link the production and dissemination of knowledge, as certain knowledge systems reinforce existing power structures and marginalize equally viable alternative viewpoints. Foucault's insight into the fundamental intertwining of knowledge and power becomes particularly salient in this context. The production and dissemination of knowledge about Islam, whether through media representations, academic discourses, or governmental policies, are shot through with power dynamics that reflect and reinforce whiteness's hegemonic ambitions, with Breivik's Manifesto reflecting one of the most extreme apotheoses of the West's epistemological incarceration of other, non-Western ways and knowing and being.

Following Edward Said (2003), one could say that Orientalism – the disparagement of Arabs as infantile, hysterical, and irrational, among others – was invented to interpellate (Althusser) the Arab/Muslim world into the West's domiciling epistemology for purposes of subjugation and control. This is reflected in the enduring tradition of the White West to silence, sanitize, diminish, and outright condemn any perceived threat, as exemplified by Breivik's notion of the "Islamic colonization of Europe."

> It is not only our right but also our duty to contribute to preserving our identity, our culture, and our national sovereignty by preventing the ongoing Islamization. There is no Resistance Movement if individuals like us refuse to contribute... Multiculturalism (cultural Marxism/political correctness), as you might know, is the root cause of the ongoing Islamization of Europe, which has resulted in the ongoing Islamic colonization of Europe through demographic warfare (facilitated by our own leaders). (Breivik, Manifesto, 2011)

To begin with, as Samuel Huntington of "Clash of Civilizations" (1996) fame himself argues, individuals have an undeniable inclination to seek out an adversary. According to Machiavelli's principles, the presence of war or the perception of an imminent threat from an enemy serves to strengthen national unity. The pursuit of self-worth, validation, and recognition necessitates the notion of an adversary to fortify collective identity. The distorted rationale behind

Islamophobia caters to this inherent need. Huntington (2004) examines American history and identifies numerous instances of designated adversaries: from "Kaisirism" to Japanese regimentation, Nazism, and communism. "The conclusion of the Cold War left America without a clear enemy. Nonetheless, the cultural gap between Islam and America's Christianity and Anglo-Protestantism reinforces Islam's enemy qualifications. And on September 11, 2001, Osama bin Laden ended America's search" (Huntington, 2004, p. 263). Ever since the Khomeini of Iran ousted the Western-friendly Shah Mohammad Reza Pahlavi of Iran in 1979, and all the way to the relatively recent rise of ISIS/ISIL, no other movement has not only overtly identified the White West as its enemy but also worked incessantly to bring about its collapse.

Black Africa has endured centuries of colonization and denigration at the hands of White Europe, yet Black Africans in Europe, particularly non-Muslims, have given no cause for White supremacists to feel threatened in their seats of perceived Übermensch dominance. Non-Muslim Africans, South-East Asians, and South Americans, among others, have demonstrated nothing approaching the perceived "Islamic colonization of Europe" that Breivik and like-minded White supremacists fixate on. In the aftermath of 911, Cornel West stated that Black people never responded to White supremacist terrorism by forming a "Black Al-Qaeda." This perhaps explains why the average European is more concerned with Muslim immigration than Black immigration. This is not to say that Black immigration is welcomed (quite the contrary), but that in a hierarchy of perceived threats to White supremacy, Islam is deemed the most perilous. The United States may not have experienced a "Black Al-Qaeda," but its rabid racism against Black people catalyzed the creation of the Black Panthers. In 1966, Huey Newton and Bobby Seale established the Black Panthers, a revolutionary Black nationalist and socialist organization, in the United States. Originally established as the Black Panther Party for Self-Defense by Huey Newton and Bobby Seale in Oakland, California, the organization aimed to confront police brutality against African Americans and agitate for Black empowerment. On April 5, 1967, 30 Black Panther members drove to the California State Assembly chamber in Sacramento to protest the Mulford Bill, which, if passed, would ban the carrying of weapons in public places and undermine the Panther's strategy. Bobby Seale read from Black Panther Executive Mandate #:1:

> The enslavement of Black people from the very beginning of this country, the genocide practiced on the American Indians and the confining of the survivors on reservations, the savage lynching of thousands of Black men and women, the dropping of atomic bombs on Hiroshima and Nagasaki, and now the cowardly massacre in Vietnam, all testify to the fact that toward people of color the racist power structure of America has but one policy: repression, genocide, terror, and the big stick…. The Black Panther Party for Self-Defense believes that the time has come for Black people to arm themselves against this terror before it is too late. (Bloom & Martin, 2016, p. 60)

In a different analogy, White supremacism resembles a smoldering volcano, constantly rumbling beneath the surface. Like sporadic puffs of smoke, its discontent becomes visible when its dominance is questioned, and immigrants clamor for equal treatment. When groups like Muslims assert their rights and demand respect for their beliefs and customs, it echoes the cataclysmic rumble of a metaphorical Mount Vesuvius, leading to destruction analogous to Pompeii's fate. Ponder the chilling prospect of the impact 1 million Breiviks could have. Unless Islam undergoes a process of "Aryanization" akin to Christianity, and whiteness is able to clothe Islam in Western garb, Islamophobia will persist as Europe's nemesis for the foreseeable future.

Primo Levi (1919–1987) was an Italian Jewish chemist, writer, and Holocaust survivor. He is best known for his moving memoirs recounting his experiences during the Holocaust, particularly his harrowing account of the year he spent as a prisoner in the Auschwitz concentration camp in Nazi-occupied Poland. In his book *The Drowned and the Saved* (2017), he writes about the violence of the tattoo, which is forbidden by the Mosaic Law yet forcefully inscribed on every Jewish prisoner in Auschwitz.

> The operation was not very painful and lasted no more than a minute, but it was traumatic. Its symbolic meaning was clear to everyone: This is an indelible mark, you will never leave here; this is the mark with which slaves are branded and cattle sent to slaughter, and that is what you have become. (Levi, 2017, p. 104)

In one sense, White supremacism seeks to domesticate, and even obliterate, the non-White body perceived as an existential threat to whiteness in every case. Primo Levi analyzes this "violence of the tattoo": "The violence of the tattoo was gratuitous, an end in itself, pure offense: were the three canvas numbers sewed to pants, jackets, and winter coats not enough?" (Levi, 2017, p. 104).

One can extend this question to contemporary metaphorical violent tattoos that mainstream White societies have been inscribing on the collective Islamic community. Measures such as outlawing the hijab, imposing culturally specific norms like handshaking or mixed-gender swimming, serve a similar purpose: they are seemingly justified under the pretext of integration or security but may feel to those on the receiving end as attempts to expunge or significantly amend Islamic identity. Levi answers his question about the necessity of the tattoos: "No, they were not enough; something more was needed, a nonverbal message, so that the innocent would feel his sentence written on his flesh. It was also a return to barbarism, all the more perturbing for Orthodox Jewish people: in fact, precisely in order to distinguish Jewish people from barbarians, the tattoo is forbidden by Mosaic law" (Leviticus 19:28) (Levi, 2017, p. 105).

Levi's perception that the tattoo was a "nonverbal message, so that the innocent would feel his sentence written on his flesh" reverberates with the experience of many Muslims who feel forcibly marked or victimized by laws and social norms that overtly or covertly seek to curb their cultural and religious practices. Rather than acknowledging and embracing cultural and religious diversity, the societal push to conform to these norms aims to imprint a new identity on the Muslim body, aligning with the majority's comfort and expectations. Levi's characterization of tattoos as a return to barbarism, especially targeting followers of Orthodox Judaism who forbid tattoos, underscores the deep offense and cultural degradation these impositions represent. For many Muslims today, similar coercive cultural assimilation tactics can feel like an injury not only to their personal autonomy but also to their religious and cultural heritage. Once again, in our quest to make sense of Breivik's killing spree and *Manifesto*, we cannot lose sight of whiteness's seemingly indefatigable policing of the myriad potential threats to its supremacy.

> He [Churchill] was not ideologically committed to destroying fascism. Fascism, including Nazis, was and is central to the elite white male dominance system, not some cancerous add-on. During the early to mid-1930s, sympathy for Hitler and other fascists was rife among that elite... many in the British establishment, including key aristocrats and newspaper owners, "were keen supporters of Hitler up until the invasion of Czechoslovakia". (Ducey & Feagin, 2021, p. 197)

Islam has now ascended the ranks as the newest opponent on White supremacy's never-ending game show of adversaries. Therefore, just as Hitler and his cronies once portrayed Jewish people as exceedingly sinister foes possessing formidable physical and mental traits, they now portray Muslims as the latest existential threat to the cherished domain of whiteness. *In The War against the Jews* (1987), Lucy S. Dawidowicz writes:

> Mein Kampf is a vision of the apocalyptic conflict between the Aryan and the Jews, of the two world systems struggling for dominion. It was his own Manichaean version of the conflict between good and evil, between God and the Devil, Christ and the Antichrist (Dawidowicz, 1987, p. 47)

Brevik's writings clearly depict the same apocalyptic conflict, albeit with Muslims replacing Jewish people.

> Time is of the essence. We have only a few decades to consolidate a sufficient level of resistance before our major cities are completely demographically overwhelmed by Muslims. Ensuring the successful distribution of this compendium to as many Europeans as humanly possible will significantly contribute to our success. It may be the only way to avoid our present and future dhimmitude (enslavement) under Islamic majority rule in our own countries. (Breivik, Manifesto, 2011)

Certainly, figures like Hitler and Breivik identified an assortment of perceived threats to White supremacy, comprising cultural Marxists, LGBTQ+ people, and feminists, among others. However, these groups, although targeted, did not receive the same heavy emphasis for "special treatment" as Jewish people and Muslims have. Perceptions of demographic threat partially explain this distinction; stereotypes often regard Jewish people and Muslims as more fertile, potentially leading to demographic changes that frighten White supremacists. Consequently, White supremacists have singled out these groups and subjected them to particularly severe and systematic forms of persecution and vilification, echoing an ominous pattern of scapegoating based on both cultural and biological myths. It is the fear of going extinct that makes the White woman's womb the ground zero of the "apocalyptic conflict." Part of the "White rage" expressed by the likes of Breivik is the perceived "unfairness" of the advantage Muslims have in "managing the wombs" of their women, framing this as a critical front in a fabricated "battle of the wombs." References to the "Muslim demographic threat" pepper Breivik's manifesto.

- Omer Taspinar predicts that the Muslim population of Europe will nearly double by 2015, while the non-Muslim population will shrink by 3.5% due to the higher Muslim birth rate.
- Muslim birth rates remain above 3, while non-Muslim birth-rates remain below replacement rate.
- The cultural Marxist/multiculturalist elites of Europe are committing high treason by allowing and justifying the Islamic demographic warfare being waged against Western European countries by the Global Islamic Ummah through mass Muslim immigration and tolerating average Muslim birth rates of 3–4.

It is precisely because of these attitudes that a shiver runs through the collective spine of womanhood when White supremacists and fascists of various kinds, from Nazis at Nuremberg rallies to antiabortionists with guns, take an interest in birth rates and fertility. Bigots are not concerned with the preferences or well-being of women; their focus rests elsewhere. Propelled by White supremacist ideologies, they are particularly anxious about the higher birth rates among Muslim populations. This fear feeds their desire to reignite a crusade and a jihad, not necessarily fought with weapons but conducted in the womb's combat zone. They view each birth within these communities not just as a demographic shift, but as a direct challenge to their vision of societal dominance, activating them to seek control over reproductive rights and influence over family planning policies, allegedly to protect their cultural and racial purity. Feminists are all too aware of the historical reality where women's bodies have been subject to intense scrutiny and examination, often through the prism of patriarchal and pseudo-scientific authority:

> Woman represents that which must be investigated and dissected
> until her secrets are relinquished. Consequently, the female body

has been subjected to the scrutinizing gaze of the human sciences far more than the male. Every hint of abnormality has been thoroughly and enthusiastically ferreted out and classified by numerous "experts" eager to provide indisputable proof of its inherent pathology. (King, 2004, p. 3)

Just as historical "experts" pursued policies to catalog and pathologize female bodies, contemporary narratives of White supremacy similarly seek to dissect and control the reproductive choices of women. King's (2004) statement, examined in the interstices between gendered power dynamics and racialized fears, uncovers the complex intersections where women's bodies become battlegrounds for assertions of dominance and control.

4. Religion's Role in White Supremacy

The problem isn't the individuals but the Islamic doctrines and culture. The problem can only be solved if we completely remove those who follow Islam. In order to do this all Muslims must "submit" and convert to Christianity. If they refuse to do this voluntarily prior to 1 January, 2020 they will be removed from European soil and deported back to the Islamic world. (Breivik, Manifesto, 2011)

It wasn't exactly a secret that many in the NS movements rejected Christendom completely and instead support Odinism. It is however understandable that they view modern humanist Christendom as weak and therefore unworthy of support (a view which I partly agree with). However, the solution is not to reject Christianity but rather to reform Christianity to re-introduce the concepts of "self-defense" as propagated by former Crusader Popes. Also, we shouldn't forget that Nazi Germany allied itself with the Ottoman Caliphate/Turkey on two occasions and supported the Christian Armenian genocides. (Breivik, Manifesto, 2011)

What to do with religion? How can White supremacy harness its age-old power over the masses? It is clear, reading Breivik's manifesto that, like the Nazis, who were not motivated by piety but lust for world domination and invincibility in Steven Spielberg's *Raiders of the Lost Ark*, Breivik perceived religion, and Christianity in particular, as a means to an end – the end being White supremacy. Extremists have long acknowledged the lasting impact of religion on societal norms and behaviors, exploring ways to channel this ancient force toward the advancement of supremacist ideologies. Paul Roland, in his book *Nazis and the Occult: The Dark Forces Unleashed by the Third Reich* (2012), gives expression to Hitler's shrewdness in intuitively discerning this need to augment the cult of his personality with transcendental forces.

> This was the true purpose of the Nuremberg Rallies. They acted as
> an insidious form of quasi-religious magic ritual, a perversion of
> both the Catholic sacrament and a pagan consecration of the
> weapons with which Nazi Germany would wage war, with
> Hitler as Priest and his inner circle in the role of acolytes.
> (Roland, 2012, p. 354)

Reading Breivik's manifesto, it is abundantly clear that he had never been a committed, practicing Christian. Breivik does not hide this fact, consistently assuring his interlocutors that his adoption of Christianity was a pragmatic decision rather than a religious conviction. I argue that a critical reading of his religious stance only makes sense if one perceives Christianity as the most potent "battering ram" in uniting a Europe emaciated by left-leaning, secular forces that have collaborated with Islam to bring about the demise of the White West. Breivik perceives contemporary Christianity as considerably reduced or "declawed" and believes that it must be restored to its former glory of earlier epochs in order to be effectively exploited for his envisioned purposes.

It comes as no surprise that extremists peruse the annals of history, as did Breivik, and seek to recreate the circumstances and emulate the personalities of select historical figures in their ambition to subdue and eliminate contemporary enemies. Consider England's Lord Protector, Oliver Cromwell. Oliver Cromwell rose to prominence during the turbulent 17th century. As a competent military leader, he played a key role in the English Civil War, leading the Parliamentarian forces to victory against the Royalists. Cromwell's military prowess earned him the title of Lord Protector, effectively making him the ruler of England, Scotland, and Ireland. However, Cromwell's legacy is also marked by his ardent religious convictions, which often bordered on fanaticism. A devout Puritan, he perceived himself as a medium of God's will, directed by a sense of divine mission to purify and reform English society.

Cromwell's religious zeal was on display in his cruel treatment of Catholics and Royalists, whom he perceived as threats to the Protestant cause. After he massacred anywhere between 2,000 and 4,000 Royalist soldiers, civilians, and Catholic priests in the town of Drogheda in Ireland in 1649, he wrote in a letter to Parliament via the Speaker:

> I am persuaded that this is a righteous judgement of God upon
> these barbarous wretches, who have imbrued their hands in so
> much innocent blood for the future, which are satisfactory grounds
> to such actions, which otherwise cannot but work remorse and
> regret. (Fraser, 1973, p. 423)

Cromwell's statement reveals an equivocation in his thought process: he acknowledges that without this belief in divine justification, such actions would naturally lead to "remorse and regret." Once again, Cromwell's struggle with truly knowing the will of God in the massacre and his determination to "read" God's actions into the ebb and flow of the war is evident in his speech to the

Parliament, leading the historian Antonia Fraser to write, "However, for once God's mercy was seen to have pursued a somewhat fluctuating course":

> That which cause your men to storm so courageously, it was the Spirit of God, who gave your men courage, and took it away again; and gave the enemy courage, and took it away again; and gave your men courage again, and therewith this happy success. And therefore, it is good that God alone have all the glory. (Fraser, 2012, p. 423)

By invoking a sense of righteous judgment, Cromwell seeks to exonerate himself and his soldiers from guilt, alleging that their deeds were essential and upheld by a higher moral and religious standard. This validation demonstrates how deeply enmeshed Cromwell's military campaigns were with his religious convictions, seeing himself as an instrument of God's will in executing judgment upon his enemies. His rigid stance on matters of faith led to policies such as the prohibition of Christmas celebrations and the persecution of religious dissenters, earning him both admirers and critics. Cromwell's complex legacy continues to be a subject of debate among historians, reflecting the enduring impact of his religious fervor on the course of English history.

Cromwell's own statements uncover an intricate engagement with his faith, where he appeared to explain events and outcomes as tokens of divine will, conveniently aligning with his political and military objectives. His inclination to interpret the successes and failures of his campaigns as indices of God's favor illustrates how he, and figures like him, spun religious narratives to serve their agendas. This manipulation is echoed in Breivik's manifesto, which similarly co-opts historical and religious symbolism, yet lacks the genuine faith that drove Cromwell. Breivik and his fellow-ideologues adopt this historical model not out of religious conviction, but as a scheme to legitimize their actions and recruit like-minded individuals.

It is vital to recognize that Oliver Cromwell and the populace of Ireland shared adherence to the same Christian faith. Nonetheless, long before Islam assumed the role of chief adversary in the ideological framework of individuals such as Anders Breivik, Catholics were disdained as the "Other" due to practices deemed heterodox by Puritans, including Mariolatry, saint veneration, and teachings on purgatory, to name a few, all subsumed under the generic "popery." In this delineation, the precedence of Catholicism predating the Reformation and Puritanism remained inconsequential. This exemplifies how religious extremism has frequently been appropriated to purify a nation of perceived deviations, corruptions, and "foreign influences," epitomized by the authority of the Pope, for instance, and to restore the nation to a conceived state of pristine purity, as evidenced by contemporary slogans such as "make America great again."

Breivik was clearly not concerned with the internecine squabbling among Christian denominations. He appears to be theologically illiterate. He half-heartedly acknowledges the significant strength of religious conviction within Islam, yet what bothers him more is Islam's perceived resilience against modernizing influences like the Enlightenment, which he believes have weakened Christianity. Breivik understood that Europe, particularly northern Europe, was too secular to use Christianity as a "crusading force," and therefore, it was necessary to "revive" and weaponize Christianity against Islam once more. Consider contemporary relations between Protestants and Catholics in the United Kingdom today, as exemplified by the annual burning of Guy Fawkes effigies during Bonfire Night in the United Kingdom. The celebration is more symbolic of cultural tradition and historical commemoration than of religious conviction or anti-Catholic animosity. In contemporary times, the event serves more as a secular celebration of unity and national identity than as an indicator of religious or sectarian enmity, reflecting the secular outlook of modern European society.

It is obvious, then, that Christianity was not central to Breivik's plan for his so-called "emancipation of Europe" but a convenient tool, "a useful idiot" – to borrow from Lenin's vocabulary – in restoring White supremacy, which was the real "holy grail" of his murderous mission. Professors of sociology of religion, Ole Riis and Linda Woodhead (2010) state that "The main way in which religions maintain emotional currency in late modern societies at a national level is by performing residual functions of a civil religion, such as dealing with collective tragedy, suffering, and death. Non-religious competitors have yet to satisfactorily fill this gap in the emotional market" (Riis & Woodhead, 2010, p. 212). On one level, this is precisely what Breivik was tapping into: deploying Christianity as a tool to "mourn" the decay and death of Norway and the broader West.

Breivik didn't merely seek to exploit Christianity's emotional resonance; he also wagered that Christianity would serve as the catalyst to incite a dormant Europe and confront the intruding forces of Islam, reminiscent of a scene from the film *Birth of a Nation* (1915). *Birth of a Nation*, which was the first film screened in the White House during President Woodrow Wilson's administration, spellbound White audiences by portraying African Americans as intimidating figures, stirring fear, and reinforcing notions of White superiority. Its glorification of the Ku Klux Klan as guardians of White civilization stirred fervent support among White audiences, rallying them around the idea of protecting their perceived racial dominance. Ultimately, for the architects of hatred, the transcendental was useful in so far as it hypnotized the masses (e.g., Albert Speer's "Cathedral of Light" consisting of 130 antiaircraft searchlights) into willing subjects and pawns in the service of White supremacy.

> They were simply swept along a tide of heightened emotion expertly and cynically stage-managed by Hitler's architect, Albert Speer, who understood the seductive power of making each member of the crowd believe that they were participating in a heroic Wagnerian pageant, and so had become part of something greater than themselves. All of the elements for invoking the dark side of the psyche were harnessed by Speer to focus the mass ranks of the Führer's followers on a single purpose: the awakening of the collective will. (Roland, 2012, p. 355)

Hence, we perceive a twofold approach in the utilization of Christianity as a tool among White supremacists: firstly, as a "priest" offering solace to those mourning the "death of God," drawing from Nietzsche's concept, and secondly, as a marshaling force rallying against the ancient nemesis of White, Christian Europe – Islam. Much like a priest heaps tribute upon the memory of the deceased, exaggerating good deeds and papering over the bad, White supremacists, such as Joseph Goebbels, excel in the art of hagiographies. In a manner evocative of a priest eulogizing the virtues of the deceased, embellishing their good deeds while glossing over their deficiencies, White supremacists, typified by figures like Joseph Goebbels, demonstrate an outstanding aptitude for crafting hagiographies. These narratives serve to mythologize and fête individuals or movements associated with their beliefs, depicting them as heroic champions of their cause.

Through eclectic storytelling and fabrication of historical facts, White supremacists construct narratives that exalt their chosen figures, enhancing their perceived righteousness and gallantry while modulating or outright overlooking their crimes. This adroit exploitation of historical narratives contributes to the propagation and normalization of supremacist ideologies, presenting them as noble and righteous endeavors worthy of awe and emulation. Once again, it is clear in the main that White supremacists have no personal commitment or investment in religion, especially the Abrahamic religions that demand the individual obey God unconditionally. White supremacism bows down to no deity – it *is* the deity. In their book *Himmler's Norge* [Himmler's Norway] (2012), historians Terje Emberland and Matthew Kott write:

> This attempt at the "sacralizing" of the ideology was something Himmler was very conscious of. The ideology in its function did not merely have a religious character, it was from Himmler's perspective intended to replace Christianity as a framework for the construction of meaning. As a statement on German upbringing declares: "It is part of the SS's mandate in the next half-century to give the German people a foundation for a new way of life through a 'non-Chistian', 'species (or race)-specific' worldview". The aim was then also, as mentioned, followed up with the establishment of a cultic-religious practice, which included, among other things, a well-developed symbol system, piety and devotional literature, solemn initiation rites and collective holidays of the order and racial community, as well as family-centered causes and rites of passage. (Emberland & Kott, 2012, p. 52)

Emile Durkheim's concept of the totem pole provides some insight into the dynamics at play in the spin and proliferation of supremacist ideologies, particularly the actions of the Nazis. In Durkheim's theory, the totem pole is a tangible expression of the collective consciousness and identity of the tribe, operating as a sacred symbol embodying its values, beliefs, and unity. Analogously, White supremacists, through their exploitation of historical narratives, hoist certain figures, nations, and ideals to a quasi-divine status, symbolizing the deification or self-worship of whiteness itself. Himmler said that he loved Norwegians on his first visit to the country in 1941. Emberland and Kott (2012) write that Himmler's SS idealized Norwegians as splendid Germanic aristocratic farmers, Vikings, and colonizers. German soldiers were charged with showing kindness toward the Norwegian population under the occupation of Norway (1940–1945). In 1941, Himmler, the head of the SS, established the maiden branch of the race-based organization Lebensborn outside of Nazi Germany, specifically in Norway. This initiative led to approximately 30,000–50,000 romantic liaisons between Norwegian women and German men (Brochmann & Kjeldstadli, 2008, p. 161). It appears that the Nazi concept of a pure Aryan national body, rooted in *Blut und Boden* (blood and soil), found its apotheosis in Norway.

The above illustrates how White supremacists concoct narratives that exalt their chosen figures, embellishing their perceived righteousness while airbrushing their crimes. This mirrors Durkheim's concept of the totem pole as an image of the tribe's collective identity and moral authority. Just as the totem pole symbolizes the tribe's unity and values, the narratives constructed by White supremacists serve to bolster and idolize their ideology, presenting it as noble and worthy of reverence. Heinrich Himmler, in his calculated efforts to "sacralize" his ideology, aimed to replace Christianity with a new worldview based on race and nationalism. This echoes Durkheim's notion of the totem pole as a consecrated symbol that galvanizes the tribe and provides a framework for meaning and identity. By launching a cultic-religious practice pivoted on racial purity and fidelity to the Nazi regime, the Nazis sought to inculcate a sense of collective identity and purpose among the German people, not unlike the function of the totem pole in tribal societies. Just as the totem pole represents the tribe's values and unity, supremacist ideologies serve to unify adherents around a shared sense of racial superiority, offering themselves as the ultimate arbiters and source of meaning.

> So, if the totem is both the symbol of god and of society, are these not one and the same? How could the group's emblem become the face of this quasi-divinity if the group and the divinity were two distinct realities? The god of the clan, the totemic principle, must therefore be the clan itself, but transfigured and imagined in the physical form of the plant or animal species that serve as totems. (Durkheim, 2001, p. 154)

I argue that the current proliferation of far-right ideology in the West, perhaps best encapsulated in the rise of Donald Trump, is symptomatic of, among others, the West's perceived crisis of faith vis-à-vis Islam. Napoleon's campaign in Egypt and Syria (1798–1801) was not the first time Western Christian forces confronted Islam after the Crusades. There were numerous exchanges and conflicts between Christian and Islamic powers in the centuries between the end of the Crusades in the late 13th century and Napoleon's expedition in the late 18th century. For instance, throughout the Renaissance and early modern periods, there were clashes between Christian European powers and the Ottoman Empire, which was an Islamic state. The Ottoman Empire presented a substantial threat to Christian Europe, particularly during its expansion into southeastern Europe and the Mediterranean region. However, Napoleon's campaign introduced modern military tactics and technology to the region. His army employed advanced weaponry such as artillery, firearms, and cavalry, which gave them a considerable advantage over local forces. Perhaps for the first time since the Crusades (Said, 1978), Muslims found themselves dismayed by the conspicuous technological disparity between their own forces and their ideological rival, the White Christian West.

In the contemporary era, however, and as Breivik's manifesto constantly refers to, Islam, to his mind, is "silently taking over Europe" through a different sort of warfare: the "jihad of the womb," unshakeable faith in the tenets of Islam, and with the support of "Trojan horses," chief among which are the ubiquitous cultural Marxists and others who are basically committing treason against whiteness, to borrow from Noel Ignatiev (2022). Nevertheless, I contend that broaching this seemingly incompatible coalition through the lens of White supremacy's methodical and strategic approach to pitting adversaries against each other – reminiscent of "Night of the Long Knives," also known as the "Röhm Putsch" in 1934 – and ultimately consolidating absolute authority sheds light on their machinations.

Space considerations preclude a thorough analysis of the historical evolution of Islamophobia in the West. Nevertheless, critical events such as the Crusades, the fall of Constantinople in 1453, and the era of colonialism acted as watershed moments, cultivating the perception that the racialized "Muslim Other" has emerged as a prime "folk devil" in contemporary Western societies (Poynting & Morgan, 2012). During the pinnacle of colonialism, European powers utilized brute military power to "manage" Islam and the Arab world, reinforced by Orientalist tropes portraying Arabs as irrational, violent, and inherently inferior (Said, 1978). Even in circumstances where Muslims were statistically marginal, such as Britain in 1881, passionate denunciations of Islam were de rigueur, exhibiting a profound animus toward the religion (Ansari, 2004). Figures like W. E. Gladstone embodied this sentiment, characterizing Islam as a menace to European peace by stating that Europeans would look in vain for peace as long as there were followers of "that accursed book" (Ansari, 2004, p. 80).

Intellectual luminaries like Max Weber perpetuated stereotypes about Islam, rendering it intrinsically martial rather than a religion of spiritual salvation (Aslan, 2005). Similarly, Francis Fukuyama's "End of History" thesis and Samuel Huntington's "Clash of Civilizations" theory gave succor to Western notions of cultural and ideological supremacy (Fukuyama, 1992; Huntington, 1996). Huntington's thesis of an inevitable clash between Islam and the West, centered on reified religious categories, reflects what Amartya Sen critiques as "civilizational incarceration" (Sen, 2006). The sociologist Reza Aslan (2005) highlights this anti-Islamic prejudice among several notable Western scholars:

> Islam has so often been portrayed, even by contemporary scholars, as "a military religion [with] fanatical warriors, engaged in spreading their faith and their law by armed might", to quote historian Bernard Lewis (1990), that the image of the Muslim horde charging wildly into battle like a swarm of locusts has become on of the most enduring stereotypes in the Western world. "Islam has never really been a religion of salvation", wrote the eminent sociologist Max Weber. "Islam is a warrior religion". It is a religion that Samuel Huntington has portrayed as steeped in "bloody borders". (Aslan, 2005, pp. 78, 79)

As alluded to previously, the proliferation of Islamophobia serves numerous psychological and political functions, including the consolidation of national cohesion and identity through the invention of an external enemy (Huntington, 2004). In the absence of a Cold War-era antagonist, Islam emerged as a suitable scapegoat, specifically following the events of September 11, 2001 (Huntington, 2004). This highlights the West's historical tendency to construct an identity parasitic, inter alia, upon the demonization of a "worthy" foe. However, as Muslim demographics grow in Europe, scholars like John L. Esposito emphasize the importance of recognizing Islam as an integral part of Western societies (Esposito & Mogahed, 2007). The globalization and migration of Muslims have altered major Western cities into culturally diverse hubs, confronting the dualistic narrative of "Islam versus the West" (Esposito & Mogahed, 2007). As such, it becomes imperative to acknowledge and engage with Islam within the framework of Western societies rather than spreading divisive "us versus them" paradigms. An arbitrary and false construct such as White supremacy is perennially condemned to labor in the laboratory of pseudo-science, much like the Nation of Islam's imaginary scientist Yakub, who "invents" White people in the laboratory.

Breivik cites Ibn Khaldun several times in his manifesto. Known as one of the founding fathers of modern sociology, historiography, and economics, Ibn Khaldun was an Arab scholar of the 14th century. His most famous contribution to social science is his work, *Muqaddimah* (Introduction), in which he fleshed out his theory of *asabiyah*. This term, often translated as "social cohesion" or "group solidarity," refers to the common bonds that hold a group or society together.

> Group feeling results only from a blood relationship or something corresponding to it. Respect for blood ties is something natural among men, with the rarest exceptions. It leads to affection for one's relations and blood relatives – the feeling that no harm ought to befall them nor any destruction come upon them. (Khaldun, 1967, p. 173)

According to Ibn Khaldun, *asabiyah* is the underlying cause of the rise and fall of civilizations. He theorized that a robust *asabiyah* leads to political growth and empire-building, whereas the deterioration of *asabiyah* results in the decline of civilizations. Ibn Khaldun argued that *asabiyah* begins in kinship bonds and small communities, typically in inhospitable settings like deserts where survival hinges on group cohesion. "Royal authority" and large-scale dynastic power are attained only through a group and group feeling. Group feeling, characterized by affection and a willingness to fight and die for each other, is the sole source of aggressive and defensive strength (Khaldun, 1967, p. 209). These groups can extend their *asabiyah* beyond kinship through shared purpose, identity, and the successful leadership that capitalizes on these shared aims to exercise political power. However, over time, as the group achieves its ambitions, becomes more affluent, and enjoys comfort, their *asabiyah* weakens, leading to its subsequent decay and likely conquest by a new group with stronger cohesion, or *asabiyah*. "The same happened to the Umayyad dynasty in Spain. Small princes seized power and divided the territory among themselves after the destruction of the Arab group" (Khaldun, 1967, p. 211). Significantly, Ibn Khaldun recognized that, while religion was a vital component of *asabiyah*, or group feeling, it was dependent on precisely the group or "we-feeling" in order to succeed.

> Religious propaganda cannot materialize without group feeling. This is because every mass (political) undertaking, by necessity, requires group feeling. Muhammad's saying, "God sent no prophet who did not enjoy the protection of his people", indicates this. If this were the case with the prophets, who are among human beings most likely to perform wonders, one would expect it to apply all the more so to others. One cannot expect them to be able to work the wonder of achieving superiority without group feeling. (Khaldun, 1967, p. 214)

Not least, Ibn Khaldun might as well have been speaking about Breivik's frustration with multiculturalism in what he perceived to be a fractured Norway when he stated, "A dynasty rarely establishes itself firmly in lands with many different tribes and groups. This is because of differences in opinions and desires. Behind each opinion and desire, there is a group feeling defending it" (Khaldun, 1967, p. 219). In addition to the various opinions, Ibn Khaldun attributes the atrophy of "group feeling," or *asabiyah*, to decadence.

> The things that go with luxury and submergence in a life of ease break the vigor of the group feeling, which alone produces superiority. Destroying group feeling renders the tribe incapable of self-defense or asserting any claims. Other nations will absorb it (Khaldun, 1967, p. 188)

Anders Breivik, in his manifesto, seems solely focused on Ibn Khaldun's fidelity to Islam, yet curiously overlooks the striking parallels between his own concerns about civilizational atrophy and Khaldun's etiology of decline, which analyzes the causes behind such decay. Breivik attributes this decline to policies advancing diversity, which he claims dilute and undermine traditional Norwegian values. According to his perspective, the demise of homogeneity in the population is an explicit threat to national identity, echoing a distorted version of Ibn Khaldun's *asabiyah* in a cultural rather than a sociopolitical context. Breivik's failure to see this is testament to a skewed worldview that is primed to cherry-pick interpretations of Ibn Khaldun's work, citing only those parts that seem to support his ideological narrative while disregarding the broader, more nuanced, and cyclic nature of *asabiyah* that could have challenged or even reversed his extremist views. Anders Breivik's selective interpretation of Ibn Khaldun's theory of *asabiyah* in his manifesto points to a premeditated oversight of the universality of this concept, which Khaldun himself applied to various societies, including both Muslim and Christian groups. Breivik broods over a civilizational regression framed within a narrative of cultural and racial homogeneity threatened by multiculturalism and immigration, distinctively targeting the perceived erosion of Norwegian values. However, his exploration notably conceals Khaldun's broader application of *asabiyah* to a range of societies, which reveals a fundamental misreading or purposeful disregard for the universal principles underlying Khaldun's theory.

Ibn Khaldun's concept of *asabiyah* is not confined to a particular religion or ethnicity but is seen as a universal phenomenon impacting all groups. Khaldun illustrates this with historical patterns from both the Islamic and Christian worlds, revealing how *asabiyah* is critical in the rise and fall of civilizations, regardless of their religious or ethnic backgrounds. He examines Muslim dynasties such as the Umayyads, Abbasids, and Almohads of Al-Andalus, showing how their decline was triggered by the diminishing of *asabiyah* within these societies. Crucially, he also extends this analysis to Christian groups, such as the Copts in Egypt, and further scrutinizes the dynamics of the Reconquista in Spain, where the Castilians, led by figures like Alfonso, succeeded in reclaiming territories due to their stronger *asabiyah* at the time compared to the fragmented Muslim rule in the region.

> According to the historiographic paradigm by which the Khaldunic conception of the state is bounded, the integrity of the state is guaranteed by its dynastic rubric and ceases with the waning and disappearance of this name: a state is Coptic, Merinid, Almohad. The structure of the individual state, therefore, is determined by the integrity of succession along a line which is almost literally a line of force: its sis a *sui generis* unit of power which appears suddenly, describes a trajectory in time, and is extinguished. (Al-Azneh, 1982, p. 35)

By focusing solely on Islamic conformity and disregarding these broader historical contexts, Breivik skews the key lesson from Khaldun's work: *asabiyah* is a vibrant force that supersedes cultural, ethnic, and religious limitations. The implications of this oversight are profound because it means Breivik fails to recognize that the challenges he attributes to Norwegian society, such as the corrosion of national values and identity, are not exclusive to Norway nor to any society undergoing multicultural shifts. An alternative interpretation of Ibn Khaldun suggests that relying exclusively on blood ties is inadequate for maintaining long-term cohesion and solidarity. Therefore, it becomes essential for communities and nations to unite around contemporary, universal values that foreground our shared humanity.

Chapter 3

Sumaya Jirde Ali: Too Bold, Too Black for White Spaces

Sumaya Jirde Ali (born 1997), a prominent Norwegian-Somali figure, has distinguished herself as an author, poet, playwright, and societal commentator, notably championing the causes of anti-racism, feminism, diversity, and equality. Raised in Bodø, in the north of Norway, following her father's migration from Somalia, she cut her teeth in the crucible of a politically active family and her own encounters with discrimination, significantly giving impetus to her literary and activist pursuits. Her wide-ranging body of work encompasses poetry compilations, including "Women Who Hate Men" and "Melanin Whiter than Bleach" as well as nonfiction writings such as "A Life in a Life Jacket: Diary Entries on Norwegian Racism," which catalogs her experiences and critiques racism within Norwegian society. Ali's contributions have earned her recognition, including the Oslo Prize for Voice of the Year and the Amalie Skram Prize, emphasizing her role as a stellar voice in contemporary Norwegian literature and social discourse.

Ali's activism has not been without trials as she has confronted persistent online harassment and fabricated accusations, particularly following public debates and expressions of dissent against political figures. Despite such hardships, Ali has remained resolute in her commitment to amplifying marginalized voices and opposing societal injustices through her writing and advocacy. Her multifaceted approach, merging literary creativity with social critique, reveals a nuanced understanding of contemporary issues, making her a crucial figure in the current dialogue surrounding racism, feminism, and social equality in Norway and beyond. On October 23, 2022, Sumaya Ali Jirde shared on her Facebook page that Atle Antonsen, a 53-year-old comedian and television host, verbally and physically bullied her at a bar in Oslo, including making comments about her skin color. Sumaya detailed the frightening incident on Facebook. Antonsen, a 53-year-old comedian and television host, reportedly confronted Ali and her friend at the establishment. He became furious, shouted at Ali, and seized her

Too Black to Be Here?, 101–144

doi:10.1108/978-1-83662-162-120251004

arm. Ali reported the incident to the police, inducing Antonsen to later apologize via Facebook. Oslo police investigated the case for hate speech and reckless conduct.

Atle Antonsen is an A-list comedian, Norwegian comedian, actor, and television personality known for his wit and comedic endowments. With a career spanning several decades, Antonsen has established himself as one of Norway's most admired entertainers, earning widespread acclaim for his performances in several comedy shows, films, and theater productions. His versatility and rapport with audiences have earned him a devoted following and myriad awards throughout his career. Beyond his comedic endeavors, Antonsen has also demonstrated his versatility by branching into television hosting and acting, further cementing his status as a talented entertainer in the Norwegian entertainment industry. Given his achievements and impeccable "progressive" and "liberal" leanings on the left in the entertainment industry, not normally associated with racism, the Sumaya incident came as a shock to many in Norway. A Retriever media archive search returned 1,528 hits since the case broke on November 15, 2022.

> According to Ali, Antonsen said "SHUT THE F… UP" once more before grabbing her arm. I tear myself away. I say that I don't understand what he's trying to say or why he's behaving this way, but then he asks me once again to shut up. Sumaya Jirde Ali claims that Atle Antonsen racially abused her. Then she claims that Antonsen said: "You are too dark-skinned to be here". Ali says she doesn't believe what she hears from Antonsen. There must have been several witnesses to the incident, and according to Ali, Antonsen must also have turned to them to ask if they did not agree that "she is too dark-skinned to be here". (NrK (a), 2022)

In his classic book *Black Skin, White Masks*, Fanon elucidates the complexities of racial identity and formulates his objective: "I believe that the fact of the juxtaposition of the White and Black races has created a massive psychoexistential complex. I hope by analyzing it to destroy it" (Fanon, 1986, p. 14). Even though it's not possible to completely get rid of the psychoexistential complex that comes with racism in Norway or anywhere else in the world, it is important to look closely at how it works as part of a larger effort to debunk and fight this persistent barrier to a truly fair, tolerant, and welcoming society. Such analysis is consistent with Martin Luther King Jr's vision of a nation where individuals are judged based on their character rather than their skin color, fostering the realization of this ideal not only in America but also in Norway, a nation that awarded Dr King the Nobel Peace Prize in 1964.

In the sterile spaces of whiteness, blackness stands out like a sore thumb, triggering reactions that seem as involuntary as an unexpected sneeze in a crowded elevator. This bizarre phenomenon bears a resemblance to a peculiar ailment, where the afflicted individuals appear utterly incapable of containing their symptoms, analogous to a contagious outbreak in an antiseptic environment. Antonsen's ability to elicit a psychosomatic response at the sight of Sumaya is not new in Norway. In 1994, Øystein Hedstrøm, a Norwegian member of Parliament, took a proactive stance by submitting a proposal on the issue of psychosomatic reactions toward nonwhites to the Norwegian parliament. Quite what Hedstrøm, a dentist by profession, hoped to achieve by forwarding this proposal is not clear. This significant action is archived in the Norwegian parliament, underscoring the degree to which blackness afflicts some White people with this "mysterious and nebulous disease."

> The proposer refers to the high risk of spreading dangerous diseases through immigration and expresses the impression that Norwegian authorities are pursuing a policy that could directly encourage HIV-infected individuals to come to Norway, as their chances of staying and receiving good treatment are significant. The economic and health consequences of such a policy could be catastrophic.
>
> Furthermore, the proposer points out that it is a little-discussed phenomenon that Norwegians develop psychosomatic illnesses due to frustration, anger, bitterness, fear, and worry caused by immigration (Hedstrøm, 2023).
> (Parliamentary Bill drafted by MP Øystein Hedstrøm, 1994/95)

It is intriguing that Sumaya writes on her Facebook page that the fact that she was in good spirits and enjoying her stroll with her friend on the way to the pub where the terrible incident occurred, exacerbated the effects of Antonsen's racism. In her own words:

> It was a rare, beautiful evening. I was with my friend, I didn't look around as I always do, and I didn't sense that feeling of vulnerability that exists in me and that can come to light unprepared. As we walked down the street, I was neither Muslim nor black, I was just a young, free woman in an exceptionally good mood. I believe this incident primarily contributes to my grief. I feel as though I am being punished for allowing myself to relax and unwind in public spaces. (Gudbrandsdalen, 2022)

Sumaya oddly berates herself for fleetingly entertaining the "outrageous" notion that her blackness wouldn't raise eyebrows in a Norway that conveniently sweeps racism under the rug with the delightful mantra of "colorblindness." Sporting her signature hijab, she accompanies her White Norwegian companion to a pub in Grünerløkka, Oslo's hipster hub. Ostensibly, their excursion personifies the epitome of "happy face" multiculturalism. What could conceivably disrupt this immaculate facade of harmonious diversity? While White individuals may perceive Sumaya's conflicted "double consciousness" (Du Bois, 1903) as unnecessary, I contend, having lived in Norway as a Black man for over 35 years, and dedicated some research to the topic, that such a state is par for the course for Black people. It is worth the while to draw insights from the work of the "Freud of Black consciousness," Frantz Fanon, in shedding light on Sumaya's regret at daring to give free reign to her blackness in White spaces. The comparison between Frantz Fanon and Sigmund Freud underscores the profound psychological insights embedded in Fanon's "transgressive" work, positioning it as indispensable for fathoming the complexities of Black consciousness. Just as Freud's theories revolutionized our comprehension of the human psyche, Fanon's analyses of colonialism and racism inform the psychological intricacies of oppression on individuals for African descent. Thus, invoking Fanon's theories provides a robust framework for examining the complex dynamics of racial identity, alienation, and liberation, essential for locking horns with the enduring challenges faced by Black communities worldwide.

> Where am I to be classified? Or, if you prefer, tucked away? A Martinican, a native of "our" old colonies. Where shall I hide? "Look at the nigger!... Mama, a Negro!... Hell, he's getting mad...". "Take no notice, sir, he does not know that you are as civilized as we." ... My body was given back to me sprawled out, distorted, recolored, clad in mourning in that white winter day". (Fanon, 1986, p. 113)

Black bodies are violently (symbolically in Sumaya's case) seized from their Black owners, only to be returned bearing a new narrative; it was an innocent quivering child who inadvertently "gave back Fanon's body," sprawled with an inscription that said Black bodies are terrifying. The Black skin is the parchment upon which white scribes (with white ink) have for centuries unloaded their fears, phobias, and fantasies. It is this haunting juxtaposition of innocence and malice – inscriptions that attribute goodness, badness, and ugliness simultaneously – etched on ebony skin that triggers a double consciousness, an epidermal schizophrenia, leading Fanon to write:

> The Negro is an animal, the Negro is bad, the Negro is mean, the Negro is ugly; look a nigger, it's cold, the nigger is shivering, the nigger is shivering because he is cold, the little boy is trembling because he is afraid of the nigger... the little white boy throws himself into his mother's arms: Mama, the nigger's going to eat me up. All round me the white man, above the sky tears at its navel, the earth rasps under my feet, and there is a white song, a white song. All this whiteness that burns me.... (Fanon, 1986, p. 114)

Fanon expresses some apprehension pertaining to the dearth of Black individuals willing to confront the profound psychological turmoil inflicted by White supremacy. He metaphorically depicts this struggle as a descent into hell where genuine transformation can emerge. Quoting Fanon:

There is a zone of nonbeing, an extraordinary sterile and arid region, an utterly naked declivity where an authentic upheaval can be born. In most cases, the black man lacks the advantage of being able to accomplish this descent into a real hell. (Fanon, 1986, p. 10)

This imagery taps into the immense challenge faced by Black individuals in confronting the psychological wounds inflicted by racial oppression. Importantly, for this catharsis to transpire, Fanon urges a confrontation with the origins of racial oppression, symbolized by the metaphor of "white scribal activity on Black skin." This metaphor gives expression to the treacherous nature of racism where Black bodies become the canvas upon which White supremacy inscribes its narratives of power and dominance. Unless we are willing to summon the courage of the mythical hero Beowulf and descend into the depths of the underwater, confronting the lurking adversaries akin to Grendel's mother Aglæc, the roots of oppression will persist unchecked, and peace will remain but a distant dream in the halls of Heorot.

In this undertaking of "racial inscription on Black skin," the Black epidermis is reduced to a mere surface upon which the narratives of whiteness are engraved, reminiscent of an ancient scribe's management of animal skin. Sumaya's experience illustrates how the racialized text, hidden like invisible ink on Black skin, becomes visible within white spaces. The necrophilia inherent in this system of racial epidermal inscription is evident in the heartbreaking autobiography of Trevor Noah, entitled *Born a Crime* (2016):

Where most children are the proof of their parents' love, I was the proof of criminality. The only time I could be with my father was indoors. If we left the house, he'd have to walk across the street from us. My mom and I used to go to Joubert Park all the time... My mother tells me once, when I was a toddler, my dad tried to go with us. We were in the park, he was walking a good bit away from us, and I ran after him, screaming, "Daddy! Daddy! Daddy! People started looking. He panicked and ran away. I thought it was a game and kept chasing him. (Noah, 2016)

Sumaya writes in her Facebook post:

Antonsen sat opposite me. There was a small table between us. I remember his grin; I remember the twinkle in his eyes. I'm no stranger to drunken men. I'm no stranger to drunken men speaking English to me. 'What are you? How are you?', says Antonsen. I chuckle and reply, 'I speak Norwegian'. (Gudbrandsdalen, 2022)

In the context of Atle Antonsen's refusal to speak Norwegian with Sumaya, a disturbing parallel raises its ugly head in terms of historical injustices, notably the

Nuremberg Laws of 1933. These laws, enacted by the Nazis, sought to strip Jewish people of their German identity by maligning them as "international Jews" and denying them the right to belong. Similarly, Antonsen's refusal to engage with Sumaya in Norwegian parallels this exclusionary tactic, perpetuating a cycle of ostracism and banishment by denying non-White individuals access to the linguistic and cultural fabric of Norwegian society, which Sumaya had mastered.

Additionally, the demand for non-White individuals to learn Norwegian while simultaneously denying them literacy in the language represents a disturbing form of racialization. By suppressing access to language, a fundamental tool for communication and integration, society, in effect, constructs barriers to belonging and participation for non-White individuals. This denial of linguistic agency serves to perpetuate their alienation from Norway's collective "we," echoing the perverse objectives of the Nuremberg Laws. Consequently, Antonsen's refusal to speak Norwegian with Sumaya not only highlights the insidious nature of the games some White people can play with language as a weapon, barring a "return" to the Garden of Eden like the two cherubim with flaming swords that ensured Adam and Eve could never return home. Antonsen's refusal reinforces the marginalization of non-White individuals, denying them the opportunity to fully participate in Norwegian society.

In a pub in Oslo, Sumaya, conspicuous by her dark skin and hijab, was observed socializing with a White female friend. To those with progressive credentials, and likely to the "delight" of populists and conservatives, Sumaya's behavior should have been lauded as an exemplary demonstration of positive integration. Antonsen must have been within earshot, and he must have heard Sumaya converse in Norwegian with her friend. No matter how integrated or "Norwegian" the non-White individual may feel, White people can always pull up the drawbridge of "nativity" and fill the moat that surrounds the castle of Norwegianness with an arsenal of categories to ward off the "enemy" – race, ethnicity, language, culture, etc. This regressive action evokes an ominous parallel with the parochial ideology of the Nazis, with echoes of their *Blut und Boden* (blood and soil) philosophy. In such a framework, the drawing up of bridges and the reinforcement of exclusionary measures correspond to a retreat into bigoted conceptions of nationality and identity, redolent of the Nazi regime's emphasis on racial purity and territorial belonging. For non-White Norwegians, confronted with such ingrained prejudices and systemic barriers, this revival of kinship or blood ties of the aforementioned *asabiyah* (group feeling) ideology of Ibn Khaldun becomes an insurmountable obstacle, leaving them vulnerable against the pervasive forces of discrimination and marginalization.

Before one is tempted to excuse Antonsen's inebriation as a pretext for speaking to Sumaya in English (while excusing his "French"), it is once again not uncommon for many nonwhites in Norway to affirm that they have had similar experiences. In the early 1990s, populists such as Carl I. Hagen employed the media like a battering ram to hammer home the message that language acquisition was essential to mostly non-White and non-Western immigrants. Immigrants were then labeled "fremmedkulturell" or literally "those from alien cultures." Speaking in a foreign language risks censure. However, with the arrival of tens of thousands of Poles and other East Europeans in Norway since joining the European Union, the previously strict requirement to learn Norwegian seems to have somewhat eased, accompanied by the "whitening" of the new wave of immigrants, particularly those from Ukraine following Russia's aggression. Earlier this year (2024), one municipality in Drammen, located 40 kilometers southwest of Oslo, wished to pass legislation accepting only Ukrainian refugees.

> In the municipal council, a clearly moved Simon Nordanger [Center Party] took the floor. He described the proposal as worthless. He cried from the podium as he said: "I have no words for what you have decided. It hurts so much that 29 people sitting in this hall are willing to sell our values", he said. "You have used the fact that some are not white enough, all others who come from other countries, who are not Western or of Western culture, are not integrable enough in Drammen". (VG, 2024)

In Antonsen and Drammen municipalities, we see a conflation of both classical and cultural forms of racism. Both clearly discriminate on the basis of pigmentation and discursively constructed cultural traits. Stuart Hall (2017a) broaches race as a discourse, a language that, is akin to a sliding signifier:

> [. . .] that its signifiers reference not genetically established facts but the systems of meaning that have come to be fixed in the classifications of culture; and that those meanings have real effects not because of some truth that inheres in their scientific classification but because of the will to power and the regime of truth that are instituted in the shifting relations of discourse. (p. 45)

In Fanon's call to "descend to hell," it is imperative that White people and nonwhites understand the need to seriously engage in an open and candid conversation about both the pigmentation aspect of racism and race employed as a discursive floating signifier. Far-right elements like Breivik and Manshaus will fill the expanding vacuum if we fail to do so. Once again, we note the salience of the perceptual category of the "white space," one where "black people are typically absent, not expected or marginalized when present" (Anderson, 2022, p. 320) in Antonsen's encounter with Sumaya. Given the alarming levels of demographic segregation in cities such as Oslo, Sumaya's experience will further convince Black people to perceive white spaces as antagonistic to Black skin.

> When the anonymous black person enters the white space, others there immediately try to make sense of him or her – to figure out 'who that is' or to gain a sense of the nature of the person's business and whether they need to be concerned. (Anderson, 2022, p. 321)

Understandably, until the recent influx of non-White people in Norway, the notion of sharing the same national borders with people who are Black and brown was still novel for many Norwegians. The numbers of Sami people, Jewish people, Romani people, Tartar (Tatar) people, and Kven people, among others, had never reached anything near the 11% of the national population that is Black and brown people in Norway today. With this burgeoning demographic, White Norwegians have some adjusting to do. Unfortunately, if the history of national minorities in Norway is anything to go by, then the future does not bode well for non-White Norwegians.

The notion of white space is evocative of the historical concept of *Lebensraum*, or "living space," which the Nazis used to rationalize their expansionist policies and the violent acquisition of territories such as the then Sudetenland (the historical German name for the northern, southern, and western areas of former Czechoslovakia), Austria, and parts of Poland, which they considered integral to the German Reich. The Nazis enforced their claim to these "German spaces" forcibly removing or subjugating populations they considered undesirable or incompatible with the Aryan ideal. Fortunately, many Norwegians supported Sumaya and refused to acknowledge Antonsen's racial and spatial entitlement. While Antonsen himself issued a muddled apology, several media outlets had to incapacitate their comment sections because of the volume of racist, Islamophobic, and misogynist abuse hurled at Sumaya.

If genuine change and transformation in race relations are to occur, then White Norwegians will have to reconsider the racial perceptions secreted in public spaces. The Sumaya–Antonsen case is crucial in that it furnished a window into the degree to which racial and spatial dominance still lurks, underscoring the ongoing struggle against systemic racism and segregation. This troubling dynamic reinforces the perception among Black individuals that white spaces remain fundamentally unpleasant and heightens the salience and persistence of racial segregation in ostensibly multicultural societies.

1. Whiteness and Complicity: Analyzing the Silence at the Bar

But this is not the worst of the matter. The worst thing about the case is how long it took for someone at the bar to react. Those who observed the incident averted their gaze, refrained from intervening, and remained silent. Only when this had been going on for many minutes did a friend of Atle Antonsen hold him down so that a crying Sumaya and her shocked friend could leave the room. One of Antonsen's friends is said to have said that "this was not a good thing to say", but he has since apologized to Sumaya Jirde Ali for being so passive (Blågestad, 2022).

You oughn't abide, sitting calm in your home,

Saying: Dismal it is, poor they are, and alone

You cannot permit it! You dare not, at all.

Accepting that outrage on all else may fall!

I cry with the final gasps of my breath:

You dare not repose, nor stand and forget.

(…)

Pardon them not – they know what they do!

They breathe on hate-glows, and evil pursue,

They fancy to slay, they revel with cries,

Their desire is to gloat, when our world is at fire!

In blood they are yearning to drown one and all!

Don't you believe it? You've heard the call!

(…)

And then they'll leave home for a rainfall of steel,

Till last they hang ragged on barbed wire will,

Decaying for Hitler's Aryan call,

That is what a man's for – after all
        – Arnulf Øverland, Dare not to Sleep [Du må ikke sove] (1936)

The renowned Norwegian writer, journalist, and activist, Arnulf Øverland (1889–1968), was fiercely opposed to the Nazi occupation of Norway during World War II through his prolific anti-Nazi poetry. Despite enduring imprisonment in Germany's Sachsenhausen concentration camp, he persisted in writing, becoming a symbol of resistance and resilience in Norway's struggle for liberation. It is a fiery and confrontational call to action against smugness and indifference in the face of injustice and subjugation. In the poem, Øverland warns against the hazards of remaining inactive and silent in the face of societal injustices. He challenges those who choose to turn a blind eye to the pain of others, pressing them to awaken to the gathering clouds of hatred and death in Europe and take a stand for what is right. The title itself, "Du må ikke sove" [Dare not to Sleep], is the social critic's marching orders to the masses given the capitulation of other moral and ethical bulwarks of society. Øverland was no stranger to courting controversy: in 1933, he was charged with contravening the blasphemy laws against Christianity in a speech entitled "Christianity, the Tenth Plague of the Land"; he was acquitted. Now, in his poem three years later, he once again resorts to a provocative intertextual hermeneutic in appropriating the words of Jesus in stating, "Pardon them not; they know what they do!" Øverland appeals to readers to stay awake, both literally and metaphorically, to stay alert and responsive to the injustices around them. Throughout the poem, Øverland employs colorful imagery and compelling rhetoric to express his message. He depicts the dread of war, poverty, and oppression, portraying a stark picture of a world tormented by suffering and injustice. Yet, amid this gloom, he offers a gleam of hope, urging readers to rise up and fight for a better future.

Sumaya Ali Jirde endured a harrowing instance of racial abuse while socializing with a friend at a pub in Oslo. The comedian Atle Antonsen brazenly broadcasted, "You are too dark-skinned to be here," with such force that the surrounding tables were compelled to register the distinct and menacing import of his words saturated with verbal violence. Regrettably, Antonsen's blatant racism elicited no countervoice that could match it. Only silence. The "I" person in Øverland's poem awoke from his slumber with the voice that urged him not to sleep but in Sumaya's case, the audience was awake yet opted to sleep, pretending to have heard nothing. Such actions constituted deliberate neglect and cowardice, as their apathy – and perhaps a distorted interpretation of Gandhi's Ahimsa – amounted to collaboration with wrongdoing through the perpetuation of silence and the preservation of the existing state of affairs, leaving a distressed individual to fend for herself.

Unfortunately, no opposing voice emerged with the fervor necessary to challenge Antonsen's blatant racism. In its place, an eerie silence prevailed. In a distressing parallel to Øverland's poetic persona, whose awakening was prompted by the imperative not to yield to slumber, Sumaya's audience remained alert, yet settled for the nirvana of contrived ignorance. This deliberate neglect and cowardice, akin to a distorted interpretation of Gandhi's principle of Ahimsa, manifested as complicity with evil through the maintenance of silence and the preservation of the status quo, leaving a vulnerable woman to navigate her vulnerability alone. While Sumaya was a relatively well-known social critic, Antonsen's towering stature, both in terms of fame and physique, perhaps cowered the involuntary listeners into silence. "Beyond Good and Evil" by Friedrich Nietzsche (1973) contests traditional moral concepts and offers a re-examination of values, advocating for the individual's quest for self-realization and self-mastery. Nietzsche critiques the dichotomy of good and evil, arguing for a more nuanced understanding of morality that transcends conservative norms. Nietzsche's quote, "Our neighbor is not our neighbor but our neighbor's neighbor – thus thinks every person" (Nietzsche, 1973, p. 104) reflects his distrust toward traditional notions of philanthropy and virtue. It suggests that people often prioritize their own welfare or the interests of those closest to them rather than widening this welfare net to include all individuals. Applying this above to the conditions surrounding Sumaya in the pub, it's probable that those around her remained silent due to a blend of factors such as fear of social consequences, a desire to avoid conflict, and the absence of a personal connection to Sumaya. They may have justified their apathy by focusing on their immediate circle of acquaintances rather than admitting Sumaya as part of their broader community. This view underpins Nietzsche's critique of traditional morality, emphasizing how self-interest and social dynamics can influence individuals' behavior, even in situations where moral intervention is warranted.

> There must have been several witnesses to the incident, and according to Ali, Antonsen turned to them to ask if they did not agree that "she is too dark-skinned to be here". (NrK, 2022)

Not only did Antonsen abuse Sumaya racially in front of the other patrons in the pub, but he also perversely invited them to agree with his declaration that Sumaya was too Black to be in the establishment. Antonsen's sinister inducement of fellow pub patrons, egging them to jointly affirm Sumaya's unwanted presence due to her skin color, echoes a deeply ingrained prejudice echoing through the ages. This insularity parallels the biblical narrative where Pontius Pilate, dreading public upheaval, inflicted physical torment upon Jesus in an unsuccessful attempt to dissuade calls for crucifixion. Antonsen, in assuming a role similar to Pilate, manipulates opinions by proclaiming not "Ecce Homo" but "Ecce Mulier" ("Behold the woman"), emphasizing Sumaya's blackness to mark her as an outsider, unfit for acceptance. In this traumatic scenario, Sumaya becomes allegorically "crucified" for her racial identity, with spectators complicit in this "crucifixion." The absence of any "Simons of Cyrene" (the African who carried Christ's cross temporarily) individuals willing to alleviate her suffering, starkly accents the systemic nature of racial oppression and the pervasive indifference among observers.

Sumaya's predicament echoes a historical legacy of exploitation and dehumanization, from the horrors of the transatlantic slave trade to the monstrous spectacle of "human zoos," for example, where 80 Africans from Senegal were exhibited in Oslo's Frogner Park in 1914 to commemorate the bicentennial of Norway's Constitution (Strandberg & Thomas, 2024). The White gaze has for centuries held dogged opinions about the place of Black bodies – where they should be seen or not seen (not in the pub, according to Antonsen), assigned to the field or the house (Malcolm X's "field/house" negro distinction), etc. The prominent Black scholar and activist, Angela Y. Davis, renowned for her lifelong commitment to social justice and radical political activism, emphasizes the distinctiveness of Black women's suffering during the transatlantic slave trade. Initially, the exploitation of Black women's labor value led to their perception as genderless. "Where work was concerned, strength and productivity under the threat of the whip outweighed considerations of sex. In this sense, the oppression of women was identical to the oppression of men" (Davis, 1981, p. 4). However, there was the added dimension of sexual exploitation:

> However, women also endured unique forms of suffering, as they fell prey to sexual abuse and other forms of brutal mistreatment exclusive to women. Expediency governed the slaveholder's posture towards female slaves: when it was profitable to exploit them as if they were men, they were regarded, in effect, as genderless, but when they could be exploited, punished, and repressed in ways suited only for women, they were locked into their exclusively female roles. (Davis, 1981, p. 4)

Davis characterizes Harriet Beecher Stowe's Black matriarchal figure Eliza in *Uncle Tom's Cabin* as "a travesty of the Black woman, a naive transposition of the mother-figure, praised by the cultural propaganda of the period, from White society to the slave community. Eliza is White motherhood incarnate, but in blackface – or rather, because she is a 'quadroon', in just-a-little-less-than-white-face" (Davis, 1981, p. 23). Thus, the supposedly "empathetic" portrayal of Black women, upon whom Stowe confers qualities amenable to White sentiments, ameliorates the true nature of slavery, even in a novel as significant as Stowe's, which according to Abraham Lincoln purportedly started the civil war. The White gaze deemed Sumaya's Black body out of order, necessitating her verbal imprisonment. Her blackness was transgressive enough, but the added element of a hijab put her beyond the pale white estimation. Stowe's novel, along with the enraged stare of Antonsen, is once again a reminder, if ever one was needed, of whiteness's discomfort with the presence of Black bodies, which has inflicted what Fanon (1986, p. 14) called a "psychoexistential complex." Davis concludes:

> The Elizas, if they indeed existed, were certainly oddities among the great majority of black women. They did not, in any event, represent the accumulated experiences of all those women who toiled under the lash for their masters, worked for and protected their families, fought against slavery, and who were beaten and raped, but never subdued. It was those women who passed on to their nominally free female descendants a legacy of hard work, perseverance and self-reliance, a legacy of tenacity, resistance and insistence on sexual equality – in short, a legacy spelling out standards for a new womanhood. (Davis, 1981, p. 25)

Yet, amid this despair, encapsulated in Sumaya's traumatic experience, there remains a glimmer of hope. Despite enduring crucifixions across time and space, blackness's resilience continues to manifest in unexpected ways. Even in regions like the Nordic countries, where racial diversity may seem incongruous with historical narratives, blackness finds conduits for resurrection and assertion. The ongoing struggle highlights the need for solidarity and active resistance against all forms of racial injustice, ensuring that each crucifixion inspires renewed determination for equality and liberation. Atle Antonsen reminds us, despite the remonstrance from most White people, that classical scientific racism is well and alive, especially among the so-called liberals and progressives. The excuse of alcohol and inebriation will simply not do. It would be absurd to argue that alcohol inherently carries properties that induce racism. One can only wonder why alcohol is not associated with promoting anti-racist sentiments. Sumaya's formal complaint to the police forced Antonsen into a mea culpa.

> I realize that I have to reevaluate my relationship with alcohol and how I communicate with people under the influence of alcohol. It is obvious that this contrasts with how I perceive myself. (Aftenposten, 2022)

Antonsen attempted to excuse his racial abuse of Sumaya in the pub by assigning blame to alcohol rather than his own racism. However, this argument fails to acknowledge that alcohol often amplifies prevailing prejudices rather than constructing them anew. Researchers who interviewed individuals seeking medical attention for injuries sustained from violence in multicultural British cities found evidence supporting this. Professor Jonathan Shepherd, director of the Cardiff University Crime and Security Research Institute (Cardiff University, 2018), highlighted a significant finding: while hate may have played a role in the attacks, alcohol acted as a catalyst. To put it another way, when alcohol impairs cognition and inhibition, it does not prompt individuals to suddenly utter racist, misogynist, or homophobic remarks from thin air. Rather, akin to lemon juice revealing invisible ink, alcohol functions as a catalyst, uncovering and highlighting the submerged biases and prejudices that lie within. This emphasizes the importance of addressing alcohol abuse not only for individual health but also for societal well-being as the researchers conclude. The common perception may lead one to believe that far-right groups, including neo-Nazis, engage in excessive alcohol consumption as an integral aspect of their ideological stance. This perceived connection between alcohol and right-wing extremism is often boosted by misconceptions suggesting that all Nazis were notorious substance abusers.

In his study entitled "A Sober Reich? Alcohol and Tobacco Use in Nazi Germany," Lewy (2006, p. 1182) writes, "Not only did the Nazi party opposed alcohol, but also physicians expressed their disdain for the drink."

> Dr. Guenther Hecht of the Racial Political Office of the Nazi Party (Rassenpolitisches Amt der NSDAP), even linked the dangers of alcohol to the race policies of the Third Reich, claiming that the lack of self-control of the "oriental people" led to the ban on alcohol in Islam, but instead the people of the East smoked hashish. The Jews were alcohol free but used cocaine or morphine to calm their nerves instead. The Aryan race had no historical need for narcotics; its bane lay in alcohol, whose market was controlled by Jews. (Lewy, 2006, p. 1182)

Hitler's personal choices regarding tobacco and alcohol consumption did not directly influence the policies of the Third Reich. While Goebbels may have used Hitler's abstinence from these substances in propaganda, it had little substantive impact on the Nazi regime's racial ideology and actions. This implies that we cannot solely attribute the fostering or prevention of racism to alcohol consumption or its absence. Instead, it underscores the complex sociopolitical factors at play in the formation and execution of discriminatory policies and actions. Therefore, attributing racism solely to alcohol consumption overlooks the deeper systemic issues and historical contexts that perpetuate prejudice and discrimination.

In the aftermath of World War II, W.E.B. Du Bois stated the following in regard to the prospect of a postwar world without racial conflict:

> It is with regret that I do not see after this war, or within any
> reasonable time, the possibility of a world without race
> conflict... The war's greatest tragedy is the treatment of Jews
> in Germany. Yet its technique and reasoning have been based
> upon a race philosophy similar to that which has dominated both
> Great Britain and the United States in relation to colored people.
> (Du Bois, 1970, p. 141)

Du Bois continues his analysis of Nazi racism, arguing that the physical differences between Jewish people and Germans could not have justified it in reality.
Not least, he dismisses any plausible hierarchy of innate abilities by saying that it
was often Jewish people who were considered superior in certain respects, fueling
jealousy. Rather, the "ideological basis of this attack was that of fundamental
biological difference showing itself in spiritual and cultural incompatibility" (Du
Bois, 1970, p. 142). We return, then, once again to that old nemesis that bedevils
race relations: classic scientific racism – the visceral kind that, aided and abetted
by alcohol, blurted the words, "You are too Black to be here." If Sumaya's
cardinal sin was to be too Black for whiteness, Jewish people were not white
enough. The Polish and Nazi leaders conceived the plan to transfer Jewish people
from Europe to Madagascar as a solution to their perceived Jewish "problem" in
Europe. Spearheaded by Reinhardt Heydrich, Himmler's deputy, the plan aimed
to deport all of Europe's 11 million Jewish people to the island of Madagascar.
However, logistical challenges and geopolitical considerations, such as the fear of
interception by the British navy, ultimately led to the abandonment of the scheme.
Despite its failure to materialize, the Madagascar Plan illustrates the extent to
which Nazi ideology sought to eradicate Jewish presence from Europe, demonstrating the depths of their genocidal intentions and the lengths to which they
were willing to go to achieve their goals (Confino, 2014). Referring to excerpts
from Goebbels about the "final solution of the Jews," Herf (2006) writes:

> The memo referred to 'more than eleven million Jews' in Europe
> who 'must be concentrated in the East' and eventually 'after the
> war, be sent to an island', such as Madagascar. There would be no
> peace in Europe until the Jews were 'excluded from the European
> territory'. (Herf, 2006, p. 146)

White capriciousness has long constrained Black mobility. White Europe
wanted to relocate the "not sufficiently White" Jewish body to Africa while the
southern White people of the antebellum USA picked up arms to deny Black
people human dignity and freedom of mobility. This tragic historical dilemma is
the backdrop to Antonsen's "You are too Black to be here" outburst. In
Shakespeare's *Othello*, the protagonist's blackness becomes a point of strife, with
his noble qualities overshadowed by racial prejudice. Othello's Black pigmentation becomes a source of conflict among the White characters in Shakespeare's
play. "Iago presents his argument to Othello under the guise of honest friendship

but with the devious aim of playing on Othello's insecurity as a Black man in a White society" (Cohen, 2021, p. 79):

> Ay, there's the point: as, to be bold with you,
>
> Not to affect many proposèd matches
>
> Of her own clime, complexion, and degree,
>
> Whereto we see in all things nature tends –
>
> Foh! one may smell, in such, a will most rank,
>
> Foul disproportion, thoughts unnatural. (3.3.230–235)

At first labeled solely by his race as "the Moor," he encounters an onslaught of racist insults from characters like Iago, Roderigo, and Brabantino, who refer to him as "thick lips," "old Black ram," "the devil" and "Barbary horse." Despite this racial bias, Othello emerges as an honorable figure, demonstrating virtues such as civility, honesty, humility, patience, bravery, heroism, and wisdom. Characters like Brabantino perpetuate a Black-and-White binary, but Othello's transformation from a racial stereotype to an individual highlights the complexity of race and identity in the play. Similarly, Antonsen's statement implies the perpetuation of this tragic historical predicament where the sole basis for deeming Black individuals unwelcome or inferior is their race. This demonstrates the enduring impact of racial bias and highlights the ongoing struggle for equality and justice.

Let us, however perversely, indulge in the utterance that Sumaya was too Black to be in the pub. What, then, is the appropriate domain for the Black female in Norway? Back to Africa, a brothel, hidden away somewhere as a domestic servant? Only the White imagination can tell. Thankfully, Sumaya has an answer. In her recent memoir published after the Antonsen affair with the telling title *A Life in a Life Jacket: Diary Entries on Norwegian Racism* (2023), Sumaya includes self-directed advice or insights gained through personal reflection.

> When you speak up, you turn the mirror and say, look at you, listen to what you say – you who have always expected to be seen, weigh your own words and scan rooms, and who have perfected navigating your own body in a kind, gentle way that tolerates that it is and remains something others must tolerate.
>
> To be able to endure and cope with racism, no matter how subtle or explicit it was, you had to constantly step outside your bodily borders, out of yourself, which made you lose yourself over time. And so today I have the difficult task of gathering your diasporic being, learning to know and love you, and knowing and loving myself. (Ali, 2023, pp. 218, 219)

According to Angela Davis, Sumaya embodies this unsubdued legacy of Black womanhood in her writing. A legacy, Phoenix-like, that rises from its own ashes after death, symbolizing renewal, regeneration, and immortality.

> It was those women who passed on to their nominally free female descendants a legacy of hard work, perseverance, and self-reliance, a legacy of tenacity, resistance, and insistence on sexual equality – in short, a legacy spelling out standards for a new womanhood. (Davis, 1981, p. 25)

Indeed, and as Sumaya so eloquently puts it, Black people have had to learn the art of "gathering their diasporic beings." This "diaspora" of the Black body was not voluntary but imposed upon us as encapsulated in Antonsen's "Too Black to be here." How did parts of our Black bodies end up in the diaspora? What were the forces that dismembered our bodies and had to be gathered and loved, as Sumaya puts it? Not only its natural resources, but the very bodies native to African soil fell under the purview of White greed.

Blackness was "stolen from Africa" in Bob Marley's memorable song "Buffalo Soldier" and, like Prometheus, who stole fire from the gods, Black bodies were forcibly taken from Africa to fuel plantations that would produce commodities such as sugar, coffee, chocolate, etc. The Black bodies that were not forcibly shipped over to the Americas were subjected to colonization in the so-called "dark continent" of Joseph Conrad's *Heart of Darkness* imagination.

When critiquing the impact of whiteness on the Black body, we are often met with the self-justifying riposte, "Well, why don't you return to Africa, if Europe is so terrible?" Seen through the unvarnished Black lens, many Africans reckon that, paradoxically, there is a higher chance of survival into old age in the White West than in Africa. Consider the historical context that dismembers the Black and brown body: Atom bombs were dropped on Japan, not Germany; Agent Orange was sprayed over Vietnam and millions killed in the war; Mohammad Mosaddegh, the Prime Minister of Iran, was ousted in 1953 in a coup d'état orchestrated by the CIA and British intelligence (Dehghan & Norton-Taylor, 2017); the United States backed dictators like Mobutu Sese Seko in Zaire (Afoaku, 1997), assassinated Patrice Lumumba in the Congo (Reid, 2023), supported the apartheid regime in South Africa (Africa Today, 1964), and bombed Iraq under false pretenses of weapons of mass destruction (Global Times, 2023). Given this nasty backdrop, Black people often reckon that facing potentially racist law enforcement in the West and other forms of discrimination still poses significantly less risk than hoping for a peaceful, prosperous life in Africa or Southeast Asia.

Immanuel Wallerstein's world-systems theory and Walter Rodney's "How Europe Underdeveloped Africa" (1972) make it clear that the legacy of Western colonialism and exploitation continues to shackle Africa. Rodney's analysis highlights how European powers exploited Africa's resources and labor for their own benefit, leading to economic, social, and political underdevelopment on the continent. Wallerstein's theory further elucidates this dynamic by framing Africa within the global capitalist world-system, where it occupies a peripheral position, exploited by core countries for cheap labor and resources. Despite achieving political independence, many African countries remain economically dependent on the West, trapped in unequal trade relationships, and burdened by debt. This ongoing exploitation perpetuates a cycle of underdevelopment and reinforces Africa's subordinate position in the global economy, underscoring the enduring legacy of colonialism and imperialism. In regard to US State Department plans for Africa in the aftermath of World War II, Noam Chomsky writes: "Some areas were of little interest to the planners, notably Africa, which Kennan advised should be handed over to Europeans to 'exploit' for their reconstruction" (Chomsky, 2003, p. 150).

2. The Silent Struggle: Fear of Racism in Everyday Interactions

These are some of the reasons why Black individuals cannot be "too Black" to exist anywhere. Sumaya, like Rosa Parks before her, challenges the oppressive scrutiny that expects them to keep moving, whether out of a pub or to the back of the bus. Black individuals are reclaiming their identities, "returning from the diaspora" and embracing self-love. They have endured their own "Rivers of Babylon," where, in their estrangement from their own Black and brown skins, they metaphorically "hung their harps upon the willows." Now, however, these exiles are finding their way back to a place of healing and self-acceptance – a sanctuary where the intrusive gaze of others can no longer displace them physically.

> In all these years, I have not defined myself as Norwegian. Presently, I not only declare that I am Norwegian-Somali, but I do so with immense pride and joy. I live out a double identity for myself every day. All that entails experience, insight, and wealth. I no longer feel the need to prove what I can do or who I am to others. I do not feel the need to explain why I and my voice have value, and why I should not have to defend my own presence and existence. (Sumaya Ali, 2023, jacket cover)

Ultimately, Sumaya and Rosa Parks were just Black individuals going about their business. There is nothing aberrational about their actions. The aberration lies in the White supremacist gaze, which has for far too long lorded over all it surveys, especially the Black female body. But the times they are a-changin'. Unbeknownst to Antonsen, Sumaya's proverbial pen was mightier than the sword. Black women who can write in the spirit of Ida B. Wells are the bane of White supremacy. Ida B. Wells learned to read and write at Rust College in Holly Springs, Mississippi. This college, founded in 1866, is one of the oldest historically Black colleges in the United States. Ida's parents, former enslaved people who were freed after the Civil War, valued education, and despite facing many hurdles, including the loss of her parents to yellow fever when she was just 16, Wells continued her education and went on to become a prominent journalist, activist, and researcher, advocating against lynching and for civil rights and women's suffrage. Frederick Douglass's master knew the "danger" of educating an enslaved person: "Learning would spoil the best nigger in the world, if you teach that nigger – speaking of myself – how to read the Bible, there will be no keeping him, it will forever unfit him for the duties of a slave" (Douglass, 2014, p. 118).

> People, however, don't think as much about the fact that it's not just Hulsker and Antonsen who make racist remarks when drunk. Racism doesn't always manifest itself through words or offensive references. Sometimes it's looks, laughter, and exclusion that greet many of us with darker skin when we interact with new people. This phenomenon occurs both during periods of intoxication and in daily life. These incidents also lead to a lot of fear.
>
> For some, this fear is variable. For others, it's constant and underlying. Because even though racism itself isn't as big of a problem as "some would have it", the fear of encountering it might be an even bigger problem. (Kuflu & Libanos, Aftenposten, 2022)

The opinion piece in Aftenposten, one of Norway's largest papers, is written by young, Black Norwegian politicians. They first referenced the Bernt Hulsker case, which was fresh in the public mind. Hulsker, a former professional football player, received an 18-day suspended prison sentence for his hate speech. The incident occurred during a COVID-19-affected Christmas party on the night of March 10, 2022, at the karaoke bar "Sing More" in downtown Oslo. The karaoke bar charged Hulsker with hate speech and rash behavior toward the bouncer Jwan Rasho following Rasho's attempt to eject him. In court, Hulsker acknowledged calling Rasho a "damn negro" and saying, "How can you ask a White man to leave?" when asked to exit the karaoke bar.

The court found Hulsker guilty on both charges. Upon reading the charges in court, the former footballer and TV personality admitted guilt to reckless behavior but not to hate speech (Dagsavisen, 2022). In court, Hulsker began his account by expressing regret to the bouncer as he had done publicly before. He explained that the participants at the Christmas party had started the evening at a restaurant, and he had "drunk too much" by the time they arrived at "Sing More" with his colleagues. Eventually, Hulsker began mimicking the British comedian John Cleese, who parodied Germans during the war by making Nazi salutes. In this chapter, with its focus on Sumaya and the Antonsen case, I refrain from teasing out or dissecting the intricacies of the Hulsker case. However, it is pertinent to note the common thread between the two cases: the widespread tendency to assign culpability to alcohol consumption as a means of lessening the severity of the transgression. I will concern myself with the authors' statement, "For some, this fear is variable. For others, it's constant and underlying. Because even though racism itself isn't as big of a problem as 'some would have it', the fear of encountering it might be an even bigger problem" (Kuflu & Libanos, Aftenposten, 2022).

What happens to the psyche of young and impressionable Black teenagers in Norway who are constantly told to integrate and participate actively in a vibrant democratic society such as Norway's, only to discover that racism is not a scourge limited to a few far-right elements, but liberals and progressives they have long admired and aspired to emulate? Undoubtedly, this disillusionment, at such a young age, will color, pardon the pun, every thought and action vis-à-vis their White counterparts. They are compelled to carry and wield these defensive weapons of expecting racist outbursts to be "shields" forever, with no distinction between peacetime and wartime. The alternative is brutal as Sumaya previously wrote about in her Facebook post:

> It was a rare, beautiful evening. I was with my friend, I didn't look around as I always do, and I didn't feel the feeling of vulnerability that exists in me and that can come to light unprepared. As we walked down the street, I was neither Muslim nor black, I was just a young, free woman in an exceptionally good mood. I believe this incident primarily contributes to my grief. I feel as though I am being punished for allowing myself to relax and unwind in public spaces. (Gudbrandsdalen, 2022)

These psychological "shields of self-defense" manifest as preemptive strategies that individuals from Black communities implement to navigate the ubiquitous threat of racism. For instance, one common manifestation is a hesitancy to form new acquaintances as Black individuals may expect to encounter prejudiced attitudes or discriminatory treatment in social interactions. Past experiences of racial microaggressions or outright hostility trigger this tentativeness, prompting individuals to limit their social circle as a protective measure against potential harm. From this perspective, the pervasive hostility of the White gaze, gestures, words, and actions has systematically marginalized those from mainstream spaces, making ghettos their final bastions. These marginalized individuals seek refuge in ghettos where they can find a semblance of safety and belonging amid a society that often fails to afford them acceptance and equity. The progression from the necessity of cognitive and emotional "self-defense" to the periphery of paranoia mirrors Joseph Conrad's reflections in *Heart of Darkness* on the Congolese, whose intentions confounded him.

> The steamer toiled along slowly on the edge of a black and incomprehensible frenzy. The prehistoric man was cursing us, praying to us, welcoming us – who could tell? We were cut off from the comprehension of our surroundings; we glided past like phantoms, wondering and secretly appalled, as sane men would be before an enthusiastic outbreak in a madhouse (Conrad, 1995)

Professor of philosophy Lewis R. Gordon employs an apt analogy to explain the grim reality of whiteness in his book *Fear of Black Consciousness* (2022) by comparing the phenomenon to "a group that crashes someone else's party and whose members tell everyone that not only are they amazing and are doing everyone a favor by crashing the party, but further that the celebration ought to be in their honor" (Gordon, 2022, p. 28). We see this time and again in the aftermath of cases such as the Hulsker and Antonsen cases. The unwelcome presence of whiteness, whose members assert entitlement and superiority while dismissing the legitimacy of their presence, abruptly and rudely intrudes upon Black people going about their business – Sumaya enjoying her day out and the bouncer, Jwan Rasho, professionally doing his job.

Lesley Gore's 1963 classic song "It's My Party" poignantly captures the intrusion that Sumaya and other people of color experience. As the lyrics unfold, we find the protagonist crying at her own birthday party, feeling upset because Judy arrives wearing her Johnny's ring. Similarly, the intrusion of whiteness into Black people's spaces – whiteness "crashing the party" (Gordon, 2022, p. 28) – can be likened to the crashing of a party, leading to silent, and sometimes overt, tears shed by Black individuals – tears that often go unnoticed and misunderstood by others. Just as the singer asserts her right to be distraught despite the occasion, marginalized individuals assert their right to autonomy and belonging, even in the face of unwelcome intrusion and dominance.

Despite demonstrable proof of racial injustice, many White individuals remain confounded by Black people's persistent focus on racism. To them, it seems unfounded, analogous to Don Quixote confusing windmills for dragons. They fail to comprehend the deep-seated and systemic nature of racism, rejecting it as an exaggeration or imagination on the part of Black individuals. Moreover, there is a prevailing belief among some White circles that Black people are excessively consumed by a culture of victimization, often disparaged as "Wokeism." This term has become the latest scapegoat for White supremacy – the new McCarthyism. It's a convenient way to discredit the legitimate grievances of Black individuals, distorting their calls for equality and justice as mere histrionics or self-victimization. On the other hand, why Black people have put up so long with this "party-crashing" behemoth is a puzzle, and Gordon (2022) hazards an explanation:

> Why does such behavior flourish even in the face of its denial? In part, it persists because it is seductive. Many people, even among those dominated, want white supremacy to be what it claims to be because that would give some meaning to their suffering through making white domination seem just. They cannot, in other words, face its truth, which is, in fact, its lie. It is a set of beliefs and institutions handed down across generations saturated with bad faith. (Gordon, 2022, p. 28)

While many Black people would dispute this assertion, several would lend credence to this conundrum. My own experience in education, from primary and upwards to university, in countries as diverse as Ghana, the United Kingdom, and Norway, has distilled anecdotal evidence of the proliferation of whiteness' seductive spell over some Black psyches. It was not uncommon to hear Black parents agonize over the fact that their children loathed their Black skins and desired to be white. In other words, the task of combating racism does not cease with its white source, it is a twofold endeavor that must simultaneously treat the victims. It goes without saying that the belief that White supremacy must be valid in order to give meaning to Black suffering is utterly false.

Anti-racist educators are duty-bound to fight what the Nigerian Nobel Laureate Wole Soyinka called the visual cataracts that have obscured a truthful apprehension of Africa and, by extension, blackness. "The darkness that was so readily attributed to the 'Dark Continent' may yet prove to be nothing but the willful cataract in the eye of the beholder (Soyinka, 2012, p. 26)." The Brazilian educator Paolo Freire draws upon Martin Hegel's argument that oppressed peoples subject themselves to the consciousness of the master and gradually lose their autonomous selves in becoming "beings for another." "The oppressed can overcome the contradiction in which they are caught only when this perception enlists them in the struggle to free themselves" (Freire, 1996, p. 31). Freire uses the Portuguese term *conscientização* to refer to the process of critical consciousness-raising or conscientization. It involves individuals critically discerning the social, political, and economic forces that shape their lives, as well as the systems of oppression that exist in society.

Through *conscientização*, people are empowered to critically examine their reality, recognize sources of oppression and injustice, and take action to alter their circumstances. It is a central concept in Freire's pedagogy, particularly in his work with oppressed communities, because it forms the foundation for empowering individuals to become agents of change in their own lives and communities. Central to this process is the notion of self-liberation through empowerment. Like Socrates, Freire and other critical pedagogues, can only play the role of midwives, asking questions and highlighting knowledge that assists in the process of birthing *conscientização*. Sumaya demonstrates this sense of self-liberation from the shackles of the seductive nature of whiteness that Gordon (2022) implicates in whiteness's staying power. In her reflexive autobiography, Sumaya writes:

> It is painful to admit that for so long you lived in a mentally and physically barren landscape, that you were taught from a young age to believe that it is those who are drowning you who will one day extend a life jacket. (Ali, 2023, p. 221)

This epiphany is commensurate with Freire's advocacy of the imperative for the oppressed to become agents of their own self-emancipation.

> The central problem is this: How can the oppressed, as divided, unauthentic beings, participate in developing the pedagogy of their liberation? Only as they discover themselves to be "hosts" of their oppressor can they contribute to the midwifery of their liberating pedagogy. As long as they live in the duality in which to be is to be like, and to be like is to be like the oppressor, this contribution is impossible. (Freire, 1996, p. 30)

Revisiting "the fear of encountering racism" as "an even bigger problem" than racism itself (Kuflu & Libanos, Aftenposten, 2022), it is apparent that such fears rooted in real but subtle and difficult-to-prove experiences were later distilled in the term microaggressions. Chester M. Pierce was an influential psychiatrist, educator, and researcher recognized for his groundbreaking work on the psychology of racism and the impact of discrimination on mental health. Born in 1927, Pierce was a trailblazer in the field of racial psychiatry, dedicating much of his career to understanding how racial and ethnic identity intersected with mental health and well-being.

Pierce is perhaps best known for his pioneering work on the concept of microaggressions. He coined the term in the 1970s to illustrate the subtle, everyday forms of discrimination experienced by minoritized groups, particularly people of color. Pierce's research stressed how these ostensibly minor slights and insults could have significant and enduring effects on individuals' mental health, contributing to feelings of invalidation, self-doubt, and psychological anxiety. Throughout his career, Pierce advocated for greater awareness of the psychological impact of racism and discrimination, emphasizing the need for systemic change to address these issues. He was also a prominent figure in the field of cultural psychiatry, exploring how cultural factors influence mental health and treatment outcomes. Pierce (1995) defines microaggressions in this way:

> Probably the most grievous of offensive mechanisms spewed at victims in racism and sexism are microaggressions. These are subtle, innocuous, preconscious, or unconscious degradations, and putdowns, often kinetic but capable of being verbal and/or kinetic. In and of itself a microaggression may seem harmless, but the cumulative burden of a lifetime of microaggressions can theoretically contribute to diminished mortality, augmented morbidity, and flattened confidence. (Pierce, 1995, p. 281)

In addition to his research contributions, Pierce was a passionate educator and counselor, training generations of psychiatrists and psychologists to identify and address the complexities of race, culture, and mental health. His work has had a continuing impact on the field of psychology, inspiring further research and advocacy efforts to promote mental health equity and social justice. Pierce (1995, p. 281) forwards an example of microaggressions: "The lone black among a group of seventy full professors is asked to move the chairs so a meeting can commence." In another example, Pierce (1995) draws attention to how Black people, as the victimized, often feel the need to engage in assuaging the fear of White people after experiencing a microaggression. A White female passenger, feeling uncomfortable seated next to two Black men on an airplane, exchanges seats with a White man nearby, demonstrating her anxiety. The Black passenger seated next to the White male passenger, subjected to racially motivated microaggressions, experiences additional stress and discomfort as he feels the need "to initiate friendly small talk, probably to make the White feel good about himself and for the black to indicate happy acceptance of the insult" (Pierce, 1995, p. 281).

Chester Pierce's theory of microaggressions provides valuable insights into how these elusive forms of discrimination generate psychological maladies. According to Pierce, microaggressions are brief, routine exchanges that transmit hostile, derogatory, or negative racial slights or insults toward marginalized groups. Pierce's theory emphasizes that these outwardly minor acts of discrimination can have significant and cumulative effects on individuals' mental health and well-being. To avoid exhaustion, Black people must carefully select which microaggressions they will grapple with.

> However, in a real sense, one's adaptation to the stress of a dominator depends on how well one defends self-image, how carefully one selects which microaggressions to defend against, to deflect, or to allow to pass. Most microaggressions have to be allowed to pass, to protect one's time, energy, sanity, or bodily integrity. Racism and sexism then are stress-related public health illnesses. They can be approached in terms of questions about segregation, quarantine, and immunization. (Pierce, 1995, p. 282)

Drawing from Pierce's theory, we can understand how racial microaggressions contribute to psychological ills through several mechanisms:

- *Cumulative Impact:* Pierce's theory highlights the cumulative impact of microaggressions in the long run. These repeated incidents of subtle discrimination can erode an individual's resilience and coping mechanisms, resulting in chronic stress, anxiety, depression, and additional mental health issues.
- *Identity Threat:* Microaggressions often target aspects of an individual's racial or ethnic identity, which comprise the bulwark upholding the sense of self. Pierce's theory suggests that these attacks on identity can lead to feelings of invalidation, self-doubt, and internalized racism, contributing to the degradation of self-esteem and psychological distress.
- *Hypervigilance:* Individuals who experience microaggressions may become hypervigilant, frequently on the lookout for further instances of discrimination or bias. This heightened state of vigilance can be draining and lead to increased levels of stress, anxiety, and emotional turbulence.
- *Social Isolation:* Microaggressions can also lead to social detachment and seclusion, as individuals may skirt certain environments or interactions where they anticipate suffering discrimination. This social isolation can impair feelings of loneliness, alienation, and depression, further impacting mental health and well-being.

Touching on the aforementioned perplexity of White people at the seemingly unwarranted Black preoccupation with racism, Pierce (1995, p. 277) reminds us, "Almost all oppressors are unmindful of the withering effects of cumulative, individual, and collective microaggressions toward victims, even honestly believing that they themselves have inflicted no damage upon socially devalued persons." Gordon (2022) alludes to this obliviousness to the cause of mental suffering, while simultaneously sensing and acknowledging the damage, when he recounts an incident in which a White colleague asked him if he had been in therapy. Finding the question odd, Gordon asked his colleague why she asked about this in the first place. Pondering on her response that he seemed "well... healthy. That's not normal," Gordon concludes:

> In a white supremacist society, the bearers of that supremacy require the normalization of pathological blackness. That colleague was saying that to belong to her world – in the sense of fitting in, to the extent that that was possible – required me to be mentally ill... To some extent... she was right. That colleague was also voicing a white need. Blacks are supposedly abnormal; therefore, for me to be "normal", pathology *must* be there. She needed to see it. (Gordon, 2022, p. 31)

In summary, Chester Pierce's theory of microaggressions helps us understand how these subtle forms of discrimination are causal in engendering psychological maladies among individuals from marginalized racial groups. By recognizing the harmful effects of microaggressions and working to address them, we can promote mental health equity and create more inclusive and supportive environments for all individuals. In the spirit of Freire, who advocated a mutual healing journey for both the oppressor and the oppressed, one cannot stop at the mere analysis of the oppressed's condition. Understanding the unseen anxiety and silent suffering of individuals like Sumaya, Nigist, and Sara leads not to the vilification or demonization of the oppressor, but to love and compassion, as the path to emancipation is a collective one that involves all shades of humanity. Freire describes the condition of the oppressed alone as "necrophilic":

> The peasant is dependent. He can't say what he wants. Before he discovers his dependence, he suffers. He lets off steam at home, where he shouts at his children, beats them, and despairs. He complains about his wife and thinks everything is dreadful. He doesn't let off steam with the boss because he believes he is superior. Lots of times, the peasant gives vent to his sorrows by drinking. (Freire, 1996, p. 47)

Perhaps this fatalistic resignation to such "necrophilic" behavior may explain the many challenges faced by people of color in Norway: psychological problems, academic failings, indulgence in criminal activity, and the ensuing high rates of prisoners of color, among others. By way of anecdotal observation, a trip to any local emergency room (legevakta) in major Norwegian cities reveals a preponderance of Black and brown people. For genuine healing and change to occur, Freire (1996) suggests a radical engagement:

> This, then, is the great humanistic and historical task of the oppressed: to liberate themselves and their oppressors as well. The oppressors, who oppress, exploit, and rape by virtue of their power, cannot find in this power the strength to liberate either the oppressed or themselves. (Freire, 1996, p. 26)

This book was conceived in this radical spirit of mutual healing.

This does not imply that White oppressors can absolve themselves of their crimes or shift the burden to the oppressed. White people also need to be conscientized to the collective cost of racism. In her book *The Sum of Us: What Racism Costs Everyone and How We Can Prosper Together* (2022), Heather McGhee refers to Vanderbilt Professor Jonathan Metzl's book *Dying of Whiteness*, where he takes stock of the cost of skyrocketing gun ownership among White people propelled by the fear of Obama's Black presidency. Despite an era of record-low crime rates in the United States, right-wing media, in conjunction with the militant National Rifle Association, aggressively marketed White fear. Ironically, the proliferation of white gun ownership saw a marked rise in White suicide rates.

> Suicide attempts with a gun have an 85 percent success rate, compared to a 3 percent rate for the most frequently used suicide method, drug overdose. White men are now one-third of the population but three-quarters of the gun suicide victims. And twice as many people die from gun suicides in America each year as from the gun homicides people have been so conditioned to fear. (McGhee, 2022, p. 239)

So much for the fears of the "Black peril." As the "browning" of the populations of the West continues unabated, the band of human colors has no choice but to find a way to coexist, or better yet, thrive, like the spectrum of colors in the rainbow with echoes of the uplifting Noahic legend of the cessation of evil, judgement, and devastation. The thesis of Eric Kaufmann's book "Whiteshift" (2018) centers on the idea that demographic changes, principally the decline of the White population in Western countries due to low birth rates and immigration, are the catalysts for a significant cultural and political shift. Kaufmann argues that this demographic transformation is leading to a resurgence of White identity politics and nationalist movements as White people seek to maintain their cultural and political dominance in the face of increasing diversity. He explores how these dynamics shape contemporary politics, social attitudes, and identity formation, proposing strategies for managing multiculturalism and addressing the concerns of different demographic groups. Some critics are worried that Kaufmann's emphasis on preserving White cultural dominance could undermine efforts to promote diversity, equality, and social justice. They argue that his emphasis on White identity politics ignores the structural inequalities and historical injustices that continue to shape society and perpetuate racial and ethnic inequalities. While the concerns about inadvertently lending succor to White supremacy are legitimate, his point about the changing demographic and the need to rethink race-relations is apposite.

The stoic Roman philosopher Lucius Seneca stated in *Letters from a Stoic*, "In certain cases, sick men are to be congratulated because they themselves have perceived that they are sick" (Seneca, 2020, p. 10). The first business of order, then, is for both White people and Black people to perceive the nature of their "sicknesses" and only then embark on the road to mutual healing. In the crucible of racial vilification, even souls such as the racially reviled Sumayas must recover the faintest embers of empathy within to engage in a battle of wills against the towering edifice of White supremacy with the aim of saving all. As Freire reminds us, "Only power that springs from the weakness of the oppressed will be sufficiently strong to free both" (Freire, 1996, p. 26). His call is one where the hands of the oppressed are to be stretched, not in supplication, docility or fear, but so that "more and more they become human hands which work and, working, transform the world" (Freire, 1996, p. 26).

3. Structural Racism and the "Original Sin"

> But is Antonsen a racist? Many people believe that Antonsen's racism is obvious – his drunkenness simply spills over into his actions. This is where it becomes important to think about structural and unconscious racism. This includes discriminatory structures, unconscious prejudices, and inherited stereotypes. In addition, there are infantile notions that "everything is funny" only when the right person says it.
>
> Many societies are full of such structures and unconscious prejudices. Our society is also rife with sources of racist statements and actions, often without the assumption that an individual acting in a racist manner is necessarily a racist in the true sense of the word. This is why such attitudes, actions, and statements can appear, in full or in other individual contexts. (Gule, Aftenposten, 2022)

Lars Gule, a retired Norwegian academic, was until recently one of the country's leading authorities in regard to the Middle East, Islam, and extremism. Gule comments on the perplexing phenomenon of White liberals who cannot be defined as ideologically committed racists yet make statements that are clearly racist. He reconciles the contradictions by invoking systemic and structural racism. To his credit, Gule invokes these concepts, which many in Norway refuse to acknowledge or tone down, as is evident in the title of his opinion piece, "The time of downplaying and explaining away should be over now." As an example of denial of the existence of systemic and structural racism in Norway, one professor, a former head of diversity studies, denounces structural racism's founding father, Eduardo Bonilla-Silva:

Embracing concepts developed by research activists with big egos and enormous ambitions, who believe their concepts and perspectives can establish completely new descriptions of reality and foster peace and justice, is naive. Both Eduardo Bonilla-Silva and Johan Galtung, the fathers of the terms structural racism and structural violence, two hugely influential researchers, undoubtedly fit into this category. My conclusion is that the concept of structural racism is quite unsuitable for analyzing discrimination and inequality in society. (Brekke, 2021)

Herein lies the crux of the problem. If a former head of so-called diversity studies in Norway dismisses structural and systemic racism as "unsuitable for analyzing discrimination and inequality in society," one can indeed understand why White liberals and the general public are ill-prepared to grapple with racism, with the result that cases such as Antonsen's rear their ugly heads at regular intervals. The insouciance is buttressed by the hubris that the shared sense of Nordic exceptionalism stands impervious to the base, uncouth manifestations inherent to racism. One cannot provide an exhaustive list of the plethora of "feel-good-factors" that feed into what I have called "the architecture of virtue" (Thomas, 2016) in Norway.

This concept can be broadly interpreted as Norway's delicate supervision of both tangible and intangible assets, both domestically and internationally, in order to unswervingly portray, uphold, and perpetuate itself as an advocate of human rights, equity, and peace. Drawing from Barthes' (1972) discourse on symbols and signs designed to propagate specific myths, examples such as the Nobel Peace Prize, extensive involvement in global peace initiatives (e.g., the Oslo Peace Accords of 1993), and sizable contributions to the United Nations Development Programme (UNDP) exemplify Norway's strategic endeavors. For instance, in 2014, Norway emerged as the UNDP's leading core contributor, allocating an impressive sum of over 112 million USD, and supporting numerous projects worldwide. While this compilation is not exhaustive, given the focus of this study on race relations, the notion of the "architecture of virtue" also extends to Norway's reception of asylum seekers and refugees, particularly those originating from Africa and Asia over the years. Marianne Gullestad, a late Norwegian anthropologist, discusses the same phenomenon in relation to the media debate about the use of the epithet "neger" [negro]" in Norway.

According to my interpretation, the neutrality of the term "Negro" is associated with the nation's perceived innocence and goodness regarding slavery, imperialism, and colonialism. Accepting Ertzgaard's [black Norwegian sprinter who objected to the use of "'Negro"] plea would imply accepting the accusation that Norway was a part of Europe, which once treated blacks "like animals and a pest". (Gullestad, 2005, p. 40)

In essence, a significant number of Norwegians exhibit a disinclination toward acknowledging the existence of systemic racism, primarily due to the trepidation that such acknowledgment could precipitate the collapse of the meticulously crafted facade of Nordic exceptionalism, akin to the proverbial house of cards. During discussions with fellow introspective Norwegians, some admitted to the existence of systemic racism in Norway. However, the horror of confronting potentially unsettling truths lurking within their own psyches constrains them to withdraw hastily to the safety of ignorance, preferring the consolation of familiar ignorance over the disquiet of confronting harsh realities. Having the ship moored and tethered to the familiar harbors of the conscience is preferable to having it untethered and at the mercy of the waves. It is preferable to anchor the ship of imagined racial inclusiveness and tolerance to the familiar shores of conscience rather than letting it drift, unmoored, at the whim of the tempestuous waves.

It was Eduardo Bonilla-Silva (1997) whose influential paper pushed for a reorientation of the study of racism toward his structural theory of racism. He asserted that whereas the prevailing discourse broached racism as a predominantly ideological phenomenon, it is essentially a structural issue. This view was prevalent, among others, because Marxist theory construed racism as an offshoot of the class struggle in which the bourgeoisie exploited class divisions along racial lines to perpetuate their hegemony. According to Bonilla-Silva's perspective, we must disentangle racism from its roots in class struggle and examine it as a social phenomenon within racial relations (Bonilla-Silva, 1997, p. 466). Therefore, we must explore racism in the interstices of practices, not in ideas. In such a framework, it would be unhelpful to dismiss racism as irrational because it has real consequences.

There are parallels with Durkheim's "social facts." Émile Durkheim (Durkheim, 1982) advanced the concept of social facts. Social facts refer to the aspects of social life that exist outside of individuals and inform their behavior. These include norms, values, customs, traditions, and institutions that exert a strong influence on individuals, shaping their actions and thoughts. Durkheim argued that social facts have a reality of their own and are not simply the outcome of individual actions but are products of collective forces within society. He emphasized the importance of studying social facts scientifically, independently of individual subjectivity, to understand how societies function and evolve. Bonilla-Silva (1997, p. 472) sketched the historical contours of the particular evolution of racism in context in a process he saw as "racialization," which infiltrates categories such as class and gender as entities with real collectivities.

> What are the dynamics of racial issues in racialized systems? Most important, after a social formation is racialized, its "normal" dynamics always include a racial component. Societal struggles based on class or gender contain a racial component because both of these social categories are also racialized; that is, both class and gender are constructed along racial lines. (Bonilla-Silva, 1997, p. 473)

From this perspective, Sumaya Jirde Ali's "racialization" makes sense. As a woman, one who was dark-skinned and hailing from a refugee background, the White male patriarchy felt threatened. Sumaya, a rising poet and influential social critic in Norway, was a formidable voice in her own right. Antonsen's perplexing and intimidating insistence regarding Sumaya's supposed hidden agenda, of which he was purportedly cognizant, serves as a notable example. Furthermore, his readiness to use physical force sheds light on the intricate racialization process that permeates gender and class categories. Harnessing Foucault's (1977) concept of the panopticon to explore how Antonsen's White gaze racialized the Black female body of Sumaya unpacks the power dynamics couched within racialized systems. The panopticon, a symbolic structure of surveillance and control, operates on the principle of relentless observation and the internalization of discipline by those under surveillance. Antonsen's gaze serves as the watchtower of the panopticon in Sumaya's case, enforcing a racialized lens that inspects and controls her body and identity to prevent her from invading the bastions of White patriarchy.

> All authorities exercising individual control function according to a double mode, that of binary division and branding (mad/sane, dangerous/harmless, normal/abnormal), and that of coercive assignment, of differential distribution (who he is, where he must be, how he is to be characterized, how he is to be recognized, how a constant surveillance is to be exercised over him in an individual way. (Foucault, 1977, p. 199)

Antonsen's assessment of Sumaya as a threat stems from the intersectionality of her identities: as a woman, a person of color, and a refugee. Her very existence, in the eyes of the White male patriarchy, challenges established power structures and norms. As previously mentioned, Sumaya's emergence as a rising poet and influential social critic amplifies this threat as her voice gains prominence and challenges the monovocal dominant narratives. Antonsen's claim that Sumaya was operating with a hidden agenda highlights the panoptic nature of racialized surveillance where the racialized subject internalizes and self-polices the reading of deviance or subversion. His willingness to resort to physical force further demonstrates the coercive mechanisms of racialization, wherein the Black female body transmutes into a site of both fascination and fear for the White male gaze. The aim was to mold a "docile" female body in Foucauldian terms.

> The human body was entering a machinery of power that explores it, breaks it down and rearranges it. A "political anatomy", which was also a "mechanics of power", was being born; it defined how one may have a hold over others' bodies, not only so that they may do what one wishes, but so that they operate as one wishes, with the techniques, the speed and the efficiency that one determines. Thus, discipline produces subjected and practiced bodies, "docile" bodies. (Foucault, 1977, p. 138)

There is a sense in which "structural racism" carries the connotation of ordering and structuring. Antonsen's attempt to incarcerate Sumaya can be analyzed through Foucault's (1977, p. 143) concept of partitioning, which draws attention to the division and control of individual bodies within disciplinary spaces, much like the famed Prussian military drills. Foucault contends that disciplinary space is divided into several sections, each relating to an individual body or element to be regulated. This division serves to eliminate vague distributions, prevent individuals' uncontrolled disappearance, and mitigate their unstable and dangerous coagulation.

> It was a tactic of anti-desertion, anti-vagabondage, and anti-concentration. Its aim was to establish presences and absences, to know where and how to locate individuals. It was a procedure, therefore, aimed at knowing, mastering and using. Discipline organizes an analytical space. (Foucault, 1977, p. 143)

In Antonsen's case, his actions reflect the racialized process of discipline and punishment etched within the system of racism in which he operates. Antonsen, as a distillation of this racialized system, learns to partition Sumaya's blackness, gender, and class, viewing it as a threat that must be controlled and contained. By attempting to incarcerate Sumaya, Antonsen seeks to impose discipline on her Black body, relegating her to a specific place within society where she can be monitored and controlled. In this manner, Antonsen's conduct is commensurate with Foucault's notion of breaking up collective dispositions and analyzing chaotic pluralities. Rather than viewing Sumaya as an individual with agency and autonomy, Antonsen reduces her to a racialized stereotype, imposing upon her the collective identity of a sinister Black woman. This parochial approach allows Antonsen to justify his attempts to discipline and punish Sumaya, as he perceives her blackness as inherently deviant and in need of punitive measures. Racialization in relation to Black individuals, then, deviously operates through weaponizing the blackness of these individuals against themselves. The ultimate aim of the kind of structure exercised by the likes of Antonsen as an extension of the White supremacist collective is to exploit the visibility of blackness to induce Black people to constrain their behavior to conform to White dictates.

> Disciplinary power, on the other hand, is exercised through its invisibility; at the same time, it imposes on those whom it subjects a principle of compulsory visibility. In discipline, it is the subjects who have to be seen. Their visibility assures the hold of the power that is exercised over them. It is the fact of being constantly seen, of being able always to be seen, that maintains the disciplined individual in his subjection. (Foucault, 1977, p. 187)

Antonsen's violent desire to "reimpose" what he perceived as "compulsory visibility" upon Sumaya parallels the coercive enforcement of hijabs on women by the Mullahcracy in Iran. Within the panopticon, White supremacy demands loyal self-monitoring from Black women, with severe repercussions for any deviation from prescribed norms. Sumaya, however, had long resisted this anticipation, refusing to kowtow to White dictates that sought to restrict and mold her blackness into a compliant, docile form. Instead, she stubbornly challenged the power dynamics inherent in the panopticon, declining the role of a passive "prisoner" and asserting her right to occupy an agency position alongside the very agents of surveillance. Antonsen's reaction, therefore, stemmed from his frustration at Sumaya's refusal to adhere to the prescribed boundaries of racialized surveillance and control. If Sumaya was left unpunished, and several other Black individuals followed in her footsteps, the entire panopticon structure would collapse, as the bluff of White supremacy would be made a gaping stock. If Sumaya went unpunished, and if others of Black extraction were to emulate her defiance, the entire panopticon apparatus would face imminent collapse, exposing the hollow facade of White supremacy.

Lars Gule is right. Antonsen and Hulsker are not racists in the sense that the neo-Nazis Joe Erling Jahr and Ole Nicolai Kvisler were. Winant (1998, pp. 760–761) operates with the following definition of racism:

> Today, a racial project can be defined as racist if it creates or reproduces a racially unequal social structure, based on essentialized racial categories; if it essentializes or naturalizes racial identities or significations, based on a racially unequal social structure; or both.

To "essentialize" is to distill or reduce something to its essential or most vital aspects. It involves identifying the core characteristics, kernel, or qualities that define a particular concept, idea, or entity while often overlooking marginal or less significant details.

There is no prior or subsequent record that gives the indication that Antonsen espoused a racist ideology in the sense defined by Winant (1998). Nevertheless, his remarks were racist because he essentialized Sumaya's physical presence to her skin color alone and to the exclusion of a myriad other characteristics and qualities: from the physical (female, age, etc., visible Muslim) to her qualifications (poet, writer, social critic, etc.). It is significant that Antonsen did not antagonize Sumaya's Islamic identity based on the hijab she wore. This must be noted because rare is the occasion when contemporary racists (the previously mentioned White "lone wolves") are simultaneously unconcerned with Islam. Neither did Antonsen explicitly pour scorn on Sumaya because she was a female. Had he suffered from misogyny, her White Norwegian friend would have suffered the same fate. The controversial Freudian slip, an unpremeditated error in speech, memory, or action that reveals an individual's subconscious thoughts, desires, or motivations, cannot explain his outburst either. Critics contest the validity of Freudian slips, asserting that factors like cognitive processing errors, linguistic patterns, or random chance, rather than subconscious causes, can account for them.

So, should we conclude that a sudden and mysterious onslaught of anti-blackness, an overpowering, otherworldly emotional blitz against blackness, momentarily blindsided or ambushed Antonsen? If so, this irrational surge of anti-Black sentiment has ensnared many, claiming even the virtuous, as chronicled in the biblical tale of Moses's siblings – Miriam and Aaron – who, too, fell victim to its relentless tide. We read in the fourth book of the Torah, or Numbers, "And Miriam and Aaron spake against Moses because of the Ethiopian woman whom he had married, for he had married an Ethiopian woman" (Numbers 12:1; King James Version). While it is certain that the "Ethiopian" woman is Black, scholars debate whether she was Nubian or the well-known Midianite, Zipporah. Significantly, the recent Netflix film, *Testament: The Story of Moses* (2024) depicts Zipporah as a Black woman, played by the Black British actress Dominique Tipper.

Scholars have noted that the biblical account does not explicitly outline the reasons for Miriam and Aaron's hostility toward Moses's wife, a description of whom is Black. However, the subsequent affliction of Miriam with leprosy suggests a divine condemnation of racial prejudice. The sudden juxtaposition of Miriam's affliction with her now repulsive "whiteness" against the backdrop of Moses's wife's "blackness" highlights a possible contempt or discrimination against her by Moses's siblings. "If she were from Nubia, this woman would have been Black, 'rendering the whitened skin of Miriam a singularly fit punishment for her objections to the Cushite wife'" (Filler et al., 2021). This incident, therefore, serves as a poignant narrative illuminating the divine condemnation of racism within the biblical context. On the one hand, some of the ancients, such as the celebrated Philo of Alexandria, demonstrate a prescient racial inclusivity in regard to the overt racism of Moses's kin. Philo, in his allegorical interpretation, differentiates Aaron and Miriam's derivative knowledge of God from Moses's lucid insight. Moses's profound understanding, inaccessible to his siblings, leads to their racism and subsequent opposition. Philo draws a curious parallel between Moses's wife's dark skin and the concept of "perfect focus," like the Black of the eyes, symbolizing Moses's unique, unmediated connection with the divine (Filler et al., 2021). On the other hand, the scholastics of the medieval era, such as Bernard of Clairvaux (1090–1153 AD) imposed their racialized hermeneutics into the biblical text: Black became synonymous with sin and evil, and Moses's disturbing marriage to a Black woman had to be rationalized:

> This notion, encouraged by the Vetus Latina reading of Songs of Songs 8:5 as "quae est ista quae ascendit dealbata" (who is she who arises, made white), was repeated in many contexts, though Bernard of Clairvaux contrasted Moses and his Ethiopian with Christ, who as the bridegroom of the Song of Songs not only humbles himself to wed a black woman but whitens her in the process (Moses could not change the color of skin but Christ could. (Filler et al., 2021, p. 1160)

No one, then, appears to be immune to the subtle influences of anti-Black racism, even in the pages of the world's most influential best-selling book of all time, the Bible. Examining the issue of anti-Black racism in the Bible further brings to mind the protest of the unnamed Black Shulammite woman in the Song of Solomon.

> I am black, but comely, O ye daughters of Jerusalem, as the tents of Kedar, as the curtains of Solomon. Look not upon me, because I am black, because the sun hath looked upon me: my mother's children were angry with me; they made me the keeper of the vineyards; but mine own vineyard have I not kept. (Song of Solomon 1:5, 6; KJV)

Matthew Henry (1662–1714), one of the most celebrated and prolific writers, best known for his *Commentary on the Whole Bible* and whose commentary is still immensely popular among evangelical Christians, stated the following about the blackness of King Solomon's lover, the Shulammite woman:

> [...] she owns she is black. Guilt blackens; the heresies, scandals, and offences, that happen in the church, make her black; and the best saints have their failings. Sorrow blackens; that seems to be especially meant... She was fair and comely; whiteness was her proper color; but she got this blackness by the burden and heat of the day, which she was forced to bear. She was sun-burnt, scorched with tribulation and persecution (Mt. 13:6, 21); and the greatest beauties, if exposed to the weather, are soonest tanned. (Blue Letter Bible, Matthew Henry's Commentary, 2024)

Allegorical denigration of blackness within a Judeo-Christian framework is not an exclusive phenomenon attributed solely to Matthew Henry; it is evident across various theological exegesis. Blackness is associated with negative attributes such as guilt, heresies, scandals, offenses, and sorrow, drawing upon Christian allegorical interpretations. The Shulammite woman experiences a metaphorical transformation from fairness (whiteness) to blackness as a result of experiencing hardships and suffering. While on the surface, this transformation may seem to convey a universal message about the effects of harsh conditions on individuals, it is important to consider how White theologians and commentators perpetuated anti-Black racism within a Judeo-Christian context. The correlation of blackness with harmful attributes such as suffering, and hardship reflects a deeply embedded bias against Black people within Western Christianity. Allegorical interpretations of biblical texts have historically rooted this bias, often figuratively linking blackness to sin, sorrow, and moral degradation. By metaphorically equating blackness with adversity and suffering, Henry's commentary reinforces the idea that color is inherently negative or injurious.

To Matthew Henry's mind, "She was fair and comely; whiteness was her proper color; but she got this blackness from the burden and heat of the day, which she was forced to bear." This postulation – the implicit notion that whiteness is normal, the "default" color of the Shulammite woman – is commensurate with the first tenet of critical race theory: "First, racism is ordinary, not aberrational – normal science, 'the usual way society does business, the common, everyday experience of most people of color in this country'" (Delgado & Stefancic, 2012, p. 7). The implication is that the Shulammite woman, someone worthy of a romantic relationship with none other than the renowned King Solomon, could never be Black. Clearly, the assumption was that Solomon himself was White, the color of virtue. The blackness of the Shulammite woman had to be found elsewhere, for instance, in the manual labor she had to endure out in the heat of the day working in the vineyard. Simply because blackness was not "normal," its presence demanded an explanation.

In the theology of clerics and divines like Matthew Henry, sin, defined as insurrection against God's laws, is figuratively equated with blackness. Historically, Western religious discourse has symbolically linked blackness to moral depravity and spiritual degradation. While contemporary Western culture has moved away from unvarnished antiblack theological speculations, remnants of this historical perspective endure, indicating that the cultural shift toward racial equality has not yet fully eradicated the deep-rooted biases of the past. Clerics and divines such as Matthew Henry metaphorically equate sin, defined as rebellion against God's laws, with blackness in their theology. This association mirrors a historical trend in Western religious discourse, symbolically linking blackness to moral corruption and spiritual degradation.

While contemporary Western culture has moved away from overtly anti-Black theological interpretations, remnants of this historical perspective persist, indicating that the cultural shift toward racial equality has not yet fully eradicated the deep-rooted biases of the past. Centuries of anti-Black theology have clearly permeated White Western countries, which share a common Judeo-Christian heritage. Pastor, activist, and lecturer at Georgetown and Harvard University, Jim Wallis wrote the New York Times bestseller, *America's Original Sin: Racism, White Privilege, and the Bridge to a New America* (2016). When Jim Wallis refers to slavery and racism as America's "Original sin," he is making a theological and moral assertion about the nascent injustices that have shaped the United States. Christian theology derives the term "original sin," implying that humanity's inherent sinfulness stems from Adam and Eve's disobedience in the Garden of Eden. By identifying slavery and racism as America's "Original sin," Wallis is accentuating that these injustices are fundamental to the nation's history and identity. Like the theological idea of Original sin, they are deeply etched and have far-reaching consequences that continue to impact society today. Wallis argues that acknowledging and addressing these historical injustices is essential for moral and social healing, as well as building a more just and equitable society.

> And the political and economic problems of race are ultimately rooted in a theological problem. The churches have too often "baptized" us into our racial divisions, instead of understanding how our authentic baptism unites us above and beyond our racial

identities. . . if white Christians in America were ready to act more
Christian than white when it comes to race, black parents would be
less fearful for their children. (Wallis, 2016, pp. 8, 9)

Several other Western nations could share similar sentiments. We can discern
the origins of ongoing racism in contemporary White society within the complex
intersections of theological, economic, and historical trajectories. This is the type
of racism that blatantly maintains Sumaya's exclusion from a bar in Oslo based
solely on her skin color. The repercussions of the "Original" sins of past generations are unquestionably manifesting themselves in the present: the chickens are
coming home to roost. A comprehensive and thorough examination of this entire
historical trajectory is imperative. In Christian theology, baptism symbolizes a
spiritual rebirth, often signifying a "death" to sin and the subsequent emergence
of a "new man [sic]." Noel Ignatiev's (2022) advocacy for a "death to whiteness"
resonates within this framework, suggesting an undoing of the structures and
ideologies that uphold White supremacy. Malcolm X's statement, "the chickens
are coming home to roost," is often cited to suggest that the consequences of one's
actions will ultimately catch up with them. In the context of the assassination of
President Kennedy, Malcolm X employed this phrase to suggest that Kennedy's
policies had led to his own demise. His lack of sensitivity clearly offended some
Black people. My argument for invoking Malcolm is to call out the hypocrisy that
dilutes and whitewashes the kind of racism that is well and alive in Norwegian
society yet perceives itself as a champion of human rights and democracy the
world over. Malcolm's pronouncement highlights the necessity of confronting and
defeating White supremacism, instead of pursuing unity with "liberals" and
"progressives" who toy with the White apparatus. Malcolm asserts that we
cannot appease fascists and racists, but we must confront them. Wallis (2016) cites
another reason for the urgency of confronting the "Original sin":

In about thirty years, the majority of Americans will be descended
from Africans, Asians, and Latin Americans. Many white
Americans are clearly not ready for that profound demographic
change in their country. The white fear of who "we" Americans
will be is at the heart of much of the resistance to immigration
reform, in my view, as well as underlying the criminal justice
controversies and other political issues such as voter suppression.
(Wallis, 2016, p. 38)

There is no doubt that the same trend is apparent in Norway too, as Fig. 2
indicates. In 2024, the Black and brown populations from Asia and Africa,
respectively, will make up close to 10% of the total population, compared to less
than 1% in the 1970s. Undoubtedly, these seismic demographic shifts have
unsettled conservatives to such an extent that they are crafting desperate and
racist policies as I write. As previously mentioned, Drammen municipality, 45 km
southwest of Oslo, crafted a controversial proposal to only accept refugees from
Ukraine, prompting Simon Nordanger from the Center Party to file a complaint
against the municipality for violating discrimination laws and constitutional
provisions.

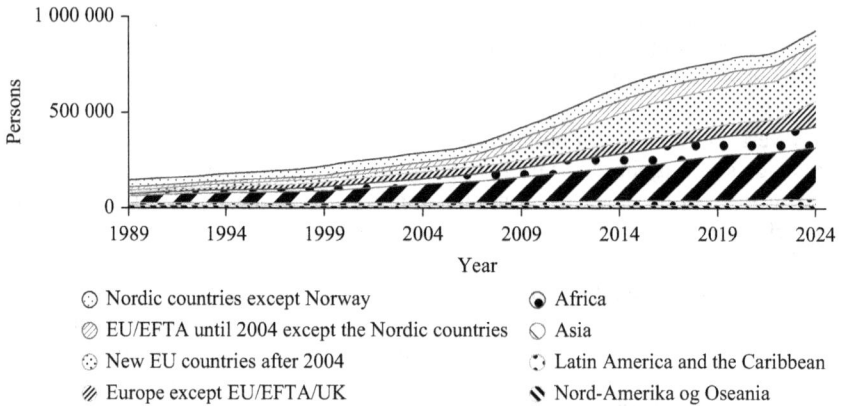

Fig. 2.   Country Background for Immigrants. *Source:* Immigrants and Norwegian-born to immigrant parents, Statistics Norway.

The narrow majority vote that passed this decision has sparked controversy because it departs from the municipality's professed values of equality and nondiscrimination. Nordanger's emotional response during the council meeting reflects the severity of the situation, conveying dismay at the willingness of some council members to compromise on these values. His objection cites discrimination laws and constitutional principles that prohibit partial treatment based on factors such as ethnicity and guarantee equal treatment under the law. Ultimately, the municipality's decision faces legal scrutiny, with the municipal lawyer suggesting that it may be in violation of both national and international regulations. This case is an illustration of mounting White fears at in light of the proliferation of Black and brown bodies in Drammen, a city with a large non-White demographic.

4. Nice Racism: The Liberal Conundrum

> I have realized that I owe you an apology from Saturday. It was thoughtless to joke around about such heavy matters... I've probably become completely blind after too many years of fooling around with this Golden thing. Anyway, I deeply apologize if I ended up hurting you. (Antonsen, NrK, 2022)

Johan Golden and Atle Antonsen are Norwegian comedians who have collaborated extensively in the entertainment industry. They are best known for their work together on various television shows, comedy sketches, and live performances. Their partnership spans a number of decades and has produced many comedic creations that have become popular among Norwegian audiences.

Golden and Antonsen share a comedic chemistry that is apparent in their performances, characterized by witty banter, sharp humor, and often irreverent satire. They have a knack for creating memorable characters and situations that resonate with viewers, showcasing their talent for observational comedy and comedic improvisation. Their cooperation has resulted in the creation of several successful television shows, including "Golden Goal," "Team Antonsen," and "Uti vår hage" [Out in our Garden]. These programs have received widespread acclaim and have solidified Golden and Antonsen's reputation as two of Norway's most beloved comedians.

Johan Golden was born in Guadeloupe, with a father from the Caribbean and a mother from Halden, who met in Montpellier, France. He grew up in Kjelsås, Oslo, while his father returned to Guadeloupe when Johan was six years old. He holds citizenship in both Norway and France (Holen, 2023). In her book, *Nice Racism: How Progressive White People Perpetuate Racial Harm* Robin DiAngelo (2021, p. 2) defines "nice racism" as referring to "White people who see themselves as *racially* progressive, well-meaning, *nice*... They might call themselves, 'woke', or even claim to be 'beyond race'. White progressives are generally on the left side of the political spectrum but can be moderates, centrists, or 'soft' conservatives." In Antonsen's rambling "apologies," reference is made to his comedic partner Johan Golden in the sentence "fooling around with this Golden thing."

While not explicitly labeled as racism, the phenomenon referred to as this "Golden thing" implies a complex dynamic where Johan Golden is represented as Atle Antonsen's buffer against accusations of racism. Antonsen uses Golden's non-White identity as evidence, arguing that he cannot be racist due to his friendship with a non-White individual. This approach mirrors a common pattern among many White individuals who identify as moderate or progressive yet face criticism for their racist actions. They often bank on a perceived sense of progressiveness, rooted in their dealings with non-White individuals, to shield themselves from accusations of racism. Rather than facing their own racial biases, they deny their culpability and attempt to shore up their image by invoking friendships with people of color who vouch for their supposed anti-racist credentials. This behavior highlights the complexities of racism and privilege, as well as the tendency for "moderate" White people to deflect accountability rather than engage in meaningful self-reflection and action to address systemic inequalities. DiAngelo refers to a lengthy excerpt from Martin Luther King's writing about his skepticism toward White moderates, which is worth reproducing in its entirety:

> I have almost reached the regrettable conclusion that the Negro's great stumbling block in his stride toward freedom is not the White Citizen's Councilor or the Ku Klux Klanner, but the white moderate, who is more devoted to "order" than to justice; who prefers a negative peace which is the absence of tension to a positive peace which is the presence of justice; who constantly says: "I agree with you in the goal you seek, but I cannot agree with your methods of direct action"; who paternalistically believes he can set the timetable for another man's freedom... Shallow

understanding from people of good will is more frustrating than absolute misunderstanding from people of ill will. Lukewarm acceptance is much more bewildering than outright rejection. (DiAngelo, 2021, p. 3)

In dissecting the dynamics of Antonsen's alliance with Golden, a sobering truth emerges: Antonsen has, whether consciously or not, leveraged his relationship with Golden to *shield* himself from accusations of racism, thereby prolonging racial inequalities. This seemingly harmonious partnership, characterized by shared humor and camaraderie, serves to disguise underlying historical tensions between races. However, upon closer examination, it reveals a troubling pattern of exploitation and tokenism. For Black people, such a relationship transmutes into a Faustian bargain, with many Black people familiar with this phenomenon of the "terror of closeness," wherein White and supposedly progressive people engage in superficial alliances with people of color without truly confronting the systemic injustices that perpetuate racial disparities. How does it feel to be the "insurance policy" of White moderates against the storms of racism that they whip up themselves? By juxtaposing themselves alongside individuals of color, such progressives create the illusion of racial transcendence, thereby absolving themselves of accountability for their own racial biases and actions.

> Progressive white people are more likely to manifest *aversive racism,* a term coined by the psychologist Joel Kovel. Aversive racism is racism that is suppressed from awareness because it conflicts with a consciously held belief in racial equality. It is a subtle but insidious form, because it allows the person to enact racism while maintaining a positive self-image ("I have lots of friends of color"). (DiAngelo, 2021, p. 7)

In regard to "nice racism," DiAngelo (2021, p. 2) that the progressive White person "may have traveled extensively, speak several languages, and live in large urban cities or smaller progressive enclaves... But because they do not see anti-racism efforts as directed at them; they 'already know all this' and are not part of the problem." We see this evident in the casual tone in Antonsen's so-called "apology": "I have realized that I owe you an apology from Saturday. It was thoughtless to joke around about such heavy matters... I've probably become completely blind after too many years of fooling around with this Golden thing. Anyway, I deeply apologize if I ended up hurting you" (Antonsen, NrK, 2022). In our earlier discussion, we explored Antonsen's rationalization centered around alcohol. However, if this behavior has persisted over many years ("completely blind after too many years"), then attributing it solely to alcohol is a diversion. The pertinent question arises: How did Johan Golden and the Norwegian audience of this brand of humor tolerate this for such an extended period, especially if it culminated in statements like "You're too Black to be here"? To his credit, Johan Golden stated the following:

> I know Atle is not racist, but what he did here was 100 percent
> racist, Golden said during the recording... It is a terribly bad day
> for everyone who believes that racism does not exist in Norway.
> They are struggling, Golden continued. (VG, 2022)

While laudable, it is crucial to note the significance of a particular media headline, which boldly stated, "Nearly one million viewers saw Johan Golden joke about Atle Antonsen" (M24, 2022). This headline once again perpetuates the association between Antonsen's racism and Johan Golden and their lighthearted banter, effectively neutralizing Antonsen's anti-Black racism and absolving him of blame. The psychological impact of such framing on White readers is evident: by portraying Johan Golden, a person of mixed race himself, as playfully mocking his close friend Antonsen, the entire incident may appear trivial and insignificant. These narratives risk downplaying the seriousness of Antonsen's racist behavior and further entrenching harmful stereotypes about race relations and acceptable forms of humor. Thus, while the headline may seem innocuous at first glance, it perpetuates a narrative that undermines the gravity of racial discrimination and its enduring impact. Golden possesses the "magical factor" which, by proxy for Antonsen, serves to exonerate him. Like a priest to whom the faithful ascribe attributes of purity and spirituality, Golden's "blackness" is called upon by the White congregation to atone and propitiate for the sins of the wayward Antonsen:

> "Magical Negro" is a term coined by the film director Spike Lee.
> The Magical Negro trope – think Morgan Freeman as God in
> several films, The Oracle in the *Matrix,* or the supernatural inmate
> in *The Green* Mile – certainly appeals to white progressives. The
> Magical Negro is a supporting stock character, most often created
> by white writers, who comes to the aid of a white protagonist in a
> film or a book. Magical Negro characters possess special insight or
> mystical powers. (DiAngelo, 2021, p. 117)

White progressives may perceive themselves as forward-thinking and progressive, yet in reality, they often contribute to regression rather than progress in the pursuit of a genuinely equitable and postracial society. Black people will have reason to never let their guard down – to ceaselessly remember their blackness – as long as they are determined to find their "Johan Goldens" to showcase their progressive credentials, along with a White collective that is more than happy to succumb to the allure of the "Magical Negro" stereotype. The true magic lies not in the guise of a mythical "Magical Negro," but in the collective effort to create a more just and equitable society for all. For non-White people such as Johan Golden, the dilemma is the further fragmentation of the authentic being of the Black person. In existentialism, "bad faith" (French: *mauvaise foi*) describes the psychological state in which individuals behave inauthentically. This occurs when they succumb to societal pressures, adopt false values, and relinquish their inherent freedom as sentient human beings. Sartre states, "In order for me to deceive myself, I must both know the truth and not know it" (Sartre, 1958, p. 64).

This ambiguity enables various forms of self-deception, as explained by Sartre through several examples, notably the case of a café waiter. In this scenario, the waiter has studiously mastered every gesture and action associated with his role, to the extent that his entire essence becomes entangled with "the being-in-itself of the café waiter" (Sartre, 1958, p. 59). However, Sartre explains that, as a being-for-itself, he cannot simply exist as a café waiter in the same manner that an inkwell exists as an inkwell or a glass as a glass. Instead, his identity as a waiter traps him in bad faith, negating his own existence as a being that surpasses his predefined role. This example vividly illustrates the pervasive nature of bad faith within the realm of human reality and existence.

In her book *How White Feminism Betrays Women of Color* (2020), Ruby Hamad writes about how the identity of indigenous women was appropriated by the Western imagination. She upends the Disney version of "the young, free-spirited" Pocahontas who saved the life of John Smith by "throwing herself between Smith's neck and her father's axe just as the Algonquian chief went to execute the Englishman" (Hamad, 2020, pp. 35, 36). Hamad (2020, p. 36) presents Pocahontas as the "noble savage" who possesses supernatural abilities like "leaping through waterfalls unscathed" and "talking to animals and painting with the colors of the wind." Again, one witnesses the deprivation of nonwhites' authenticity. They are divested of whatever attributes they possess and can only be perceived through a White-centric lens that confers whatever characteristics are amenable to White supremacy. Johan Golden may be funny, but he is fully aware and no doubt understands the inauthentic, contrived condition of "bad faith" that his celebrity status demands of him. Hamad unveils the real Pocahontas:

> The real Pocahontas was only ten years old when the middle-aged Smith landed in Jamestown, Viriginia. The two never had a sexual relationship, and it's highly unlikely she ever saved his life given the only record of that incident is in Smith's own highly embellished writing in which he presents himself as the object of many a Native maiden's affections and claims to have been saved more than once... The Princess Pocahontas myth represents a passive sex symbol, the "Good Indian" who unites the white man and the Native, the civilized and the savage.... (Hamad, 2020, p. 36)

Hamad (2020) argues that the White appropriation of the Pocahontas myth is meant to affirm the superiority of White society over the native one. White society recruits her with the intention of conquering, assimilating, and destroying Native American culture. "Even her 'princess' status was a fabrication (it is not a role that exists in Native cultures) that imbues the Pocahontas legend with gravity and weight, making her enthusiasm for White society all the more meaningful" (Hamad, 2020, p. 37). Then, are all Black and White relationships doomed to the inauthentic phenomenon of "bad faith"? Seen through the lens of history, White progressives have time and again saddled non-White people with bad faith. Despite the celebrated Black entertainer, Sammy Davis Jr's unwavering support for John F. Kennedy during his presidential campaign, including campaigning alongside Sinatra, Davis Jr faced exclusion and discrimination when Kennedy snubbed him from his inauguration festivities. This snub came after Davis's interracial marriage to the Swedish actress May Britt, which sparked controversy and even death threats due to its defiance of prevailing societal norms.

The concepts of self-deception and ressentiment closely link to bad faith. Central to existential thought is the idea of freedom and choice. Bad faith, in its essence, signifies self-deception. While outright lying to oneself represents a clear example of bad faith, Jean-Paul Sartre's study of the concept delves into nuanced forms of equivocation and concealment of truth. Sartre theorizes that individuals often engage in behaviors aimed at evading the truth, particularly when it relates to their own freedom and the responsibilities it entails. As an ardent advocate for both freedom and truth, Sartre devotes substantial attention to dissecting, elucidating, and condemning instances of bad faith throughout his philosophical oeuvre. Indeed, bad faith emerges as a central tenet in his philosophical discourse and subtly permeates his literary works across various stages of his career. Within Sartre's framework, the concept of bad faith serves multiple purposes:

- It provides insight into the widespread adherence to beliefs that Sartre considers patently false.
- It supports his argument about the distinct nature of consciousness compared to nonconscious entities.
- As a cornerstone of his existential psychoanalysis, it becomes an essential tool for understanding both real human experiences (such as his biographical studies of Genet and Flaubert) and fictional narratives (as seen in his character development in works like "The Childhood of a Leader" and "No Exit").
- Implicitly in his early writings and explicitly in later ones, bad faith operates as a moral critique, identified as a vice to be overcome and juxtaposed with the virtue of "authenticity."

When contextualized within the dynamics of race relations and social justice, the notion of bad faith can shed light on how White progressives inadvertently perpetuate systemic inequality. By relying on individuals to play the role of the "acceptable" non-White friend, White progressives may unknowingly reinforce harmful stereotypes and contribute to the internalization of inauthentic identities by non-White individuals. This perpetuation of bad faith ultimately hinders progress toward a truly equitable and postracial society as it obscures the truth of racial dynamics and perpetuates existing power imbalances. A White-and-Black alliance does not have to be suspect as in the case of Antonsen and Golden. What is important, however, is the degree to which the partnership is characterized by genuine freedom and authenticity for both to be themselves and not act in "bad faith." If Golden's friendship is invoked and solicited to assuage accusations of racism, with Golden kowtowing, then his nonwhiteness is "unfree" – lived in the service of whiteness and hence a form of colonization, what Hamid Dabashi called the "comprador intellectual."

> To sustain the legitimacy of the predatory empire, the comprador intellectual must also do her or his share in re-accrediting the hitherto discredited ideologues of the imperial project. The comprador intellectual speaks with the voice of authenticity, nativity, and Orientalized oddity. He is from "there", and she "knows what she is talking about", and thus their voices carry the authority of a native informant. (Dabashi, 2006)

To maintain the legitimacy of the exploitative empire, the comprador intellectual assumes the responsibility of rehabilitating the previously discredited proponents of imperial ideology. Perceived as a native informant, the comprador intellectual draws authority from their purported insider perspective, speaking with an air of authenticity and exoticism. However, they tailor their narratives for a Western audience that is predisposed to embracing orientalist narratives rather than crafting them in isolation. While these writers draw from their intimate cultural knowledge, they must recognize the ethical implications of their work as their critiques of other cultures can inadvertently perpetuate harmful stereotypes.

We return, then, to Fanon's "I propose nothing short of the liberation of the man of color [and woman, we may add] from himself" (Fanon, 1986, p. 10). In his book *Anti-Semite and Jew* (1948), Sartre asks "'What is a Jew?' but 'What have you made of the Jews?'." In the same vein, the question is not who Black and brown people are, but what White people have made of them. When White society largely shapes individuals' understanding of themselves through caricatures and stereotypes, what level of authenticity can they expect to possess? Their authenticity isn't a matter of rediscovering some lost essence of their being, analogous to correcting a spelling error with whiteout. Rather, preconceived identities and modes of behavior, inauthentic and designed to conform to the expectations and biases of White people, often confine non-White individuals in White-dominated societies. This imposition of predetermined identities denies non-White individuals the opportunity to express themselves authentically, perpetuating a cycle of cultural erasure and distortion.

In the Disney classic, *The Lion King*, the wise monkey Rafiki asks Simba, "Who are you?" This pivotal question prompts Simba to embark on a journey of self-discovery, ultimately leading him to salvage his lost heritage and rightful place as king. Non-White individuals, battered by "bad faith," cannot simply return to a romanticized past in Africa or elsewhere, as their identities have been heavily influenced and shaped by the oppressive narratives imposed upon them by White society. Instead, they need to start living authentically by challenging, recognizing, and deconstructing the narratives White people have crafted for them, which portray White people as the protagonists and nonwhites as the antagonists. A good place to begin is to demand that people of color co-write the script for the future.

Years ago, in my role as a high school teacher, I implemented a pedagogical approach that challenged and destabilized racist narratives in English textbooks in Norway (Thomas, 2017). Drawing on concepts from postcolonial theory, I employed a contrapuntal pedagogy to engage students in critical readings of texts saturated with orientalist and racist tropes. While acknowledging the potential inaccessibility of academic texts by scholars such as Said, Fanon, Bhabha, and Spivak for my English as a Foreign Language (EFL) students, I devised practical tasks that sensitized them to discourses of othering. For example, I prompted students to analyze the ethnic origins, occupations, and gender of the main characters in short stories, encouraging them to identify and discuss positive and negative stereotypes. Subsequently, I challenged students to rewrite alternative narratives from the perspective of marginalized characters, empowering them to reclaim their voices and challenge racialized representations.

One such exercise involved studying the text "Blackout" (Roger Mais) alongside excerpts from Solomon Northup's memoir "Twelve Years a Slave." By juxtaposing the harrowing experiences of Solomon Northup with the themes in "Blackout," students gained a deeper understanding of the historical context of slavery and its enduring impact. Furthermore, I used critical discourse analysis strategies to examine premodifiers associated with main characters, sparking discussions about the portrayal of nonwesterners in literature. Moving forward, I emphasized the importance of incorporating multi- and intercultural studies into teacher-training programs to equip educators with the tools necessary to address issues of cultural representation in the classroom. Furthermore, I advocated for greater diversity among teaching staff to challenge Orientalist hegemony and create inclusive learning environments. Ultimately, my aim was to create space for diverse perspectives and narratives, thereby challenging and subverting neocolonial power structures embedded within the educational system. Until Black and brown people learn to speak in the authentic voice of Steve Biko, who fearlessly penned these words to the Abe Bailey Institute for Inter-racial Studies, South Africa, in 1971, we will not know what an authentic life is. The title of the book *Steve Biko: I Write What I Like* (2017) reflects Biko's "good faith":

> In an effort to answer these questions one has to come to the painful conclusion that the liberal is in fact appeasing his own conscience, or at best is eager to demonstrate his identification with the black people only so far as it does not sever all his ties with his relatives on the other side of the color line. Being white, he possesses the natural passport to the exclusive pool of white privileges from which he does not hesitate to extract whatever suits him, Yet, since he identifies with the blacks, he moves around his white circles – white-only beaches, restaurants, and cinemas – with a lighter load, feeling that he is not like the rest. Yet at the back of his mind is a constant reminder that he is quite comfortable as things stand and therefore should not bother about change. Although he does not vote for the nationalists (now that they are in the majority anyway), he feels secure under the protection offered by the Nationalists and subconsciously shuns the idea of change. (Biko, 2017, p. 71)

Biko's critique emphasizes the importance of authenticity and a genuine commitment to racial equality. He points out the hypocrisy of liberals who claim to identify with Black people but are unwilling to sever ties with their own privileges or challenge the status quo. This is commensurate with the idea that White progressives may unknowingly perpetuate systemic inequality by relying on superficial alliances and tokenism. Ultimately, Biko's assertion that authentic change requires a willingness to confront discomfort and challenge the status quo aligns with his call for genuine racial solidarity and the rejection of superficial alliances.

> Why then do they persist in talking to the blacks? Since they are aware that the problem in this country is white racism, why do they not address themselves to the white world? Why do they insist on talking to blacks? (Biko, 2017, p. 70)

Until individuals, particularly White progressives, are willing to engage in this process of self-reflection and action, systemic inequality will persist.

Chapter 4

Adoption Imperialism: The Johanne Ihle-Hansen Case

Nettavisen, a Norwegian online media source, gained access to text messages written by Johanne Zhangjia Ihle-Hansen, a 17-year-old adopted daughter from China, tragically murdered by her White Norwegian brother, Philip Manshaus, in 2019. These messages, spanning from June 1, 2019, to August 9, 2019, uncover crucial information leading up to the incident. Especially, the last message was sent the day before she was murdered. Philip feared Johanne would side with non-White individuals in the impending race war, which served as his motivation for killing her.

> Philip talks about race and purity of blood. Obviously, it is the whites who are considered to be human.
>
> Philip is so racist and hateful. I don't feel safe.
>
> He listens to a speech about how dirty and disgusting the Chinese are as a race. Can you understand what I'm going through? This is madness.
>
> My mother told my father about Philip. Then the next day, he (Philip) removed the articles from the wall. Then he had a good talk with my mother. It didn't seem real. She didn't think so either. Philip hardly ever talks to her. (Nettavisen, 2020)

Known as "Joey" among friends, Johanne Zhangjia Ihle-Hansen (2002–2019) tragically passed away at the age of 17. Born in China on June 18, 2002, she arrived in Norway when she was nine months old. On August 10, 2019, her own brother, Philip Manshaus, killed her at her home in Eiksmarka, roughly half an hour's drive west of Oslo, solely because of her non-White heritage (South China Morning Post, 2020).

Too Black to Be Here?, 145–182

doi:10.1108/978-1-83662-162-120251005

Manshaus aimed to spare their White Norwegian parents from the race war he believed was imminent. Following the murder of his sister, he proceeded to Al-Noor Mosque in Bærum to inflict harm on as many people as possible. Philip Manshaus entered the Al-Noor Islamic Centre in Bærum, Norway, armed with firearms, determined to inflict harm on as many people as possible. However, a 65-year-old mosque member thwarted his attack, neutralizing him before any casualties occurred. The police subsequently captured Manshaus. His motives for targeting the mosque stemmed from his extremist beliefs and racist ideology, as he sought to perpetrate violence against Muslims in line with his White supremacist views.

The final autopsy report revealed that Johanne was shot and killed with four shots while sitting in her bed, with no signs of struggle. She sustained three shots to the head and one to the chest, all of which were fatal and fired in rapid succession (PM News, 2019). A blanket covered her after the murder. She had disclosed to both her boyfriend and friends that she noticed changes in Philip's behavior prior to the shooting and felt afraid. She particularly reacted to his display of Nazi symbols in his room. Sandvika High School held a memorial service for the 17-year-old classmate on Tuesday following her death. The Muslim community and members of the Al-Noor Islamic Center were invited to participate in the funeral. Amna Moammar, a representative from the mosque, delivered a eulogy, referring to Johanne as a hero who likely prevented further loss of life that day. Johanne was deeply committed to antiracism. Instead of flowers, her family requested contributions to the Youth Department of the Anti-Racism Center, Agenda X.

The exploration of racial ambiguity and the racialization of non-White adopted children in Norway, through the lens of the classic novel *The Autobiography of an Ex-Colored Man* by the African American author, James Weldon Johnson (1995), offers a moving and intricate narrative. A predominant theme of the novel is the concept of racial passing, whereby individuals of mixed-race heritage attempt to "pass" as White with a view to gaining social acceptance and economic opportunities denied to them as Black Americans. The protagonist struggles with the decision to pass as White or embrace his Black identity, ultimately choosing to pass for the sake of societal advancement. Johnson examines the psychological and emotional toll of racial identity, as well as the internal conflicts faced by individuals caught between two worlds, through striking storytelling and introspective narration. The novel explores themes of race, identity, belonging, and the societal pressures that shape individual lives. *The Autobiography of an Ex-Colored Man* is considered a seminal work of African American literature and a groundbreaking exploration of racial passing in American society. It has received acclaim for its touching portrayal of the complexities of race and its durable relevance in discussions of identity and social justice.

Just as the protagonist of Johnson's novel contends with the desire to "pass as white" despite his mixed-race identity, non-White adopted children in Norway often face a similar paradox. Raised in predominantly White environments, they might learn to perceive themselves as "Norwegian" despite their physical appearance, which contradicts the concept of racial assimilation. Philip's tragic death of Johanne and the collective awakening of non-White adopted individuals in Norway draw a compelling parallel. The murder of Johanne serves as a pivotal moment, unveiling a truth long suppressed or denied. The racially motivated murder of Johanne served as the catalyst many non-White adopted individuals needed to forge a sense of solidarity in confronting their racial identity and rejecting the facade of whiteness imposed upon them, analogous to the day Johnson's mixed-race character cruelly discovered his "nonwhiteness."

> One day near the end of my second term at school the principal came into our room, and after talking to the teacher, for some reason said, "I wish all of the white scholars to stand for a moment". I rose with the others. The teacher looked at me, and calling my name said, "You sit down for the present, and rise with the others". I did not quite understand her, and questioned, "Ma'am?" She repeated with a softer tone in her voice, "You sit down now, and rise with the others". I sat down dazed. I saw and heard nothing. When the others were asked to rise, I did not know it. When school was dismissed, I went out in a kind of stupor. A few of the white boys jeered me saying, "Oh, you're a nigger too". I heard some black children say, "We knew he was colored". "Shiny" said to them, "Come along, don't tease him, and thereby won my undying gratitude. (Johnson, 1995, p. 6)

The decision of many non-White adopted individuals to no longer "pass as White" reflects a broader movement toward reclaiming their racial identity and asserting their voices. The call to detonate the façade of belonging speaks to the necessity of authenticity and self-affirmation in the face of societal pressures to correspond to a White-centric narrative. Through this lens, *The Autobiography of an Ex-Colored Man* becomes a powerful tool for examining the complexities of racial identity and belonging, particularly within the context of adoption and racial assimilation in Norway. Johnson's exploration of racial passing and the consequences of racial betrayal resonates deeply with the experiences of non-White adopted individuals navigating their own sense of identity and belonging in a predominantly White society. Malcolm X's haunting reflection on his adoption of the surname "X" within the Nation of Islam serves as a compelling parallel to the experiences of non-White adopted children in Norway and the broader West.

> My application had, of course, been made and during this time I received from Chicago my "X". The Muslim's "X" symbolized the true African family name that he never could know. For me, my "X" replaced the white slave master name of "Little" which some blue-eyed devil named Little had imposed upon my paternal forebears. The receipt of my "X" meant that forever after in the nation of Islam, I would be known as Malcolm X. Mr. Muhammad taught that we would keep this "X" until God Himself returned and gave us a Holy Name from His own mouth. (Malcolm X, 1964, p. 229)

Just as countless African Americans, like Malcolm X, wrestle with the deletion of their ancestral identities and the imposition of names enforced on to them by the slave trade, non-White adopted children often confront a different and yet somehow similar struggle with their own sense of identity and belonging. The assumption of the surname "X" indicates a retrieval of agency and autonomy over one's identity, a dismissal of the names enacted by oppressive systems of power. In the context of the Nation of Islam, it signifies a mutiny against the enslavement of the past and liberty to believe in "the religion of Black people," a connection to a heritage concealed by the legacy of slavery and colonialism. This act of renaming personifies a hopeful vision of the future, one rooted in the promise of spiritual renewal and self-determination.

In a similar vein, non-White adopted children may find themselves conflicted with the intricacies of identity formation, situated within the intersection of the past, present, and future. While their past may not be entirely unfamiliar, as evidenced by traces of cultural heritage like Johanne's middle name, "Zhangjia," they nevertheless navigate a landscape fraught with ambiguity and longing. Television crews invariably entwine themselves with the quest to uncover their origins, often characterized by emotionally taxing expeditions to adoption facilities and, potentially, encounters with birth mothers. These programs exploit the insatiable public appetite for entertainment, representing a form of national voyeurism. The commodification of infants from economically disadvantaged, non-White nations initially manifests this voyeurism, with subsequent financial transactions facilitating the spectacle of their "reconciliation" with their biological parents.

The agonizing tension between the ever-present past and the elusive future characterizes the experiences of both African Americans and non-White adopted children. Like Malcolm X's "X", which serves as a placeholder until the celestial revelation of a Holy Name, non-White adopted children occupy a liminal space of in-betweenness, incessantly negotiating the contours of their identity in a world shaped by racial hierarchies and historical injustices. Ultimately, Malcolm X's narrative illuminates the transformative power of self-naming and identity assertion in the face of systemic oppression. His journey resonates with the experiences of non-White adopted children, accenting the shared struggle for self-recognition, dignity, and belonging in societies marked by racial prejudice and exclusion.

For adopted youth like Johanne, the challenge of recovering a preadoption identity is elusive. Adopted children face an exceptional struggle compared to nonadopted nonwhites in Norway, who can rely on familial ties to maintain their identities and resilience. Johanne's journey began when she arrived in Norway from China at the tender age of 9 months, thrust into a society vastly different from her birthplace. What sets Johanne's experience apart is the absence of the familial and cultural anchors that normally sustain non-White individuals in Norway.

Her Norwegian family primarily shaped her identity formation, serving as the sole source of love, belonging, and self-identity. The treachery Johanne faced cuts deep. As her own brother turned against her based solely on the color of her skin, her pigmentation, and somatic traits, which should have been inconsequential to the love and support she received from her family, became the catalyst for her untimely demise at the hands of her own brother. Racial prejudice's over-whelming influence shatters familial bonds, epitomizing the "terror of closeness" through this rupture in ties. Johanne's tragic fate serves as a harrowing reminder of how skin color, in its stark simplicity, can supersede even powerful familial bonds, leading to dire consequences.

> I ran downstairs, and rushed to where my mother was sitting with a piece of work in her hands. I buried my head in her lap and blurted out, "Mother, mother, tell me, am I a nigger? I couldn't see her face, but I knew the piece of work had fallen to the floor, and I felt her hands on my head. I looked up into her face and repeated, "Tell me, mother, am I a nigger?" There were tears in her eyes, and I could see that she was suffering more for me. (Johnson, 1995, p. 8)

The disturbing excerpt from Johnson's *The Autobiography of an Ex-Colored Man* captures a moment of profound realization and distress for the central character, echoing the potential experiences of non-White adopted children in Norway. Imagine the shock and confusion when these children, reared in pre-dominantly White households, face the callous reality that their "race" carries negative connotations in society. In the Norwegian context, White supremacists demonstrate a Manichaean worldview, embodied in a dualistic classification system devoid of nuanced distinctions in skin color. This dichotomy categorizes individuals into two distinct groups: Nordic/Aryan White people and nonwhites. Consequently, the terminological delineation into "non-White" and "White" serves to encapsulate this stark racial partition. Johanne's case illustrates this phenomenon. Her radicalized brother could not see beyond her Chinese heritage – stigmatized as the "yellow peril" – which, in his view, invalidated any claim she had to Norwegian identity. To him, her ethnicity overshadowed her upbringing and connection to Norwegian culture. This narrow-minded perspective strained their relationship and left her feeling alienated from her own family. This underscores the pervasive and encompassing nature of White supremacist doc-trine, which perceives any variation from its racial hierarchy as a potent challenge to its hegemonic authority.

White supremacy, as a socio-political construct, operates as an exclusivist and immutable prototype, predicated on the perpetuation of racial domination under the guise of purported racial superiority. Its inelasticity imagines it as an insur-mountable condition, compelling nonwhites worldwide to collectively unite and resist it. The conceptualization of White supremacy, ingrained in a binary racial taxonomy, unconsciously fosters unanticipated bonds of affinity among non-White groups, such as non-White adopted children and non-White immigrants, despite the absence of inherent commonalities. Pierre Bourdieu's concept of symbolic violence, in which dominant groups impose arbitrary categories and hierarchies that perpetuate social inequalities, provides an understanding of these contrived bonds imposed upon previously nonexistent "groups." White supremacists, by engineering a rigid group formation process based on racial categorization, perpetrate symbolic violence as they impose artificial distinctions where none inherently exist, as "race" itself is a capricious construct, what Stuart Hall calls a floating signifier.

According to Bourdieu, symbolic violence operates through the imposition of symbolic systems and norms that legitimize and perpetuate existing power structures. In the context of White supremacy, this crystallizes as the construction of racial hierarchies that privilege whiteness while ostracizing non-White identities. By straightjacketing individuals into discrete racial categories and designating differential value and privilege based on these categories, White supremacists perpetuate systemic oppression and injustice. White supremacists' symbolic violence prompts minoritized communities to demand solidarity. Recognizing the arbitrary nature of racial classifications and the constructed nature of racial hierarchies, marginalized groups unite in their collective struggle against racial oppression and injustice. This solidarity transcends superficial differences and underscores the shared experience of navigating and resisting systemic discrimination. Through collective action and resistance, marginalized communities challenge the hegemony of White supremacy and strive toward a more just and equitable society.

"Norway Behind the Façade" (TV2, 2023) aired on Norway's TV2 in January 2023, shedding light on the experiences of adopted Norwegians and revealing the troubling fact that their biological parents had been actively searching for them. In many cases, these individuals were unaware of their adoption and the efforts made by their birth parents to find them. Many activists persistently lobbied for Norwegian authorities to investigate the occurrence of irregularities and potential illegalities surrounding adoptions. They emphasized the importance of admitting any unlawful activity and revealing the truth, particularly in light of the financial gains made by some unscrupulous entities involved in adoptions. Bufdir [the Norwegian Directorate for Children, Youth, and Family Affairs], responsible for adoption oversight, responded by recognizing the need for an investigation, drawing attention to disconcerting findings from similar inquiries conducted in other countries. These findings, ranging from corruption to counterfeit documents, underscore the urgency of addressing systemic issues within adoption processes. Bufdir suggested that an external and independent party should conduct the investigation for reasons of impartiality and credibility. However, the government rejected this proposal, citing budgetary constraints. Instead, Bufdir was ordered to utilize existing resources for an internal review, with the understanding that any necessary funding reallocations would be proposed by the organization itself. Despite these developments, the call for a comprehensive investigation into adoption practices persists, fueled by concerns over potential human rights violations and the need for transparency and accountability within the adoption system.

Structural racism refers to the ways in which societal institutions, policies, and practices systematically disadvantage certain racial or ethnic groups while privileging others. In the case of Norway's adoption scandal, structural racism becomes manifest through the exploitation of poverty and corruption in the

Table 1. Overview of Adoptions to Norway Since 1972.

Country	1972–2022	1972–2015 (20 Other Countries)	Total
Colombia	4,079		
China	1,454		
The Philippines	774		
Ethiopia	693		
India	595		
Chile	313		
Peru	139		
Madagascar	36		
Vietnam	11		
Other countries		1,508	9,602

Source: Adopsjonsforum (2022).

global South to facilitate the adoption of Black and brown children by White Norwegian families (see Table 1). Norway, as a wealthy Western state, perpetuates a system where it benefits from the vulnerabilities of countries in the global south to fulfill the desires of its citizens for adoption. Norway's reputation as a prototype of Nordic exceptionalism often cloaks its collusion in perpetuating structural racism, as in the adoption scandal. The adoption process, which involves importing children from predominantly non-White countries, highlights how Norway capitalizes on the racialized power dynamics between the global North and South. The White parents who opt to adopt Black and brown children often reside in social and cultural environments shaped by their own White habitus. This habitus, comprising their ingrained norms, values, and behaviors, is primarily influenced by their experiences within White-dominated spaces. They live, work, and socialize among other White individuals, rarely encountering meaningful interactions with racial diversity or confronting the systemic racism ingrained within their environments.

> Racial choices are obviously not limited to housing. They affect almost everything whites do. From the friends they have, schools they attend, churches they patron, jobs they hold, the leisure activities they enjoy, or the seat they choose on a train or bus. All these things reinforce systemic racism... Whites develop practices to preserve their advantages... Whites racial isolation shapes their lives from birth to death as life course analysis shows and creates the basis for "collective action" (Bonilla-Silva, 2022, p. 837)

Commensurate with the above, the environments in which these White parents reside are ill-equipped to shield non-White children from the racism and discrimination that they will inevitably encounter. These environments have neither the motivation nor the opportunity to address the systemic racism that pervades society. The White habitus perpetuates a racialized worldview that may inadvertently marginalize or overlook the unique needs and experiences of these vulnerable children. Without exposure to diverse perspectives and experiences, White parents may struggle to fully understand or empathize with the challenges faced by their adopted children. They may inadvertently perpetuate racial biases or reinforce societal stereotypes, contributing to the alienation or otherization of their non-White children within their own families. In the aftermath of Johanne's murder, many non-White adopted young adults shared the until-then taboo topic of racism. One such individual was Vicente Mollestad, who writes:

> On August 10, a twenty-two-year-old white man attacked a mosque in Bærum, armed with shotguns. While the attempt to damage the mosque fails, the arrest and search of the family home reveal the murder of his stepsister, a transnationally adopted girl from China, aged 17. Upon our arrival in Norway, the new world embraced us, yet the reality we inhabit reveals naive desires and, in the worst scenario, deadly lies. They spoke of us as equals. About "belonging", not as strangers or immigrants. We repeated words to ourselves. But the idea of us as innocent, trusting, dream-fulfilling children became more complicated as we mutated into more frightening and alien beings through puberty and adulthood. The hair grew long, black, and unruly. The skin, dark and undeniably different. The body no longer resembled the image of a child but bore the features of a stranger. It was a stranger to our surroundings, a stranger to ourselves, and sometimes a stranger to those closest to us. (Dagbladet, 2019)

Vicente mirrors the experiences of numerous transnationally adopted individuals, who, despite entering "new worlds" with promises of equality and belonging, frequently face a harsh reality. His opinion piece suggests that the earlier welcome fades as the physical and cultural differences become more noticeable with age. A growing sense of alienation replaces the sense of equality and belonging. This distancing is not just social but also internal, causing the adopted individuals to feel detached from their surroundings, themselves, and even those closest to them. The societal anticipation that these children would effortlessly integrate into their new homes without facing the challenges of racism and identity conflict is Panglossian. As they grow, their physical differences become markers and loci of otherness, often exposing them to the evils of racism and exclusion. The term "fatal lies" in Vicente's op-ed may refer to these misleading assurances of complete acceptance, the illusion of assimilation, regardless of one's background or appearance.

During the Cold War, US citizens adopted 10,000 German children, including Peter F. Dodds, from a German orphanage. *Outer Search Inner Journey* (1997), his memoir, is the first book by a foreign-born adoptee on international adoption. As a prominent figure in the movement to ban international adoption, Dodds has delivered keynote speeches at adoption conferences in New Zealand and Canada, and has appeared in interviews on television, radio, and online platforms. Dodds does not pull any punches when he writes in his article entitled *The Parallels between International Adoption and Slavery* (2015).

> Adoption is, in and of itself, a violence based in inequality. It is candy-coated, marketed, and packaged to seemingly concerned families and children, but it is an economically and politically incentivized crime. It stems culturally and historically from the "peculiar institution" of Anglo-Saxon indentured servitude and not family creation. It is not universal and is not considered valid by most communal cultures. It is a treating of symptoms and not of disease. It is a negation of families and an annihilation of communities not imbued with any notion of humanity due to the adoptive culture's inscribed bias concerning race, class, and human relevancy. (Dodds, 2015, p. 77)

Clearly, the lack of racial diversity within their social circles and communities may limit the resources and support available to White parents in navigating the intricacies of transracial adoption. Without access to culturally skilled guidance or diverse role models, White parents may face significant challenges in fostering a strong sense of cultural identity and belonging for their adopted children. In essence, the White habitus of adoptive parents underscores the need for intentional efforts to address and dismantle systemic racism within adoption practices and broader society. It highlights the importance of creating environments that actively embrace diversity, promote cultural humility, and prioritize the well-being and dignity of all individuals, regardless of race or ethnicity.

White Norwegian families seeking adoption often justify their actions by contending that the children will have better lives in Norway than in their countries of origin. This justification, however, reflects a form of egotism that prioritizes the desires of the adoptive parents over the well-being and rights of the children. By reducing complex social, economic, and cultural issues to crude narratives of rescue and redemption, White Norwegians perpetuate a patronizing attitude that buttresses racial stereotypes and undermines the agency and dignity of the children and their birth families. Furthermore, Norwegian authorities often dismissed or ignored the objections and concerns raised about the adoption process, thereby perpetuating structural racism. However, the government started to pay attention due to the magnitude of these scandals, exacerbated by the racist murder of Johanne.

In the fall of 2022, the Norwegian Minister for Children, Kjersti Toppe, stated that there were no indications of illegal adoptions in Norway. However, the newspaper, VG (2024), has verified that this is not accurate. Since the 1970s,

Norwegian authorities have received at least 88 alerts about possible illegal adoptions, including one addressed directly to Toppe. Minister Toppe now concedes that the Norwegian government should have taken action on adoption issues earlier, and her administration is currently addressing this. VG's extensive investigation revealed that diverse watchdogs, embassies, international bodies, and the media have constantly raised alarms about the risks of child trafficking and blunders in adoption papers, with some alerts originating from adoption associations. Seven adoptees suspected of misconduct in their adoption cases contacted the Norwegian Directorate for Children, Youth, and Family Affairs (Bufdir) in 2022, in addition to the 88 alerts. Following several exposés by VG over the past year about illegal adoptions from various countries, Bufdir is considering a temporary halt to all adoptions in Norway.

Minister Toppe had declined to apologize to those affected by the illegal adoptions, stating that she preferred to wait for the results of a public inquiry, which is expected to conclude by the end of 2025. Seven adoptees suspected of wrongdoing in their adoption cases contacted the Norwegian Directorate for Children, Youth, and Family Affairs (Bufdir) in 2022, in addition to the 88 alerts. Following numerous exposés by VG over the past year about illegal adoptions from various countries, Bufdir is considering a temporary halt to all adoptions in Norway.

The government's refusal to allocate adequate resources for a comprehensive investigation into adoption practices demonstrates a lack of accountability and transparency. By prioritizing budgetary constraints over the need for truth and justice, Norwegian authorities uphold systems that perpetuate racial inequalities and injustices. The adoption scandal in Norway exemplifies structural racism, exploiting the country's privilege and power to the detriment of marginalized communities in the global south. It emphasizes the need for a critical examination of how racialized dynamics operate within supposedly progressive societies, as well as the imperative for accountability and justice in addressing systemic injustices. Peter Dodd considers adoption a peculiarly Anglo-Saxon phenomenon that caters for, among others, the "white savior" craving, and implicates White supremacy:

> Pro-slavery arguments were ultimately based on racism, the belief whites were superior to blacks, and this cemented the arguments of slavery defenders. Pro-international adoption arguments are ultimately based on nationalism, a sense of national consciousness exalting the United States above all others. Nationalism binds the arguments of international adoption defenders. American nationalism provides a moral justification for a system that extracts children from their homelands, places them on the adoption market where they are sold to American parents and raised under the Christian banner. In my opinion, White Supremacy has given way to Adoption Imperialism. (Dodd, 2015, p. 79)

Using Cheryl Harris's (1995) theory of "whiteness as property" to analyze the Norwegian adoption scandal provides a critical perspective on the structural racism present in international adoption practices. Harris's theory posits that whiteness is a form of property that produces material and symbolic benefits, adding value under legal, economic, and social systems that preselect for White interests and identities. In light of the Norwegian adoption scandal, "whiteness as property" is evident in how the country's adoption practices interact with global racial dynamics. The unending debate and postponements in addressing the irregularities in adoption practices, such as Minister Toppe's refusal to apologize or effectively investigate until a public inquiry is complete in 2025, demonstrate how systems of power protect investments in whiteness. This delay and the lack of proactive measures can be seen as a way to uphold the status quo, which privileges White Norwegian families desiring children while disregarding the rights and voices of the children from marginalized communities, who are often of different racial backgrounds.

The valorization of White, Nordic identities within these adoption processes can also be seen as an extension of Harris's concept, where whiteness ensures control over valuable resources – here, the capacity to adopt children from less privileged nations. This privilege is further reinforced by international adoption arguments that often revolve around a tacit Eurocentric pride, believing that Western nations provide better futures for these children, clandestinely undervaluing the children's original cultures and communities. Such a stance reflects a form of "adoption imperialism," as termed by Peter Dodd, which replaces overt White supremacy with a subtler but equally pervasive form of racial and nationalistic superiority.

Furthermore, the practice of adopting children from the global South to fulfill familial desires in the West can be critiqued as a modern incarnation of colonial entitlement to the bodies and futures of people of color. This echoes historical entitlements to property rights in White legal frameworks that allowed for ownership and control over others deemed to be property, including enslaved people. The critical backlash and subsequent consideration by Bufdir to suspend all adoptions highlight the growing recognition of these racial and ethical complexities. However, the slow response and the lack of immediate rectification measures accentuate how deeply embedded these racial privileges are. The societal and governmental foot-dragging in addressing these issues directly and promptly may reflect an unconscious protection of whiteness as a privileged identity that "deserves" to be parented, irrespective of the ethical or racial implications. Thus, the Norwegian adoption scandal, when viewed through Harris's framework, highlights the ways in which whiteness as property operates not just in maintaining racial boundaries within a nation but also in how nations interact with each other. It exposes the need for a more equitable global framework that respects the rights and identities of all children and their cultures, rather than perpetuating a market driven by racial and nationalistic superiority.

Thus, a white person "used and enjoyed" whiteness whenever she took advantage of the privileges accorded white people simply by virtue of their whiteness – when she exercised any number of rights reserved for the holders of whiteness. Whiteness as the embodiment of white privilege transcended mere belief or preference, it became usable property, the subject of the law's regard and protection. In this respect, whiteness, as an active property, has been used and enjoyed. (Harris, 1995, p. 282)

1. Muffled Voices: Silenced Norwegian Adoptees

An analysis of the Norwegian media landscape's handling of adoption themes, using the Retriever database, unpacks a significant shift beginning in the 1980s. An examination of the headlines reveals a curious fixation on adoptees' well-being, characterized by a "fetishized" obsession. Researchers scrutinize every aspect of the adoptee experience for signs of pathology. Consider point number 8: "Internationally Adopted Children Rarely Become Punks, Nordlys Morgen (Oct. 18, 1999)." The panoptic "mania" in regard to adoptees mirrors the dynamic of "The Truman Show," where Truman's life was meticulously curated to cater to the entertainment needs of a concealed audience. Likewise, the media's relentless focus on adoptees' well-being seems to serve a voyeuristic clientele, baying for more, with every aspect of the adoptees' lives scrutinized for public consumption. Below are a few illustrative examples:

- Course on Internationally Adopted Children, *Aftenposten Morgen* (September 18, 1990).
- Adopted Children Still Get Insurance. *VG* (September 18, 1993).
- Korean Children From Across Norway: At a Camp by the Beach, *Aftenposten Aften* (August 4, 1994).
- Mostly From Colombia *VG* (May 12, 1996).
- The Discomfort of Being Adopted, *Bergens Tidende Morgen* (October 13, 1997).
- Adopted Children Succeed in the Education System, *NTB Text* (July 6, 1998).
- Learning Difficulties Among Adopted Children, *NTB Text* (November 2, 1998).
- Internationally Adopted Children Rarely Become Punks, *Nordlys Morgen* (October 18, 1999).
- New Study on Internationally Adopted Children: The Most Talented and Best at Most Things, *Aftenposten Morgen* (February 5, 2000).
- Internationally Adopted Children Not Allowed to Donate Blood *Nordlys Morgen* (July 9, 2000).
- More Suicides Among Internationally Adopted Children, *NTB Text* (January 15, 2002).

Drawing from postcolonial studies, Gayatri Spivak famously asked the question, "Can the subaltern speak?" Spivak's inquiry questions the notion that dominant discourses can accurately represent the voice of marginalized or oppressed groups. Spivak's critique applies to the adoption and media representation context, where predominantly White media outlets, catering to a predominantly White readership, construct narratives of rescue and salvation. This narrative perpetuates the idea that White adoptive parents, and the Norwegian nation as a collective are "saving" Black and brown adoptees from misery in their homelands and providing them with better lives in Norway. Race scholars bemoan the parochial nature of such a "dialogue":

> A key to understanding the social context of much stereotyped thinking about racial matters is the fact that most whites live in what might be termed the "white bubble"—that is, they live out lives generally isolated from sustained and intensive equal status contacts with African Americans and other Americans of color. (Feagin & O'Brien, 2003, p. 25)

This narrative serves to reinforce the superiority and benevolence of the White savior figure, while simultaneously sidelining the voices and agency of the adoptees themselves. White media gatekeepers often render adoptees as passive recipients of this purported salvation, filtering their voices and experiences through their lens. Reni Eddo-Lodge's book *Why I Am No Longer Talking to White People About Race* (2020) critiques the bias of some White individuals to divert discussions about racism away from analyzing whiteness as the root cause. Their discomfort leads them to steer the conversation toward topics such as Black identity, identity politics, or the idea of unity and shared humanity. Eddo-Lodge expresses frustration with this diversion tactic, emphasizing that addressing racism necessitates confronting the implications of White identity.

The experiences of adoptees in Norway, particularly those from non-White backgrounds, can relate to this sentiment. In discussions about adoption and adoptee welfare, there may be a preference to focus narrowly on the adoptees themselves, their identities, and their integration into Norwegian society. However, this overlooks the deeper structural issues related to race, identity, and power dynamics that influence their experiences. Similar to Eddo-Lodge's observation, conversations about adoptees in Norway may unconsciously silence discussions about whiteness and its role in shaping adoption policies, societal perceptions, and the lived realities of adoptees. The avalanche of White media coverage incessantly appears to seek to reassure the White reader that the adoptees are adjusting well and even thriving. This effervescence of jittery reporting, I argue, conceals a fear: the fear of the inconvenient truth coming to light if we allow the adoptees to speak for themselves. By shifting the focus away from whiteness, these discussions may fail to address systemic inequalities and the ways in which race intersects with adoption experiences. Therefore, just as Eddo-Lodge advocates for focusing on White identity when addressing racism, there is a need to focus on whiteness in conversations about adoption in Norway. This entails critically examining how White privilege and power dynamics shape the adoption process, media representations, and societal perceptions of adoptees.

By focusing on whiteness in these discussions, we can work toward a more nuanced understanding of adoption experiences and advocate for more inclusive and equitable adoption policies and practices.

So, what would the subalterns say if they could speak? Fortunately, adoptees' voices have been filtering through more distinctly and unapologetically in recent years, with the murder of the adopted Johanne Zhangija Ihle-Hansen triggering a seismic shift in public consciousness and debate. This heart-breaking event served as a catalyst for adoptees to assert their agency and demand recognition, sparking nationwide exchanges about the challenges and vulnerabilities faced by adoptees in Norway. It has prompted a reckoning within society and the adoption system itself, forcing stakeholders to listen, acknowledge, and address adoptees' voices and concerns in an unprecedented manner. Many, accustomed to Spivak's "White men saving brown women from brown men" syndrome, were shocked by what they had to say. For instance, the 42-year-old journalist and award-winning author, Brynjulf Jung Tjønn, who was adopted from South Korea at age 3, states in an interview in the national daily Aftenposten (2022):

> I have always felt like one second-class Norwegian. Much of it has to do with the fact that I have received so many questions and comments about my appearance. So, I always dreamed of being a white, Norwegian man, says Tjønn. When the coronavirus was identified in China, Tjønn experienced that several individuals took detours to avoid bumping into him and the children. I was also asked if I had been to China lately. I laughed it off, as I often do. Now he wants to talk about it out loud to be adopted. It is in many ways peculiar, he believes.

Herein lies the paradox: while the Norwegian media has long obsessed with the success of the non-White adopted in Norway, adoptees such as Brynjulf have been obsessed with being White so much so that he has published a collection of poems with the title "White, Norwegian Man." Georgina Lawton is a British-Irish-Nigerian writer whose personal narrative is the subject of a nonfiction book: *Raceless: In Search of Family, Identity, and the Truth About Where I Belong* (2021). Part-memoir, part-socio-political discussion, the book focuses on the construct of racial identity in homes, exploring Lawton's experience of being mixed-race in a White home with two White parents without knowing why, and discovering she was the product of a brief liaison between her mother and her birth father. After the latter died, a DNA test revealed that she was more than 40% Nigerian. She is a *Guardian Weekend* columnist who regularly contributes to the paper and also writes about travel, race, and identity for other publications. Georgina verbalizes the suppressed and almost "taboo" subject of talking about race and difference in a White-dominated world such as Brynjulf's when she states:

> It was none of anyone's business where I was "from". But race didn't care about my family lore, or my parents' inability to discuss our differences. Race was dogged in its desperate pursuit

of me; it could not be ignored, it was inescapable. And as much as I tried to brush it off, as much as I tried to believe what I was told, race attached itself to me, a little more, year on year. I first became cognizant of my role as the perpetual outside at the age of five, when a classmate showed me a nifty little skin-scratching technique to temporarily turn myself lighter. (Lawton, 2021, p. 12)

The juxtaposition between the Norwegian media's fascination with the success of non-White adoptees and the psychological struggles faced by adoptees like Brynjulf sheds light on the complex dynamics of racial identity within adoption narratives. While the media portrays a narrative of accomplishment and integration (assimilation in reality) for non-White adoptees, individuals like Brynjulf grapple with feelings of otherness and a yearning to wistfully conform to White norms, as evidenced by his collection of poems titled "White, Norwegian Man".

Georgina Lawton's personal journey, as explored in her book "*Raceless*", further complicates this dynamic. Raised in a White household with White parents, Lawton's experience of being mixed-race and her ensuing discovery of her Nigerian legacy through a DNA test highlight the abiding impact of race and identity in shaping one's sense of self. Lawton movingly articulates the unrelenting intrusion of race into her life, despite attempts to ignore or deny its significance, emphasizing the inescapable nature of racial identity. Lawton's reflection on her childhood experience of trying to lighten her skin highlights the persistent influence of societal norms and pressures to conform to whiteness, even from a young age. Her assertion that "race attached itself to me, a little more, year on year" speaks to the enduring impact of racial identity and the challenges faced by individuals navigating racialized spaces. In verbalizing the silenced conversation about race and difference in primarily White environments, Lawton confronts the discomfort and taboo associated with discussing racial identity. Her narrative serves as a powerful reminder of the importance of acknowledging and addressing the complexities of racial identity within adoption narratives and broader societal contexts, such as that of Brynjulf.

In the book, he describes the physical and biological sides of giving birth. "Mother never got mastitis"; "Father never cut my umbilical cord". I have a Norwegian name, Norwegian parents and family. But I have a look that doesn't fit in with everything. People perceive me as simultaneously Norwegian and foreign. As an adopted person, you are perceived as both Norwegian and foreign, and as such, you lack a personal history. A research report from the Norwegian Institute of Public Health from 2021 shows that there is a high prevalence of mental disorders, ailments, and health challenges for adopted children. Three out of four elderly people stated in the report that they have had one or more adopted children who have struggled with psychological problems during their upbringing. (Aftenposten, 2022)

Brynjulf's evocative words provide a poignant insight into the complex experiences of adoptees in Norway, particularly in relation to issues of racial identity and belonging. His description of feeling out of place despite having Norwegian parents and family highlights the inner turmoil adoptees face in reconciling their physical appearance with their cultural and familial surroundings. W.E.B. Du Bois famously described the dual consciousness, where individuals navigate conflicting identities and perspectives, in this sense of being both Norwegian and foreign. W.E.B. Du Bois's concept of "double consciousness" intricately captures the experience of individuals who negotiate multiple cultural identities. Central to Du Bois's work, "double consciousness" articulates the psychological and social reality confronted by African Americans and other marginalized groups within predominantly White societies.

It elucidates the sensation of possessing two opposing identities and self-perceptions, shaped by one's own racial and cultural heritage as well as the dominant White culture. Du Bois argued that African Americans continuously struggled with the perceptions of the dominant White society, resulting in a pervasive awareness of their dual existence. This awareness engendered a profound sense of "twoness," wherein individuals perceived themselves through their own lens while simultaneously considering how they were viewed by the White majority. Consequently, African Americans navigated and reconciled these contrasting identities, often experiencing internal conflict, tension, and a profound sense of "double consciousness."

> The history of the American Negro is the history of this strife – this longing to attain self-conscious manhood, to merge his double self into a better and truer self. In this merging, he wishes neither of the older selves to be lost. He would not Africanize America, for America has too much to teach the world and Africa. He would not bleach his Negro soul in a flood of white Americanism, for he knows that Negro blood has a message for the world. He simply wishes to make it possible for man to be both a Negro and an American, without being cursed and spit upon by his fellows, without having the doors of Opportunity closed roughly in his face. (Du Bois, 1990, pp. 8, 9)

However, the application of Du Bois' concept of double consciousness diverges for adopted children compared to Black Americans. While Black Americans may grapple with the legacy of slavery, Jim Crow laws, and the Civil Rights movement as aspects of a unique historical trajectory germane to their collective identity, adoptees lack a shared heritage or historical narrative to anchor their "disorganized" sense of self. Instead, their identity is fragmented and often devoid of a tangible connection to their roots. This lack of a shared past hinders the distillation of a cohesive adoptee identity and obstructs the development of solidarity against racism and discrimination. Georgina Lawton movingly gives expression to this "fragmented self" when she does a DNA test and discovers her Nigerian heritage.

> Forty-three per cent of *me* was from *there.* My genetic make-up
> had been decoded, my blackness was laid out in front of me, the
> region boldly highlighted before. *Nigeria.* It had always been
> within me, I thought, I'd just never been able to access it. All of
> a sudden, I had a racial identity which was my own: I was
> apparently from west Africa, whatever that actually meant. It
> was almost everything I'd wanted to know and yet it was a stark
> departure from my former life. I didn't know how to feel. Should I
> have been happy? Relieved? Instead, I felt properly sorry for
> myself, and started to cry? (Lawton, 2021, p. 17)

Additionally, the diversity among adoptees in terms of language, culture, and
geographic origin further complicates attempts at shaping a shared identity.
Unlike Black Americans, who may share a common heritage from the "moth-
erland of Africa," adoptees come from miscellaneous backgrounds and may lack
a unifying cultural or historical reference point. This diversity is not amenable to
efforts at cultivating a sense of solidarity and collective identity among adoptees,
as their experiences and backgrounds vary widely. Additionally, the research
report from the Norwegian Institute of Public Health highlights the prevalence of
mental health challenges among adoptees, accenting the profound impact of
adoption experiences on psychological well-being. This underscores the importance of addressing the unique needs and challenges faced by adoptees, including
issues related to identity, belonging, and mental health support. Overall, Brynjulf's narrative, coupled with insights from Du Bois' concept of double consciousness, sheds light on the nuanced experiences of adoptees in Norway and the
complexities inherent in navigating racial identity and belonging within the
context of adoption. It stresses the need for greater recognition of adoptees'
experiences and the development of support systems that address their unique
needs and challenges.

Whiteness functions as an unmarked norm that privileges and shields White
individuals from the everyday experiences of racism and microaggressions,
according to Charles Mills's theory of the "Racial Contract," a system of White
supremacist social and political control. White parents may adopt non-White
children out of a genuine desire to parent and provide love and care. However,
their misrecognition of their own complicity in perpetuating systems of racial
inequality, as well as their naive belief that their whiteness will serve as a buffer
for their adopted children from racism, highlight a fatal flaw in their understanding of race and identity.

> Thus, in effect, on matters related to race, the Racial Contract
> prescribes for its signatories an inverted epistemology, an
> epistemology of ignorance, a particular pattern of localized and
> global cognitive dysfunctions (which are psychologically and
> socially functional), producing the ironic outcome that whites
> will in general be unable to understand the world they
> themselves have made. (Mills, 1997, p. 18)

According to anthropologist Marianne Gullestad, the term *innvandrer* (immigrant) in Norway has negative connotations and is frequently associated with antiblackness. Regardless of their actual nationality or citizenship status, this term carries assumptions and stereotypes about non-White individuals. The misrecognition lies in the belief that non-White adoptees can somehow transcend their racial identities and assimilate into whiteness, thus escaping the stigma and discrimination faced by other immigrants or refugees. However, despite growing up in White households, adoptees cannot erase their racial identities or protect themselves from societal racism. "Innvandrer is today more than just a word in the dictionary; it is a rhetorically powerful concept." "Within such a frame of analysis, innvandrer has become a stigmatizing way of labeling 'them'... The meaning of the word now seems to oscillate between an implicit code based on 'Third World' origin, different values from the majority, 'dark skin', working class (unskilled or semi-skilled work)" (Gullestad, 2005, p. 50).

The misrecognition of adoptees' racial identities and the mistaken expectation that they can fully participate in whiteness overlook the pervasive nature of racism and the ways in which racialized bodies are marked and othered in society. Despite their familial and cultural ties to whiteness, adoptees bear a heavy price for this misrecognition, experiencing the same forms of discrimination and marginalization as other non-White individuals. Ultimately, this highlights the urgent need for White parents, and society as a whole, to critically examine their own racial biases and actively work toward dismantling systems of oppression and inequality.

When Brynjulf, adopted from South Korea, spends a lifetime in Norway wishing he was White, it is an indictment of White society's inability or unwillingness to dismantle the values secreted into this whiteness to the detriment of other ways (and colors) of being. The "one-drop rule" in the United States is illustrative of how White supremacy operates through mechanisms of racial misrecognition, aimed at policing the borders of whiteness and reinforcing White bloodlines. This rule, which originated during the era of slavery and Jim Crow segregation, dictated that a person with any amount of African ancestry, even as little as one drop of "black blood," would be classified as Black and subjected to the social, legal, and economic ramifications of racial discrimination.

> Many people believe that determining who is "black" is rather easy, a task simplified by the administration of the one-drop-rule. Under the one-drop rule, any discernible African ancestry stamps a person as "black". White supremacists hoped that by definitively categorizing as "African", "black" "Negro", or "colored" anyone whose appearance signaled the presence of an African ancestor, the one-drop rule would protect white bloodlines. It mirrored and stoked Negrophobia by proclaiming that even the tiniest dab of Negro ancestry was sufficiently contaminating to make a person a "nigga". (Kennedy, 2008, p. 12, 13)

Mills's (1997) thesis on White misrecognition posits that White individuals often fail to acknowledge their complicity in perpetuating systems of racial inequality and privilege. Instead, they may naively believe in the meritocracy and colorblindness of society, conveniently overlooking the ways in which racism operates on both individual and structural levels. White-dominated institutions enforced the "one-drop rule" in the United States, a stark illustration of this misrecognition, and White individuals upheld it to maintain the purity and superiority of whiteness. Race has long been a problematic topic in Norway, often replaced with rewordings such as "ethnic" and "cultural" differences in educational research until recent years (Thomas et al., 2023). This hesitation to acknowledge race stemmed from its association with bigotry and the belief in inherent racial differences, which underpinned notions of White supremacy. Despite this, minority groups in Norway, including the Sami people, Jewish people, and Tartar (Tatar) people, faced state-sponsored discrimination based on classical racist ideologies.

For instance, historical reports reveal how racism against the Sami people in the 1800s manifested through practices like body snatching and skull measurements, aimed at denigrating them as inferior people. Norwegian society denied the Sami people full acceptance despite their ethnic whiteness, citing their perceived biological, cultural, and ethnic "otherness" (e.g., Mongolian blood). This exclusion mirrors the earlier denigration and subsequent integration of Irish whiteness in the United States, as explored in Noel Ignatiev's "How the Irish Became White."

During Norway's nation-building phase from 1814 to 1940, racial hierarchies were deeply rooted, influenced by Enlightenment-era ideologies. Norwegians endorsed notions of racial superiority, particularly regarding the "Germanic," "Nordic," or "Norwegian" races. The state disparaged minority groups like the Sami people and Kven people as biologically inferior, and targeted the Romani people for forced assimilation and sterilization. The state's assimilationist policies, including the forced removal of Romani children and the sterilization of Romani women, underscored Norway's colonialist mindset, despite lacking formal colonies. Particularly, this colonial mindset permeated the Sami areas, systematically marginalizing indigenous rights. In essence, Norway's history reflects a deeply entrenched racial hierarchy that marginalizes minority groups based on perceived biological, cultural, and ethnic differences. The legacy of this racialization continues to impact Norway's social fabric, especially in light of the challenges faced by adopted individuals.

The deeply entrenched racial hierarchy in Norway's history, characterized by notions of racial superiority and discriminatory policies targeting minority groups, has created a racially hostile atmosphere that continues to affect adopted individuals today. Despite this legacy, many adoptive parents may misrecognize or overlook the systemic racism faced by their children, perpetuating a cycle of racial misrecognition and marginalization. Wallis (2016, p. 74) asks the question, "'How did you all become "White people" when you came to America?' English, Italians, Swedes, Irish, Dutch, Germans, and the rest were never a common ethnic group in Europe. There is no such thing as a white race in Europe. . ." The question of how to "die to whiteness" (Ignatiev, 2022) is salutary, so Brynjulf would not have to wish he was a White man.

2. Adopted Identities: Bunad's Role in Norwegian Diversity

> To me, the bunad represents the essence of what it means to be Norwegian, coupled with national pride. There is something solemn about the costume. Personally, I felt the opposite when I was 15. I was unsure about who I was and what I stood for. The bunad underscores the fact that one has an identity. Did I have one? Why bother carrying a bunad when I do not feel prepared to do so? The bunad often represents where you come from. Not seldom do you hear the question, Where is your bunad from? In my mind, I reformulated the question as: Where are you from? I had no clear answer to this. I just wanted to remove the bunad as quickly as possible. (Andrea Bratt Mæhlum, adopted at the age of 6 from Costa Rica, NrK, 2017).

> When Gry [adopted from South Korea] was 12 years old, she had a bunad; today she can't imagine going in it. She has become aware that she can provoke people – Norway for Norwegians, she says. It's a matter of concept. Does a Norwegian have to look traditionally Norwegian or be born to Norwegian parents? I feel Norwegian more than anything else. I have nothing else to compare it to. But I probably felt more Norwegian when I was younger. (Aftenposten, 1990)

The bunad is Norway's traditional costume. Bunad embroidery and patterns intricately correspond to specific regions and are reserved for special occasions such as National Day celebrations, weddings, rites of passage such as Christian confirmations in both the Lutheran and Christian humanistic traditions, child baptisms, formal galas, events, and funerals. More than half of the Norwegian population possesses either a bunad or a folk costume (Grinder & Martinsen, 2014). This apparel, often adorned with exquisite embroidery and decorations, carries enormous symbolic significance. Remarkably, Norway boasts circa 450 distinct bunads, each representing a distinctive provincial heritage through varied patterns, motifs, and colors.

The bunad is intimately associated with rural communities and preindustrial Norway and imbued with the ethos of national romanticism, which found its apotheosis in the dissolution of the union between Norway and Sweden when the former became an independent country in 1905. Throughout centuries of political subjugation, as Norway found itself playing second fiddle to Denmark and later Sweden, the bunad surfaced as a potent symbol of the nation's resilience and unyielding spirit. It became a steadfast emblem of autonomy, transcending shifting political landscapes and symbolizing the indomitable essence of the Norwegian people. Much like the enduring myth of Scottish defiance woven into the elaborate tartan patterns and immortalized in the saga of Braveheart, the bunad became synonymous with Norway's unwavering determination and unconquered identity (Thomas et al., 2022). Adoptees, such as Andrea Bratt Mæhlum (2019), are caught in the crossfire of cultural identity, inclusion, and the unintended exclusivist message conveyed by the bunad. "Exclusivist" in the sense that the bunad, in the puritan mind, clearly corresponds to distinct regions in Norway and thus proclaims, in the spirit of Johann Gottfried von Herder, that identity is coextensive with physical terrain. In one sense, Andrea's struggle echoes the debate about whether ethnicity is fixed or mutable.

> Fredrik Barth's seminal studies on ethnic boundary-making elucidated the social plasticity of ethnicity as an aspect of relations between groups and not an essentialized congenital attribute that marks an individual from birth. In contrast to Herder who promulgated a theory of ethnicity that neatly followed the contours of the cultural landscape. (Thomas et al., 2016, p. 215; Wimmer, 2013)

The loyal devotees of the bunad tradition, often nicknamed the "bunad police of Norway," exhibit aversion toward individuals with "non-native" skin tones like Andrea's, unwaveringly refusing to adorn Black and brown skin with the revered attire, reserving it exclusively for those with white skin. Her account sheds light on how the figurative weight of the bunad, laden with notions of Norwegian heritage and national pride, can consciously or unconsciously challenge individuals whose racial identity does not align with the implicit whiteness integral to its imagery. The vibrant colors and provincial associations of the bunad, while rich in cultural significance, may inadvertently cement a narrow conception of Norwegian identity that rejects those whose skin color does not sit easily with the tacit implications of whiteness.

Andrea covets a sense of belonging with a fervor that only the adopted heart can know. Yet, analogous to the mesmerizing allure of the ring in Tolkien's epic saga, "Lord of the Rings," she is keenly aware of the bunad's ability to evoke the disapproval of a faction within the White Norwegian community – a disapproval similar to the malevolent gaze of Sauron, albeit manifested through the lens of racism. Amin Maalouf (2001, p. 9) cautions against the misleading nature of the concept of identity, labeling it a "false friend." He delves beyond mere official categories like sex, nationality, and profession, airing concern for the diverse array of elements that constitute one's identity. Maalouf emphasizes the necessity for reciprocity from the majority and observes how certain aspects of identity surface depending on the context; for instance, religion may come to the forefront when under threat.

His insight that "the secret dream of most migrants is to be taken for natives" (Maalouf, 2001, p. 38) resonates deeply with the longing of minorities like Andrea to be embraced as Norwegians, capable of proudly donning the bunad like their counterparts. Andrea's experience as an adopted individual from Costa Rica highlights the dissonance between the bunad's symbolism and her own sense of identity. For individuals like Andrea, who struggle with questions of belonging and self-identity, the inextricably and implacably linked bunad to "White" geographical locations and its role as a symbol of national pride creates a dilemma.

We encounter a heart-wrenching dilemma as we survey the plight of adoptees like Andrea, who must navigate not only the complexities of adoption but also the pressure to embrace the national costume of their adopted homeland. It's a dual process of adoption, where the adoptee must not only assimilate into a new family and culture but also grapple with the expectation to internalize its traditions, including donning the revered national costume. Yet, what recourse exists when the proposed costume fails to resonate with the intricate fabric of an adoptee's identity? How does one reconcile the contrasting threads of heritage and upbringing, merging them into a cohesive whole that adequately reflects their "double consciousness"? Consider the Sami people with their characteristic Kofte, the Scots with their distinct tartan, or Native Americans and Hawaiians whose histories leap boldly off colorful quilts in patchwork designs and patterns, all emblematic of cultural identities deeply etched in tradition and history. Unfortunately, for the adopted, there is often no comparable sartorial representation of their hybrid identity. Instead, they rely on the guardians of their adopted lineage to extend the mantle of belonging, tentatively grafting the "foreign sapling" onto the familial tree.

In visualizing a costume that speaks to the complex identity of adoptees, one might imagine a tapestry woven from a kaleidoscope of patterns, colors, and embroidery – a visual ode to the multilayered nature of their existence. Each thread is a tribute to their heritage's rich tapestry, knitted with the vivid hues of their adopted culture. This "tartan, quilt, kofte, or bunad of the adopted" would transcend the limitations of tradition, embracing the complexities of identity with open arms. In a world where the concept of identity is as fluid as the shifting sands of time, it would not merely be a costume, but a declaration – an assertion of resilience, adaptation, and belonging. Hybridized identities, such as that of British author, Bernadine Evaristo, the 2019 Booker Prize winner, born to an English mother and Nigerian father, understandably gravitate toward other hybridized identities resonating with the vibrant colors of quilts rather than parochial garments that bespeak exclusive identities.

> During my childhood I seem to have been subconsciously drawn to people who were different, without realizing that a pattern was emerging. My best childhood friend was half-Iraqi, although she didn't really look it; ditto another friend who was half Greek. My first teenage boyfriend was dark-skinned Hungarian Jewish, while the second was white English but raised in South Africa. By the time I went to drama school in 1979 I was finally able to get to know black women other than my sisters, with a record-breaking

five of us in the same college. Now that I had found them, we bonded over our experiences of being perceived as outsiders and the struggle to feel that we belonged, when the overriding message from our society was that we did not. (Evaristo, 2021, p. 27)

We can view Andrea's and other adoptees' experiences through the lens of social capital theory, specifically in relation to bonding and bridging social capital. Evaristo's narrative illustrates the inherent value of both types of social capital in fostering connections and resilience among marginalized individuals. These "marginalized" individuals happen to comprise the majority of the world's population, as John Edgar Wideman reminds us in his introduction to W.E.B. Du Bois's *The Souls of Black Folk*. "Us turns out to be most people on earth, people of color, emigrants, refugees, mixed bloods, exiles, the poor and the dispossessed, women and men who didn't count, who were unseen and unheard" (Du Bois, 1990, p. xii).

In Evaristo's recollection, we see the emergence of bonding social capital as she subconsciously gravitates toward individuals who share similar experiences of difference and "outsider" status. This proclivity to form connections with those who understand the convolutions of identity and belonging reflects the strength of bonding social capital in creating a sense of solidarity and support within marginalized communities. For adoptees like Andrea, these bonds with individuals who share a common background of adoption or cultural dislocation provide a vital source of validation and understanding amid societal messages of exclusion. Additionally, Evaristo's multiethnic circle of friends illustrates the power of bridging social capital by surpassing cultural and racial divides. By forging connections with individuals from diverse backgrounds, Evaristo and her friends bridge social boundaries, fostering empathy, understanding, and mutual respect. This bridging social capital not only enriches their personal relationships but also contributes to the development of more inclusive and diverse social networks. In Norway, this bridging capital is evident in emergence of diverse associations such as Norwegian-Colombian Association which serves as a conduit for cultural exchange and mutual support between the adopted Colombian community and the broader Norwegian society, fostering understanding and connection across diverse backgrounds.

> Through events and activities, the Norwegian-Colombian Association (NCF) functions as a gathering point and social network where adopted Colombians meet and exchange experiences and knowledge. We want the association to be a forum for topics connected with adoption, such as identity, return journey, culture and knowledge of Colombia. (Norsk-Colombianos Forening, 2015)

Shared experiences of otherization and the struggle to fit in act as catalysts for bonding and building social capital, enabling individuals to thrive. Through such avenues, individuals like Andrea find validation, support, and a sense of belonging that resists superficial markers of identity. In this way, social capital theory offers a valuable framework for understanding the dynamics of community-building and resilience among adopted individuals, highlighting the importance of both bonding and bridging social ties in navigating the complexities of identity and belonging.

Consider Andrea's experience within the context of Wimmer's (2013) typologies of boundary-making, particularly the concepts of "contraction" and "blurring." In the case of contraction, individuals like Andrea may withdraw from a designated ethnic group – in this instance, the Norwegian identity represented by the bunad – due to its exclusionary nature. On the other hand, blurring leads to de-emphasizing ethnic categories and pursuing affiliation with nonethnic-based identities. Andrea's discomfort with the bunad's exclusive associations with whiteness may prompt her to seek connections based on shared experiences or values rather than ethnic heritage. In this way, Andrea may navigate her sense of belonging by transcending the limitations imposed by traditional ethnic boundaries. Wimmer's notion of boundary as both a categorical and behavioral dimension sheds light on Andrea's struggle. While the bunad serves as a categorical boundary, delineating between "us" and "them" based on ethnic identity, Andrea's decision to remove it represents a behavioral boundary – a rejection of the prescribed script that accompanies the garment. This disconnect between societal classification and personal action underscores the complexity of identity negotiation for individuals like Andrea.

Ultimately, Andrea's experience highlights the tension between social representation and personal identity construction. Drawing on Bourdieu's insights, Wimmer emphasizes the pursuit of not only favorable social representations but also the power to legitimize one's own understanding of social reality. Andre's reluctance to conform to the bunad's exclusive identity reflects her quest for authenticity and recognition within a social context that may not fully embrace her diverse identity. Andrea's inclination to remove the bunad when she was 15 and was about to be confirmed in the Lutheran tradition reflects her desire to distance herself from a cultural marker that fails to encompass her identity as a person of color. At the time, Andrea could not have known that the purported originality of the bunad as a costume sui generis to regions in Norway was a canard. It was in the first decade of the 19th century, spurred by national romanticism, that interest in the bunad and the old Norse language emerged. It was in the interstices of these national romantics' molding of a distinct Norwegian subject that the bunad was also of interest. Neumann (2000) shows how the project of delineating "real" and "historical" folk attire, such as the bunad, was an eclectic process "[...] activist Hulda Garborg trusted her own aesthetics, as counterdistinctive to actual use, when deciding what to represent as real/of the people and what to suppress. 'We want to dress modern European cultural thought in Norwegian folk costume (bunad)'" (Nerbøvik, 1998, p. 333; Thomas et al., p. 167).

Friedrich Nietzsche's critique of the purported profundity of German identity in *Beyond Good and Evil* comes to mind. "There was a time when it was common to call the Germans 'profound'... The German soul is above all manifold, of diverse origins, put together and superimposed rather than actually constructed: the reason for that is its source. A German who could make bold to say 'two souls, alas, within my bosom dwell' would err very widely from the truth, more correctly, he would fall short of the truth by a large number of souls'" (Nietzsche, 1973, p. 174). Nietzsche is deliberately disrespectful when he shows how fluid German identity is, highlighting how it is always changing and growing. At the same time, he shows it as "profound" and therefore involuntarily exclusive, mostly by leaving out people like Andrea who don't fit within its predetermined parameters. The discussion surrounding the bunad in the context of Norwegian nationalism highlights the complex interplay between authenticity, representation, and exclusion within the construction of national identity. Nietzsche is relentless in unpeeling the so-called profundity of the German soul:

> And as everything loves its symbol, the German loves clouds and all that is obscure, becoming, crepuscular, damp and dismal: the uncertain, unformed, shifting, growing of every kind he feels to be "profound". The German himself *is* not, he is *becoming,* he is "developing". "Development" is thus the truly German discovery and lucky shot in the great domain of philosophical formulas – a ruling concept which, in concert with German beer and German music, is at work at the Germanization of all Europe. (Nietzsche, 1973, p. 175)

Nietzsche's critique of German identity, wherein he challenges the purported profundity of national identity by emphasizing its inherent multiplicity and complexity, is indeed ahead of its time. His assertion that the German soul is composed of diverse origins and manifold influences speaks to the fluidity and plurality of identity, countering the notion of a singular, monolithic national identity. If this was true in Nietzsche's time, it is incontrovertibly more so today. Neumann's (2000) analysis of the bunad as a symbol of Norwegian identity reveals the eclectic and subjective nature of the process of identifying "real" and "historical" folk attire.

Hulda Garborg's assertion that the bunad should capture modern European cultural thought underlines the contrived nature of a national identity that aligns with certain aesthetic and cultural ideals, while suppressing aspects considered incongruent with this vision. While it may not have been the explicit intent of the creators of the bunad tradition, it is important to acknowledge that many Norwegians welcome the inclusion of nonwhites in wearing the bunad. Nonetheless, the vocal segment of the population, which rejects individuals like Andrea from belonging, polices the boundaries of identity through the bunad. This narrative marginalizes those, such as Black and brown individuals like Andrea, who do not fit within its predefined standards.

In essence, the citation stresses the strain between the fabricated nature of national identity and the lived experiences of individuals whose identities challenge easy labeling. It serves as a reminder of the need to critically examine the narratives and symbols that purport to symbolize a collective identity, recognizing the inherent diversity and complexity of human experience. In reality, then, those who do not "grant" belonging to nonwhites in the use of national costumes such as the bunad are fearful of the relentless dynamism of identity. Like the river of Heraclitus, culture, identity, etc., ceaselessly march on, always amalgamating foreign elements along the way, always changing, never to sit still. The "bunad police," then, can be likened to a futile attempt that desperately seeks to perpetually engrave and capture Nietzsche's "profound" German concoction, which never existed. Now that others (i.e., nonwhites in Norway) wish to "engrave" their stories into the bunad to carve out a space for themselves, the purists are infuriated like religious prophets, condemning the sins of the people and calling on them to return to the "old sacrosanct ways." Nietzsche laments the fading appreciation for the cultural giants of the past, as well as the loss of a sense of European destiny and hope.

> The "good old days" are gone, in Mozart they sang themselves out... Mozart was the closing cadence of a great centuries-old European taste. Beethoven is the intermediary between an old mellow soul that is constantly crumbling and a future over-young soul that is constantly *arriving;* upon his music there lies that twilight of eternal loss and eternal extravagant hope... But how quickly *this* feeling is now fading away, how hard it is today even to *know* of Rousseau, Schiller, Shelley, Byron, in whom *together* the same European destiny that in Beethoven knew how to sing found its way into words! (Nietzsche, 1973, p. 177)

This dynamic demonstrates how identity is fluid and evolving, resisting confinement to rigid definitions or boundaries. Attempts to preserve a static, homogeneous identity through symbols like the bunad ultimately prove futile in the face of the ever-changing landscape of the human experience. The resistance to welcoming non-White individuals into wearing the bunad reflects a deeper anxiety about cultural change and the loss of traditional norms. It highlights the importance of challenging entrenched narratives and symbols that reinforce exclusion and marginalization, and instead embracing a more inclusive and dynamic understanding of identity.

In her book *The History of White People* (2010), Princeton Professor of American History, Nell Irvin Painter uncovers the historical contours of the invention of the White race and its all-encompassing hegemony. Not unlike the evolution of the bunad, Painter (2010) highlights the role of Ralph Waldo Emerson (1803–1882), whom she dubs "the philosopher king of American white race theory" (Painter, 2010, p. 151). Something of an imagined "glorious" past had to first be imbued into the category of Anglo-Saxon and then, like the "Holy Grail," trace its whereabouts from the miasma of history and place it like a crown upon the head of America. "The American was the same as the Englishman, who was the same as the Saxon and the Norseman. This 'Saxon' supplied the key word exiling the Celtic Irish—white though they may be—from American identity" (Painter, 2010, p. 183). One could argue in one sense that the "custodians" of the purity of the bunad perceive it as the "Saxon" or "Viking" who "exiles" non-whites such as Andrea from the commonwealth of Norwegian whiteness. Painter (2010) shows how Emerson had to negotiate a dilemma in his efforts at imbuing Anglo-Saxon whiteness with supremacist merits.

> Scandinavia might work as the ancestral home of northern whiteness, but Scandinavia of the 1850s created a dilemma: it was backward and really quite poor – a little nothing beside the British behemoth. How could Emerson reconcile that reality with his need for Scandinavian racial (hence permanent) brilliance? If the Norsemen endowed Britain with all its "Saxon" greatness, how to explain the relative obscurity of contemporary Scandinavia? Why had not the Norwegians and Danes launched the industrial revolution, grown rich on worldwide commerce, and colonized the globe? (Painter, 2010, p. 168)

Painter (2010) discusses the concept of Anglo-Saxon identity, which illuminates the myth of bunad authenticity and its role in patrolling the borders of whiteness in the context of Wimmer's (2013) theory of contraction and blurring of identity boundaries. Painter's study underscores the construction of the yearning for a "glorious" past around the Anglo-Saxon identity category, which subsequently projected onto American identity as a symbol of racial superiority. This Anglo-Saxon identity construction served to exclude nonwhites, such as the Celtic Irish (despite their obvious whiteness), from the American identity, effectively contracting the boundaries of whiteness. Similarly, one could argue that the caretakers of bunad purity identify it as the "Holy Grail" of Norwegian whiteness, with roots in the "glorious" past of the Vikings and Saxons. This perception serves to remove non-whites, like Andrea, from the commonwealth of Norwegian whiteness, reinforcing a narrow and exclusionary definition of Norwegian identity.

Furthermore, Painter's analysis of Emerson's dilemma in imbuing Anglo-Saxon whiteness with supremacist merits illuminates the complexities inherent in the construction of racial identity. Similarly, the myth of bunad authenticity reflects a struggle to reconcile the reality of modern Scandinavia with the fanciful image of a racially superior past. The relative obscurity and poverty of 19th-century Scandinavia pose a dilemma for those seeking to champion the myth of bunad authenticity, challenging the notion of Scandinavian racial brilliance. So how did Emerson reconcile the irreconcilable?

> Here Emerson resorts to a favorite metaphor: the fruit tree. Scandinavia, he surmises, lost its best men during the Dark Ages – lost them to England and never recovered: "The continued draught of the best men in Norway, Sweden and Denmark to their piratical expeditions exhausted those countries, like a tree which bears much fruit when young, and these have been second-rate powers since. The power of the race migrated and left Norway permanently exhausted." (Painter, 2010, pp. 168,169)

Painter, concludes, "It is a lame theory, and Emerson does not lean on it heavily" (Painter, 2010, p. 169). In contrast, contemporary "Emersons," who appear to be oath-bound to ensure that only those who "fulfill the criteria" for wearing the bunad, lean on the theory of "bunad purism" heavily. Just as the "guardians of bunad sanctity" cling to the notion of preserving whiteness within the bunad, Emerson upheld a theory of White racial brilliance from the Vikings to the Americans. Both narratives hinge on the idealization of a perceived past greatness, whether it's the valorized image of the Viking ancestry or the projection of Anglo-Saxon superiority onto American identity. In both cases, there's a fear of losing that perceived greatness in the face of shifting demographics or historical realities, leading to efforts to preserve and defend the purity or brilliance of whiteness within their respective cultural symbols.

3. Stealing Identity: White Adoption's Toll

> When she found her biological mother, she used the name Kine Samanthie Priyangika Fiskerstrand Oterhals. The Norwegian first name is now gone, and Priyangika Samanthie Kraggerud has in recent years become a clear, critical voice to Norwegian adoption abroad. She believes, among other things, that the structures around adoption violates children's rights, that adoption is not in the best interest of the child and that poverty is not a real reason for adoption. (Romsdalsbudstikke, 2022)

Priyangika was born in Sri Lanka in 1992 and adopted in Norway at just seven weeks old. At the time she was interviewed, her life became the subject of a documentary film shown at one of Europe's biggest documentary festivals, CPH-DOX, Copenhagen, Denmark. The theme that runs through the entire newspaper interview, with the apt title "My Adoption Was Illegal," is one of stolen identity and a battle to reclaim some semblance of agency. At the outset of the interview, Priyangika asserts that even the documentary film about her life has distorted her reality.

> In an interview in *Klassekampen* [newspaper] on Saturday, Priyangika says that the film is the director's story, and not hers. She asserts that the film primarily depicts her as a pity figure, with minimal exploration of the challenging aspects of adoption. Still, she doesn't denounce the film, and hopes it can be a catalyst for debate. (Rbnett.no, 2022)

Using critical race theory's (CRT's) tenet of subversive storytelling, we can explore the narrative of Priyangika's mission to retrieve her truth as an act of resistance against the hegemonic discourse perpetuated by White adoption practices. At 20 years old, Priyangika embarks on a journey to wrestle back some semblance of control over the narrative of her own life, which was forcibly taken from her at the moment of adoption. This act of self-assertion emerges as a subversive act within the framework of dominant power structures that have historically silenced and disregarded voices of color. Maya Angelou captures something of what Priyangika must feel in *I Know Why the Caged Bird Sings* (1969): "If growing up is painful for the Southern black girl, being aware of her displacement is the rust on the razor that threatens the throat" (Angelou, 1969, p. 6). The metaphor of the razor's rust symbolizes the corrosive nature of becoming fully conscious of the consequences of displacement. The discovery of concealed or distorted identities can be deeply traumatic for adopted children in Norway. The rust of discovering that lies have obscured their true heritage is akin to the sharp pain of Angelou's razor edge. This perception destabilizes their sense of self, causing emotional turbulence and a profound sense of loss.

Subversive or counter storytelling in CRT refers to a methodological approach that queries dominant narratives and power structures by centering the perspectives and experiences of marginalized individuals and communities. Developed by scholars such as Derrick Bell, Richard Delgado, and Kimberlé Crenshaw, counter or subversive storytelling seeks to unearth and disrupt the ways in which mainstream narratives often sideline, silence, or distort the lived realities of people of color (Bell, 1995; Delgado & Stefancic, 2012). Priyangika's brave decision to reclaim her name, shedding the imposed Norwegian identity and embracing her Sri Lankan heritage, indicates a radical departure from the assimilationist pressures imposed upon transracial adoptees. By asserting her full name, including her given name from birth, she disrupts the erasure of her cultural identity and challenges the notion of whiteness as the normative standard to which all others must conform. Malcolm X describes this act of self-naming as a form of resistance, a refusal to conform to the dominant White narrative. The above is captured in Chinua Achebe's sentiment:

> At the university, I read some appalling novels about Africa (including Joyce Cary's much praised *Mister Johnson*) and decided that the story we had to tell could not be told for us by anyone else, no matter how gifted or well-intentioned. (Achebe, 2016)

Lord Macaulay (1800–1859) was a British colonial administrator and scholar who played a substantial role in shaping British policy in India during the 19th century. His quotes reflect his colonialist outlook and his quest to impose British language, culture, and values on the Indian population as a means of asserting British dominance and control. The quote "A single shelf of a good European library was worth the whole native literature of India and Arabia" sums up Macaulay's belief in the superiority of Western culture and knowledge over indigenous Indian and Arab traditions. Such secretions into the Western discursive space reflect the colonialist view that European civilization was intrinsically superior and that native cultures were inferior and in need of enlightenment and upliftment by the British.

In envisioning "a class of persons, Indian in blood and color, but English in taste, in opinions, in morals, and in intellect," Macaulay articulated his strategy of creating a native elite who would be indoctrinated with British values and perspectives. This class of individuals would serve as liaisons between the British colonial administration and the Indian population, enabling the implementation of British policies and maintaining British control over India.

Priyangika's brave journey to confront her past, reclaim control of, and chronicle her own narrative as an adult, while acknowledging the complexities of adoptee experiences, compels us to confront uncomfortable parallels with Lord Macaulay's colonial ambitions, albeit in the modern incarnation of adoption. Though the scope and aims may vary, the underlying structures and outcomes bear a troubling resemblance. This strategy mirrors the transracial adoption approach, which often raises children from marginalized communities in predominantly White environments and indoctrinates them with Western values and culture. Like Macaulay's vision for India, this process aims to create a select group of individuals who are perceived as "civilized" and "assimilated" into dominant Western society, while cementing the hierarchical power dynamics between colonizers and colonized.

Any expression of grievance or assertion of stolen heritage by an adoptee is swiftly met with a volley of dismissive responses, reminiscent of the colonial apologia employed by figures like Macaulay. The refrain of ingratitude, "But we rescued you from a wretched fate," immediately greets adoptees brave enough to voice their sense of loss and cultural erasure. This echoes Macaulay's rationalization of British colonization as a benevolent bestowal of European "civilization" upon the colonized. Subsequently, adoptees like Priyangika find themselves stripped not only of their identity but also of the right to feel shock, sorrow, or rage. Their emotions are subjugated to the White gaze, compelled to appease not only the expectations of their adoptive parents but also the collective conscience of an entire nation, what I call "colonial emotional choreography."

Much like the scripted reality of "The Truman Show," even their tears must conform to the expectations of an audience, carefully tailored for "viewer ratings." This is evident in the patronizing interrogation Priyangika faces in the interview: "Do you understand that other foreign adoptees disagree with you?" (Rbnett.no, 2022). The adoptee, much like the colonized subject, is infantilized and denied agency. They silence their voices, diminish their narratives, and undermine their autonomy. They are demoted to a state of perpetual dependency, deemed incapable of discerning what is in their own best interest. Instead, they are instructed to defer to the wisdom of contemporary "Macaulay's" reinforcing the paternalistic dominance of Western ideologies over the lived experiences and self-determination of adoptees from marginalized backgrounds. Angela Davis gives expression to the conundrum of historical revision vis-à-vis slavery.

> When the influential scholar Ulrich B. Philips declared in 1918 that slavery in the Old South had impressed upon African savages and their native-born descendants the glorious stamp of civilization, he set the stage for a long and passionate debate. As the decades

passed and the debate raged on, one historian after another confidently professed to have deciphered the real meaning of the "peculiar institution." (Davis, 1981, p. 1)

Ultimately, both Macaulay's colonial project in India and the practice of transracial adoption involve the imposition of Western values and culture on non-Western populations as a means of maintaining control and perpetuating colonialist ideologies. While White Westerners may vigorously deny any comparisons between the two, a critical examination reveals the underlying similarities, consciously or unconsciously, in their objectives and methods of cultural imperialism and dominance. In *The Minute* (1835), Macaulay wrote, "A single shelf of a good European library was worth the whole native literature of India and Arabia." *India Today's* web desk writes in an op-ed entitled *A Minute to acknowledge the day when India was "educated" by Macaulay* (2018) with regard to Macaulay's *The Minute*. However, a member of the Program on Liberation Technology at Stanford University, who has previously contributed to rights-based campaigns in India, wrote in Macaulay's *Minute on Indian Education*.

> His characterization of Indian languages and traditions is openly racist and represents an important danger that any discourse on institutions can get into. At the surface, it may look like the discourse on institutions today is different, especially with an emphasis in some quarters that societies are different and that each need to develop institutions that suit themselves. But we only need to scratch beneath the surface to see manifestations of racism and notions of "White man's burden" that embody the discourse on institutions today. (India Today, 2019)

Moreover, Angelou's quote alludes to the systemic issues at play, including the White privilege guilt of Norwegian parents who may not have suitably vetted the adoption procedure. The focus on their own interests, rather than safeguarding the integrity of the adoptee, reflects a broader societal tendency to prioritize convenience and comfort over the well-being of marginalized individuals. This laxity perpetuates cycles of injustice and reinforces existing power imbalances. The dilemma of adopted children in Norway echoes the experiences of minoritized people of color wrestling with identity theft and erasure. Just as the Southern Black girl faces the terrible reality of her displacement, adopted children confront the disconcerting truth about their stolen identities. This understanding not only challenges their sense of self but also underscores the broader societal issues of privilege, accountability, and the need for systemic change.

> My mother was from a middle-class family in the south and lived a traditional Buddhist life until her father, who was the main breadwinner, died. This led the family into poverty and made the mother vulnerable. She and her siblings had to leave school

at an early age in order to contribute to the household, says Priyangika. Priyangika believes that her mother fell victim to the illegal adoption market after an unwanted pregnancy, and that she didn't know her child had been adopted abroad. On the other hand, she thought she would get her child back after two years. She spent many years of her life searching for Priyangika. You don't get an insight into this through the documentary, but [the mother's] story shows that it was never about a lack of love or a desire to raise me, says Priyangika. (Romsdalsbudstikke, 2022)

There is no doubt in Priyangika's mind: she was stolen from her mother and her roots in Sri Lanka. What is even more shocking is the claim that the adoption system in Norway collaborated in this theft. If true, this is not the first time Black bodies were "stolen from Africa" (southeast Asia in this instance), in the words of Bob Marley's memorable song "Buffalo Soldier." Not least, once again, we observe the duplicitous machinations of denial or silencing. The discovery of the slave ship *Fredensborg* wreck off the coast of southern Norway in 1974 revealed a long-silenced dark chapter in Norway's history. Norway has conveniently over-looked or denied its complicity in the transatlantic slave trade during its time in the Danish Union (1380–1814), contributing to a collective national amnesia. The media's coverage of this discovery, or omission, mirrors this erasure, paying minimal attention to the crucial role Norwegians played in the brutal trafficking of human lives.

It is estimated that around 40% of the crew on board the slave ships were Norwegian, and recent scholarship implies that the number of enslaved people transported may have been much higher than previously acknowledged (Hopkins, 2013; Stawski, 2018). Additionally, there were approximately 100 enslaved people in Norway, a fact rarely discussed in mainstream Norwegian history narratives. The deliberate suppression of this information mirrors the tactics employed to conceal Norway's involvement in the transatlantic slave trade.

The recent resurgence of global movements like Black Lives Matter and Rhodes Must Fall has forced Norway to face up to its hidden history of slavery and colonialism. These movements, together with the release of a documentary about Norway's "Hidden Slave Trade" (Thomas & Hof, 2024), have brought the issue to the forefront of national discourse. The detailed preservation of records, diving finds, and excavations related to the Fredensborg slave ship has provided irrefutable evidence of Norway's culpability in the exploitation of African lives.

Between 1670 and 1804, 110,000 enslaved people were transported from Africa to the Americas [the Danish West Indies (Saint Thomas, Saint Croix, and Saint John)] on ships belonging to the Danish-Norwegian kingdom. Stawski (Citation2018) disputes these numbers, claiming a figure that is six times higher, making the Denmark-Norway slave trade not the 7th but the 5th largest slave-trading nation, surpassed only by Portugal, Great Britain, and France. (Thomas & Hof, 2024, p. 13)

The media's role in shaping public perceptions of Norway's past is salutary in understanding the contemporary significance of historical injustices. By acknowledging and confronting its role in the transatlantic slave trade, Norway can begin to address the legacy of racism and inequality that continues to affect adoptees today. The parallels between the experiences of enslaved people and adoptees, such as Priyangika, highlight the enduring impact of colonialism and the importance of salvaging and accenting marginalized voices in the telling of history. Michel Foucault's knowledge-power nexus, where power structures shape and control knowledge production, provides a lens through which to view Priyangika's journey to uncover the truth about her adoption experience. Foucault's concept of "archaeology of knowledge" involves digging beneath the surface of dominant discourses to reveal the underlying power dynamics and truth regimes at play.

> In societies like ours, the "political economy" of truth is characterized by five important traits. "Truth" is centered on the form of scientific discourse and the institutions which produce it; it is subject to constant economic and political incitement (the demand for truth, as much for economic production as for political power); it is the object, under diverse forms, of immense diffusion and consumption (circulating through apparatuses of education and information whose extent is relatively broad in the social body, notwithstanding certain strict limitations); it is produced and transmitted under the control, dominant if not exclusive, of a few great political and economic apparatuses (university, army, writing, media); lastly, it is the issue of a whole political debate and social confrontation ("ideological" struggles). (Foucault, 1980, pp. 131, 132)

The five dimensions of Foucault's knowledge-power nexus are easily traceable in Priyangika's case. The "scientific" dimension is evident in the myriad "studies" and "reports" imbued with scientific credibility, assuring the public that adoptees are successful despite experiencing issues that, on the whole, are not insurmountable. Unfortunately, the "economic" element is the most glaring and perverse, as Black and brown bodies are once again the subject of commercial exchanges. Despite numerous scandals over the decades, an almost unanimous cross-party alignment supports the continuation of adoptions from the global south, lending this dubious enterprise a "political" gravitas. Only recently, some adoptees' initiative has sparked discussions about suspending adoptions. However, fortunately, Foucault's knowledge-power nexus evinces internal contradictions in the "ideological struggles" thrown up by individuals such as Priyangika and others who interrogate this "regime of truth." Once again, Foucault highlights the central role of capitalism in producing and maintaining truth regimes.

> "Truth" is linked in a circular relation with systems of power which produce and sustain it, and to effects of power which it

induces and which extend it. A "regime" of truth. This regime is
not merely ideological or superstructural; it was a condition of the
formation and development of capitalism. (Foucault, 1980, p. 133)

The power to define and interpret the architecture of adoption in Norway lies
with those who hold institutional and cultural authority, such as government
agencies, adoption agencies, and mainstream media. These entities have historically perpetuated a narrative that frames adoption as a benevolent act that
benefits all parties involved. In Priyangika's case, her courageous decision to
question the narrative surrounding adoption in Norway is an act of resistance
against the power structures that have historically defined and controlled the
discourse around adoption. As previously mentioned, the media's involvement in
the "regime of truth" becomes clear when they inform Priyangika that other
adoptees disagree with her. By mining her own experiences and critiquing the
prevailing truth regimes that portray adoption as a virtuous act, she is engaging in
a form of Foucauldian archaeological inquiry.

However, Priyangika's narrative challenges this dominant discourse by
revealing the complexities and injustices inherent in the adoption system. Her
insistence on speaking her truth disrupts the power dynamics that seek to silence
dissenting voices and maintain the status quo. In Foucauldian terms, Priyangika's
act of resistance can be seen as a form of "power/knowledge," where power
operates through the production and dissemination of knowledge. By reclaiming
her narrative and challenging the truth regimes that have marginalized adoptees
like herself, she asserts her agency and disrupts the hegemonic control over
adoption discourse. Ultimately, it is not the physician, but the patient who must
confirm or deny whether the cure is having its desired effect. The stoic philosopher
and statesman Lucius Seneca writes to his friend Lucillus in *On Sharing Knowledge* that "in certain cases, sick men are congratulated because they themselves
have perceived that they are sick" (Seneca, 2020, p. 10). He goes on to state that
the progress he has made through reading the writings of Hecato is that he has
begun to be a "friend to himself." "That was indeed a great benefit; such a person
can never be alone. You may be certain that such a man is a friend to all of
humanity. Farewell" (Seneca, 2020, p. 11). Ultimately, the adoptees who are
clearly traumatized must be agents of their healing, with the aim of being "friends
to themselves." In discovering the ugly truth about her background, Priyangika
states, "I feel that I have found a balance and acceptance of my own story, but it
has taken time" (Rbnett.no, 2022).

She has on several occasions demanded that Norway investigate
all foreign adoption cases. The Norwegian authorities have
previously replied that they do not see the need. There are no
indications of the need for such an investigation in Norway, but if
the need arises to take a closer look at individual cases, the
adoption authority will naturally intervene in the case, said State
Secretary Ingvild Arntsen (KrF) to Vårt Land in March last year.
(Rbnett.no, 2022)

The response of the Norwegian authorities is an example of Foucault's "regime of truth." In their minds, they "do not see the need" for investigating the legality of adoption cases in Norway. Precisely what Foucault asserts:

> It's not a matter of emancipating truth from every system of power (which would be a chimera, for truth is already power) but of detaching the power of truth from the forms of hegemony, social, economic, and cultural, within which it operates at the present time. (Foucault, 1980, p. 133)

In her book *White Privilege: The Myth of a Post-Racial Society* (2018), Professor of Education, Kalwant Bhopal, writes:

> There is also evidence to suggest that many white people do not see the disadvantages that black people face due to racism and often dismiss those disadvantages as being attributed to racism; this in itself can be seen as a covert or unconscious form of racism. McIntrye calls this 'white talk'. White talk is a negative strategy used by white people to circumvent their own role in perpetuating racism. (Bhopal, 2018, p. 23)

It is imperative to challenge regimes of truth, such as Norwegian officialdom, which "does not see the need" to investigate crimes of human trafficking. In his memoir *The Beautiful Struggle* (*2016*), Ta-Nehisi Coates writes about his father, Paul, who "went to Vietnam dreaming of John Wayne, but came back quoting Malcolm X" (Coates, 2017, p. 138). His father was a "Conscious Man" who went beyond reading books, which were amenable to his views.

> It was a feeling, an ingrained sense that something significant in our lives had gone wrong. My father was haunted. He was bad at conjuring small talk; he watched very little TV because, once Conscious, every commercial and every program must be strip-mined for their deeper meaning, until they lay bare their role in this sinister American plot. (Coates, 2016, p. 54)

Priyangika's journey parallels that of Coates' father in *The Beautiful Struggle*, evolving into what could be fittingly described as a "Conscious Woman." Initially, societal narratives that depicted adoption as a virtuous act without acknowledging the skullduggery and injustices integral to the adoption system may have shaped Priyangika's understanding of her own adoption. However, through her experiences and critical reflection, Priyangika begins to challenge these "regimes of truth" and interrogate the power dynamics at play. Like Coates' father, Priyangika becomes progressively conscious of the deeper implications of her adoption and the systemic issues surrounding it. She recognizes that her adoption story is not just a personal narrative but one entangled with broader structures of power and privilege. She begins to question the truth about the regimes propagated by governmental institutions and societal norms regarding adoption, realizing that they often serve to maintain existing power dynamics rather than prioritize the well-being of adoptees and their families.

Priyangika's transformation into a "Conscious Woman" involves actively engaging in an archaeology of knowledge, as described by Michel Foucault, to unpack the hidden truths and power relations underlying her adoption experience. She investigates her own history and the wider historical context of adoption in Norway, seeking to wrest back her narrative from the dominant discourse that seeks to silence or erase certain aspects of her identity and experience. Moreover, Priyangika's consciousness-raising journey involves connecting her personal experiences with broader social issues, such as racism, colonialism, and the commodification of bodies. She recognizes the intersecting oppressions that shape her adoption story and advocates for a more inclusive and just understanding of adoption that centers on the voices and experiences of adoptees themselves.

No matter how disturbing the inferences may be, the phenomenon of White individuals seeking out children of color, such as Johanne and Priyangika in marginalized regions of the world, demands thorough scrutiny. As dissenting voices against this system swell, their collective outcry is reaching a crescendo. Frantz Fanon, eternally vigilant and penetrating in his analysis, is never shy of hypotheses concerning the psychological dynamics at play within the depths of both Black and White consciousness:

> The soul of the white man was corrupted, and, as I was told by a friend who was a teacher in the United States, "The presence of the Negroes beside the whites is in a way an insurance policy on humanness. When the whites feel that they have become too mechanized, they turn to the men of color and ask them for a little human sustenance". At last, I had been recognized, I was no longer a zero. (Fanon, 1986, p. 129)

The excerpt from Frantz Fanon's writing highlights a key aspect of his analysis regarding the relationship between White individuals and people of color, particularly Black individuals. Fanon suggests that the presence of Black individuals serves as a sort of antidote to the dehumanization and mechanization that White individuals experience. He implies that White individuals, in their pursuit of technological advancement and societal progress, may lose touch with their own humanity. However, when they interact with people of color, especially Black individuals, they seek a connection to a more authentic and human essence.

In the context of the analysis provided earlier, which discusses the phenomenon of White individuals seeking out children of color for adoption, Fanon's statement sheds light on the underlying dynamics. We can interpret the "White craving for colored children" as an attempt by White individuals to rekindle a sense of humanity they believe they may have lost. Adopting children of color may allow them to reaffirm their own humanity and escape the dehumanizing effects of their own societal structures and norms. Alternatively, one could argue that it's not a desire for Black and brown children, but rather limited access to

White children that propels the Norwegian child adoption industry. This perspective, however, risks reinforcing the notion of trading in Black and brown bodies due to the shield of White privilege protecting White children. Such a stance is untenable for progressive White people, a category to which Norway often aspires. Thus, it's more plausible to continue with the premise that the inhumane dynamics of vulture capitalist demand and supply dictate that only Black and brown bodies are readily available for adoption. To this, we can incorporate Fanon's provocative yet plausible notion that the dystopian nature of vulture capitalism is somewhat assuaged (at least in the perception of White individuals) by the presence of colored babies, serving as a form of "insurance on their humanness."

Furthermore, Fanon's assertion that the presence of Black individuals serves as an "insurance policy on humanness" suggests that White individuals may rely on interactions with people of color to validate their own sense of self-worth and morality. In this context, the text mentions the growing dissent against the adoption system as a rejection of the instrumentalization of people of color for the benefit of White individuals. The voices challenging the system are pushing back against the notion that the humanity of people of color exists solely to serve the needs and desires of White individuals. But what kind of "insurance policy on humanness" would that be? It can only be one that further amplifies the very ugliness of racism, which Fanon stated inflicted "a massive psychoexistential complex" through the juxtaposition of the White and Black races (Fanon, 1986, p. 14). W.E.B. Du Bois parodies this pseudo-humanizing sentiment:

> "My poor, un-white thing! Weep not nor rage. I know, too well
> that the curse of God lies heavy upon you. Why? That's not for me
> to say but be brave! Do your work in your lowly sphere, praying
> the good Lord that into heaven above, where all is love, you may,
> one day, be born – white! I do not laugh. I am quite straight-faced
> as I ask soberly: "But what on earth is whiteness that one should so
> desire it?" Then always, somehow, some way, silently but clearly,
> I am given to understand that whiteness is the ownership of the
> earth forever and ever, Amen! (Du Bois, 2021, p. 18)

W.E.B. Du Bois's parody becomes the perverse reality for the adopted colored individual in Norway. Rather than be filled with gratitude for deliverance from "the Black Hole of Calcutta," it is the mockery of White supremacy expressed by Du Bois that becomes the lot of the adopted: humanity is equated with whiteness, which is why Brynjulf, adopted from South Korea, dreamed of being a White man in Norway. The satirical tone in Du Bois exposes the fallacy of white supremacy, revealing how it diminishes the humanity of non-White individuals by suggesting that their ultimate aspiration should be to become White. The passage highlights the absurdity of valuing whiteness as a form of divine blessing, equating it with ownership and dominion over the earth. In the context of adoption, this analysis exposes the insidious nature of the adoption industry when it perpetuates the idea that adopting children of color somehow validates the humanity of White individuals. By positioning colored children as a means for White individuals to reaffirm their own humanity, the adoption institution reinforces racist power dynamics and perpetuates the cycle of dehumanization. Ultimately, this reflection on the concept of whiteness and its association with ownership and superiority serves to challenge the very foundations of racism and the systems that uphold it. It prompts a critical examination of how racial dynamics intersect with institutions like adoption, revealing the need for systemic change to address the inherent injustices perpetuated by such systems.

Conclusion

This study considered four distinct cases with a view to exploring and better understanding the complexities surrounding race, privilege, and identity in Norwegian society. The cases shed light on the persistent manifestations of racism, White privilege, and systemic oppression in Norway. From the tragic and highly publicized murder of Benjamin Hermansen to the silent struggles faced by minoritized individuals in everyday interactions, the study underscores the urgent need for critical reflection and action to dismantle structural inequalities. By confronting painful truths, rather than invoking colorblindness and interrogating the complicity of dominant groups, the work challenges readers to engage in meaningful dialogue and advocate for genuine inclusivity and social justice. Through its penetrating exploration of White supremacy, the paradoxes of liberalism, and adoption imperialism, among others, this book serves as a poignant call to action, accenting the imperative of shared responsibility in fostering a more equitable and inclusive society.

The murder of Benjamin Hermansen serves as a stark reminder of the deadly consequences of unchecked racism and White supremacy. Despite Norway's reputation as a progressive and egalitarian society, the country is not exempt from the sinister influence of racial prejudice and discrimination. The case highlights the urgent need for greater awareness and education surrounding issues of race and ethnicity, particularly within White communities. In his book *The Life of Rosa Parks: Mine Eyes Have Seen the Glory*, Douglas Brinkley writes that:

> Rosa Parks did not wake up on the morning of December 1, 1955, primed for a showdown over civil rights with the local police. A lifetime's education in injustice – from her grandfather's nightly vigils to the murder of Emmitt Till – had strengthened her resolve to act when the time came. What arose in Parks that fateful evening was her belief in what Dr. Martin Luther King, Jr., often said: that "some of us must bear the burden of trying to save the soul of America". (Brinkley, 2000, p. 109)

Too Black to Be Here?, 183–190

Copyright © 2025 Paul Thomas.

Published by Emerald Publishing Limited. This work is published under the Creative Commons Attribution (CC BY 4.0) licence. Anyone may reproduce, distribute, translate and create derivative works of this work (for both commercial and non-commercial purposes), subject to full attribution to the original publication and authors. The full terms of this licence may be seen at http://creativecommons.org/licences/by/4.0/legalcode

doi:10.1108/978-1-83662-162-120251006

Just as Rosa Parks was not preparing for a pivotal moment in civil rights history on the morning of December 1, 1955, Benjamin Hermansen did not wake up foreseeing the tragedy that would befall him. However, the injustices surrounding them affected both individuals, leading to Benjamin's death. For Benjamin Hermansen, his education in injustice began early with subtle encounters with racism and discrimination, steadily building up to more plain forms of prejudice and violence. As a person of color growing up in a predominantly White society, he encountered microaggressions, stereotypes, and systemic barriers that shaped his worldview and understanding of race relations, much as the stories of Emmett Till's brutal murder influenced Rosa Parks. All these were omens of the dangers posed by unchecked racism and White supremacy in society. Benjamin Hermansen's heartbreaking murder, in the context of Brinkley's quote about bearing the burden of trying to save America's soul, is emblematic of the ongoing struggle for racial justice and equality. We must all embrace the prophetic call of Dr. Martin Luther King Jr. against the forces of racism and hatred that continue to plague communities worldwide.

Rosa Parks' actions catalyzed the civil rights movement while Benjamin Hermansen's legacy inspired efforts to combat racism and White supremacy in contemporary society. His story can serve as a reminder of the importance of education, empathy, and solidarity in confronting prejudice and building a more just and inclusive world for future generations. Finding avenues for anti-racist activism that are not dependent on a tragic event like Benjamin's murder is our task. Watershed events like Benjamin's murder can serve as wake-up calls and stimuli for action, but relying solely on such triggers can result in a cycle of immobility and crisis. Instead, adopting a culture of nonstop education, dialogue, and advocacy can help sustain momentum in the fight against racism. This involves actively seeking out opportunities to learn about systemic injustices, challenging one's own biases, and advocating for change in various spheres of influence, from personal interactions to institutional policies. By fostering a proactive mindset and embracing the responsibility to confront racism in all its forms, individuals and communities can work toward creating a more equitable and just society, without waiting for tragedy to compel them into action.

Moreover, Benjamin's story underscores the complex dynamics of racial identity and the challenges faced by those who are targeted by racism. It underscores the importance of educational initiatives that facilitate open and honest discussions about race, privilege, and power, empowering students to confront and dismantle systems of oppression. Furthermore, the transformation of one of Benjamin's murderers, Joe Erling Jahr, from a neo-Nazi indoctrinated youth to a penitent individual underscores the potential for education to combat hate and promote reconciliation. It highlights the power of education to challenge extremist beliefs and cultivate understanding and empathy among individuals from diverse backgrounds. In approaching the topic of racism and its consequences, I, as a Black educator in Norway, draw inspiration from the Brazilian educator Paulo Freire's radical notion that both the oppressed and the oppressor must engage in a mutual process of liberation for the benefit of all.

> It is only when the oppressed find the oppressor out and become involved in the organized struggle for their liberation that they begin to believe in themselves. This discovery cannot be purely intellectual but must involve action; nor can it be limited to mere activism but must include serious reflection: only then will it be a praxis. Critical and liberating dialogue, which presupposes action, must be carried on with the oppressed at whatever the stage of their struggle for liberation. (Freire, 1996, p. 47)

Benjamin's story vividly illustrates the intricate dynamics of racial identity and the formidable challenges confronted by those subjected to racism. Benjamin's narrative shines a light on the transformative potential of education. Not only the journey of one of Benjamin's murderers, Joe Erling Jahr, but countless others have been transformed through dialogue and empathy, which serve as a powerful testament to the transformative power of education. It exemplifies how education can combat hate and facilitate reconciliation, even in the face of extreme extremism.

In studying the aftermath of Anders Breivik's ghastly attacks, it becomes evident that his actions were not merely an isolated event but rather a manifestation of deeper societal issues deeply seated in White supremacy. Breivik's fixation on whiteness, as evidenced by his manifesto and actions, underscores the profound impact of racial ideology on individual behavior and collective consciousness. Additionally, the public discourse surrounding Breivik's mental state and motivations reflects a broader pattern of denial and misrecognition of White supremacy within Norwegian society. Breivik's despotism underscores a deeply unsettling but crucial reality that demands our attention if we are to seriously lock horns with the insidious problem of White supremacy. It prompts us to grapple with a fundamental question: what drives individuals to commit acts of mass violence in the name of their skin color? Moreover, why is this phenomenon predominantly associated with White societies? It is indeed rare, if not unheard of, to encounter instances of individuals from racial groups traditionally marginalized by White supremacy – such as Black, Asian, or Indigenous communities – committing atrocities in the name of their racial identity. This begs the question: what sets apart White supremacy as a unique and pervasive force capable of inspiring such extreme acts of violence? One explanation lies in the historical construction and distillation of whiteness itself. The concept of race, as we understand it today, is largely the dénouement of colonialism and imperialism, with White Europeans establishing racial hierarchies to justify their domination over non-White peoples. Whiteness became identical with power, privilege, and superiority, shaping the very fabric of society and influencing perceptions of oneself and others.

As a result, individuals socialized in White supremacist societies internalized notions of racial superiority from an early age whether consciously or unconsciously (Bonilla-Silva, 1997). This indoctrination perpetuates a sense of entitlement and supremacy among White individuals, instilling a belief in their inherent superiority over other racial groups. When demographic shifts, social progress, or perceived cultural dilution challenge or threaten this perceived supremacy, some individuals may resort to violence to assert and preserve their privileged status. It was Aimé Césaire who provocatively stated that "Hitler is not dead" (in Fanon, 1986, p. 90) in regard to the lasting legacy of Adolf Hitler and the ideology of Nazism. Hitler's racism was characterized by a belief in the superiority of the Aryan race, considering them the epitome of humanity and the sole creators of civilization.

He viewed Aryans as the bearers of divine genius and essential to the advancement of human culture while depicting other races as inferior and destined for subjugation or extinction as evidenced in *Mein Kampf* (1939):

> Every manifestation of human culture, every product of art, science and technical skill, which we see before our eyes today, is almost exclusively the product of the Aryan creative power. This very fact fully justifies the conclusion that it was the Aryan alone who founded a superior type of humanity; therefore, he represents the architype of what we understand by the term: man. He is the Prometheus of mankind, from whose shining brow the divine spark of genius has at all times flashed forth, always kindling anew that fire which, in the form of knowledge, illuminated the dark night by drawing aside the veil of mystery and thus showing man how to rise and become master over all the other beings on the earth. Should he be forced to disappear, a profound darkness will descend on the earth; within a few thousand years human culture will vanish and the world will become a desert.

In saying that "Hitler is not dead," Césaire was asserting that the ideology and legacy of Hitlerism – characterized by racism, fascism, and genocide – continue to persist long after Hitler's demise. Ultimately, addressing the legacy of Hitler requires confronting the underlying beliefs and structures that sustain supremacist ideologies. Recognizing that Hitler's death did not extinguish the Übermensch philosophy allows the West to better understand the persistence of racial injustice and work toward building a more equitable and inclusive society. The West can only truly eradicate Hitler's ideology by actively challenging and dismantling its legacy. Césaire contended that Western colonialism, imperialism, and racial hierarchies deeply embedded the roots of Nazism, which went beyond the individual figure of Hitler. By declaring that "Hitler is not dead," Césaire was drawing attention to the ongoing influence of White supremacy, colonial violence, and racial oppression in the postwar world. He sought to remind people that the atrocities committed under Hitler's regime were not isolated events of the past but part of a broader pattern of racial injustice and exploitation that persisted in different forms.

Anders Breivik's relevance in light of Aimé Césaire's statement lies in the examination of how Breivik's actions reflect the perpetuation of White supremacy and its violent manifestations. Césaire's assertion that "Hitler is not dead" speaks to the enduring legacy of racism and the persistence of ideologies that promote the superiority of certain races over others. Breivik's acts of terrorism, fueled by his belief in the supremacy of the White race, serve as a contemporary example of this ongoing struggle against racial oppression. Just as Hitler's ideology sought to establish Aryan dominance, Breivik's actions aimed to preserve what he perceived as the superiority of White Europeans. Therefore, by analyzing Breivik's motivations and the societal conditions that enabled his radicalization, we can better understand the continued relevance of Césaire's statement and the need to confront and dismantle systems of White supremacy.

> I feel that I can still hear Césaire: When I turn on my radio, when I hear the Negroes have been lynched in America, I say that we have been lied to: Hitler is not dead, when I turn on my radio, when I learn that Jews have been insulted, mistreated, persecuted, I say that we have been lied to: Hitler is not dead; when, finally, I turn on my radio and hear that in Africa forced labor has been inaugurated and legalized, I say that we have been certainly been lied to: Hitler is not dead. (Fanon, 1986, p. 90; Quoted from memory – *Discours politiques* of the election campaign of 1945, Forte-de-France)

Furthermore, the parallels between Hitler's rhetoric and that of modern White supremacist movements are striking. Both propagate notions of racial superiority, advocate for the marginalization or elimination of perceived "inferior" races, and espouse a distorted worldview, rooted in hate and intolerance. The resurgence of neo-Nazi groups, hate crimes targeting minority communities, and the propagation of racist ideologies online all echo Hitler's vision of a racially homogenous society. Moreover, the impact of White supremacist ideology extends beyond individual acts of violence to permeate societal structures and institutions. Discriminatory policies, systemic inequalities, and cultural narratives that perpetuate racial hierarchies all serve to uphold the legacy of White supremacy. These entrenched systems of oppression pose a grave threat to social cohesion, justice, and democracy. In light of these realities, it is imperative that the West confront the threat of White supremacy with the same urgency and determination as it would if Hitler were alive today. This entails implementing robust measures to combat hate speech, dismantle extremist networks, and address the root causes of racial inequality. It also requires fostering a culture of inclusivity, empathy, and solidarity that rejects supremacist ideologies in all their forms. Césaire, who was always startlingly blunt, would have asked White Norwegians today whether:

> [...] at bottom, what he cannot forgive Hitler [replace with Breivik] for is not *the crime* in itself, the *crime against man,* it is *the humiliation of man as such,* it is the crime against the white man, the humiliation of the white man, and the fact that he applied to Europe colonialist procedures which until then had been reserved exclusively for the Arabs of Algeria, the "coolies" of India and the "niggers" of Africa. (Césaire, 2000, p. 36)

The story of Sumaya Jirde Ali's traumatic experience of racial abuse at the hands of Atle Antonsen in a pub in Oslo sheds light on the enduring silence and complicity that often accompany acts of injustice. Despite Antonsen's brazen display of racism, characterized by his declaration that Sumaya was "too dark-skinned to be here," the surrounding witnesses failed to intervene or speak out against his actions. This silence, reminiscent of Arnulf Øverland's call to action in his poem "Dare not to Sleep," reflects a disturbing acquiescence to injustice and a reluctance to confront bigotry. In the face of Antonsen's verbal violence, the absence of a countervoice speaks volumes about the pervasive nature of racism and the challenges of confronting it in society. Instead of challenging Antonsen's racism, those present at the pub chose to remain silent, complicit in perpetuating the status quo and leaving Sumaya to come to terms with her vulnerability alone. Marcus Garvey was a Jamaican-born political leader, publisher, and orator who became a prominent figure in the early 20th-century Pan-African movement, advocating for Black self-reliance, empowerment, and economic independence. He founded the Universal Negro Improvement Association (UNIA) and promoted the idea of a unified global African diaspora. A 100 years ago, he wrote the following:

> Later on, they changed their belief or opinion, but at all times, the conscience of certain people dictated to them that it was wrong and inhuman to hold human beings as slaves. It is to such a conscience in white America that I am addressing myself. Negroes are human beings – the peculiar and strange opinions of writers, ethnologists, philosophers, scientists, ambitions, desires, just as other men, hence they must be considered. Has white America really considered the Negro in the light of permanent human progress? The answer is NO. (Garvey, 2004, p. 161)

Marcus Garvey's citation underscores the apparently never-ending struggle against racism and discrimination faced by people of color, such as Sumaya Ali Jirde, and calls attention to the need for a shift in societal attitudes toward recognizing the humanity and equality of all individuals. In light of Sumaya Ali Jirde's experience of racial abuse at the hands of Atle Antonsen, Garvey's words resonate deeply. His assertion that "Negroes are human beings" challenges the dehumanization and marginalization experienced by Black individuals in societies where racism persists. Sumaya's ordeal serves as a stark reminder of the pervasive racism that continues to plague communities, despite advancements in science, technology, social consciousness, and awareness. Garvey's question, "Has White America really considered the Negro in the light of permanent human progress?" prompts reflection on the systemic injustices and inequalities perpetuated by structures of power and privilege. Sumaya's encounter with racism highlights the failure of society to fully acknowledge and address the humanity of Black individuals, perpetuating a cycle of discrimination and marginalization.

In addressing White America's conscience, Garvey calls for a reckoning with the deeply ingrained prejudices and biases that perpetuate racism and inequality.

Sumaya's experience in the Norwegian context is a testament to racism's transnational nature, defying borders and eras, and serves as a call to action to confront these injustices and strive toward a society that values and respects the dignity and worth of all individuals, regardless of race or ethnicity.

Finally, the tragic case of Johanne Ihle-Hansen sheds light on the pervasive nature of racism within Norwegian society, as well as the transnational dimensions of structural racism inherent in adoption practices. Johanne's murder by her White brother, Philip Manshaus, driven by White supremacist ideology, underscores the urgent need to confront racism in all its forms. The experiences of non-White adopted people like Johanne, as well as the broader systemic issues revealed by the adoption scandal, demand comprehensive action to dismantle structural racism and ensure the rights and dignity of all individuals, regardless of race or ethnicity. Acknowledging past failures and considering a temporary halt to adoptions by the Norwegian government is a step toward accountability and justice, but there is still much work to address the deep-rooted inequalities perpetuated by racial prejudice and discrimination.

Investigations and reports uncover the adoption scandal in Norway, revealing a disturbing reality where wealthy Western nations commodify and transport children from predominantly non-White countries, often disregarding their rights, well-being, or cultural identity. This phenomenon reflects a form of neo-colonialism, where Western countries, driven by desires for parenthood or altruistic motivations, engage in practices that perpetuate systemic oppression and exploitation in the global South. The structural racism inherent in adoption practices becomes evident through the disproportionate impact on marginalized communities in countries of origin. Economic disparities, coupled with corruption and a lack of oversight, create fertile ground for the exploitation of children for adoption purposes. The adoption process itself, framed as a benevolent act of rescue and salvation, often masks underlying power imbalances and reinforces racial hierarchies that privilege Western adoptive parents while disregarding the agency and rights of children and their birth families.

Moreover, the racial dynamics within adoptive families, as exemplified by Johanne's murder, underscore the inadequacy of existing frameworks in addressing the complexities of transracial adoption. White adoptive parents, ill-equipped to navigate issues of racial identity and cultural heritage, may inadvertently perpetuate racial biases or contribute to the alienation of their non-White children within their own families. This highlights the urgent need for comprehensive support systems and resources to facilitate meaningful engagement with cultural diversity and promote the well-being of transracially adopted individuals.

The adoption scandal has broader implications than individual cases, extending to systemic failures in adoption oversight and regulation. The revelation of irregularities and potential illegalities surrounding adoptions underscores the imperative for accountability and transparency within adoption processes. Addressing the root causes of structural racism within adoption practices requires more than just temporary measures or reactive responses. It necessitates a fundamental reevaluation of the underlying power dynamics, economic inequalities, and cultural biases that perpetuate exploitation and marginalization. This includes prioritizing the voices and experiences of affected communities, implementing robust oversight mechanisms, and promoting ethical and equitable adoption practices grounded in principles of social justice and human rights. In the previously mentioned book *Raceless* (2021), Georgina Lawton, a mixed-race author, encapsulates the common yearning among adopted individuals for their transracial identity to be acknowledged, a yearning that can surpass even the most fundamental biological needs for food and shelter. "Belongingness can be almost as compelling a need as food," placing it on the same level as physiological requirements in Maslow's (1968) hierarchy (Baumeister & Leary, 1995).

> "I am black", I repeated, with more confidence. "I need you to acknowledge that, Mum. I need to hear you say it, because I'm not about to go another second longer trying to be something I'm not"... "There's nothing wrong with that, Mum", my brother said... "Yes, you're... well, of course there isn't. You're ... black." I breathed a sigh of relief as the words I'd waited a long time to hear made themselves at home in my house for the first time. The part of me we had tried to ignore for years had audaciously entered the room – and I wasn't about to let anyone close the door on it again. (Lawton, 2021, p. 116)

References

Abcnyheter. (2012). Hvorfor ble jeg ikke skutt? *abcnyheter*. https://www.abcny heter.no/nyheter/2012/05/25/152158/hvorfor-ble-jeg-ikke-skutt

Achebe, C. (2016). *An image of Africa: Racism in Conrad's heart of darkness* (Vol. 57). The Massachusetts Review.

Adopsjonsforum. (2022). https://www.adopsjonsforum.no/userfiles/Formidling/tabell %20-%20ankomne%20barn%201972-2022.pdf

Adorno, T. W., & Horkheimer, M. (2022). Elements of anti-semitism. In L. Back & J. Solomos (Eds.), *Theories of race and racism: A reader* (pp. 368–373). Routledge Student Series.

Afoaku, O. G. (1997). The U.S. and Mobutu sese seko: Waiting on disaster. *Journal of Third World Studies*, *14*(1), 65–90. https://www.africabib.org/rec.php?RID=P00 001034&DB=p

Africa Today. (1964) Partners in Apartheid: U.S. policy on South Africa. *Africa Today*, *11*(3), 2–17.

Aftenposten. (2001, January 28). Kjempet mot rasisme - ble offer selv. *Aftenposten*.

Aftenposten. (2011). Terrorsiktet kjøpte seks tonn kunstgjødsel. *Aftenposten*. https:// www.aftenposten.no/norge/i/jdR0L/terrorsiktet-kjoepte-seks-tonn-kunstgjoedsel

Aftenposten. (2022). Antonsen beklager etter å ha blitt anmeldt for hatytringer: – Må revurdere mitt forhold til alkohol. *Aftenposten*. https://www.aftenposten.no/article/ ap-pQBdaw.html?mon_ref=retriever-info.com

Al-Azneh, A. (1982). *Ibn Khaldun*. Franc Cass.

Alcoff, L. (2015). *The future of whiteness*. John Wiley & Sons.

Ali, T. (2002). *The clash of fundamentalism: Crusades, Jihads, and modernity*. Verso.

Ali, S. (2023). *Et Liv i Redningsvest: Dagboksopptegnelser om norsk rasisme*. Cappellen Damm.

Almendingen, B. (2008). Politianmelder Gjems-Onstad. *Nettavisen*. https://www.nettavisen. no/artikkel/politianmelder-gjems-onstad/s/12-95-1981725#am-comments

Althusser. (2014). *On the reproduction of capitalism: Ideology and ideological state apparatuses*. Verso Books.

Amartya, S. (2006). *Identity and violence: The illusion of destiny*. Penguin Books.

Anderson, E. (2022). The white space. In L. Back & J. Solomos (Eds.) *Theories of race and racism: A reader* (pp. 320–335). Routledge.

Angelou, M. (1969). *I know why the caged bird sings*. Virago.

Ansari, H. (2004). *The infidel within: Muslims in Britain since 1800*. C. Hurst & Co.

Askheim, S. (2023). *Erik Gjems-Onstad*. Store Norske Leksikon. https://snl.no/ Erik_Gjems-Onstad

Aslan, R. (2005). *No God but God: The origins, evolution and future of Islam*. Arrow Books.

Baldwin, J. (2017). *Notes of a native son*. Penguin Random House UK.

Balibar, E., & Wallerstein, I. (1991). *Race, nation, class ambiguous identities*. Verso.

Bangstad, S. (2013). Eurabia comes to Norway. *Islam and Christian–Muslim Relations, 24*, 369–391.

Barthes, R. (1972/1957). *Mythologies* (pp. 302–306). Annette Lavers (Trans.). Hill and Wang.

Baumeister, R. F., & Leary, M. R. (1995). The need to belong: Desire for interpersonal attachments as a fundamental human motivation. *Psychological Bulletin, 117*(3), 497–529.

BBC. (2002). *Neo-Nazis guilty of Oslo race murder*. http://news.bbc.co.uk/1/hi/world/europe/1765620.stm

Bell, D. (1995). Brown v. Board of Education and the interest convergence dilemma. In K. Crenshaw, N. Gotanda, G. Peller, & K. Thomas (Eds.), *Critical race theory* (pp. 20–29). The New York Press.

Bhopal, K. (2018). *White privilege: The myth of a post-racial society*. Policy Press.

Biko, S. (2017). *I write what I like*. Picador Africa.

Blågestad, K. (2022). Det verste med saken om Atle Antonsen er ikke Atle Antonsen. *Fædrelandsvennen*. https://www.fvn.no/mening/kommentar/i/xgre1p/det-verste-med-saken-om-atle-antonsen-er-ikke-atle-antonsen

Bloom, J., & Martin, W. E. (2016). *Black against empire: The history and politics of the Black Panther party*. University of Califronia Press.

Blue Letter Bible. (2024). Matthew Henry's commentary. https://www.blue letterbible.org/Comm/mhc/Sgs/Sgs_001.cfm?a=672005

Bonilla-Silva, E. (1997). Rethinking racism: Toward a structural interpretation. *American Sociological Review, 62*(3), 465–480.

Bonilla-Silva, E. (2022). What makes systemic racism systemic? In L. Black & J. Solomos (Eds.), *Theories of race and racism: A reader* (3rd ed.). Routledge.

Brand, A. (2023). "What's wrong with blackface?": Theorizing humor ecologies and blackface as satire. *Communication and Critical/Cultural Studies, 20*(2), 215–233.

Breivik, A. (2011). 2083 a European declaration of independence. *Internet Archive*. https://archive.org/details/2083-a-european-declaration-of-independence

Brekke, T. (2021). Strukturell rasisme og andre alt-i-ett-begreper. *Idunn. Tidsskrift for samfunns-forskning, 62*(1), 94–98.

Brinkley, D. (2000). *The life of Rosa parks: Mine eyes have seen the glory*. Phoenix.

Britannica. (2023). Gregor Strasser. *Encyclopedia Britannica*. https://www.brita nnica.com/biography/Gregor-Strasser

Brochmann, G., & Kjeldstadli, K. (2008). *A history of immigration: The case of Norway 900-2000*. Universitetsforlaget.

Brustein, W. (1996). *The logic of evil: The social origins of the Nazi party, 1925-1933*. Yale University Press.

Buggeland, S. (2001). De var på menneskejakt. *VG*. https://www.vg.no/nyheter/innenriks/i/8wwd8w/de-var-paa-menneskejakt

Cardiff University. (2018). Alcohol acts as igniter of hate crimes. https://www.cardiff.ac.uk/news/view/1041409-prejudice-more-likely-to-be-acted-on-when-people-are-drunk

Césaire, A. (2000). *Discourse on colonialism*. Monthly Review Press.

Chomsky, N. (2003). *Hegemony or survival: America's quest for global dominance*. Penguin Books.

Coates, T. (2015). *Between the world and me*. Text Publishing.

Coates, T. (2016). *The beautiful struggle*. Verso.

Coates, T. (2017). *We were eight years in power*. Penguin.

Cohen, P. (2021). *Othello: Race and class*. Yale University Press.

Confino, A. (2014). *A world without Jews: The Nazi imagination from persecution to genocide*. Yale University Press.

Connelly, J. (1999). Nazis and Slavs: From racial theory to racist practice. *Central European History*, *32*(1), 1–33.

Conrad, J. (1995). Project Gutenberg. https://www.gutenberg.org/files/219/219-h/219-h.htm

Crenshaw, K. (1995). Race, reform and retrenchment: Transformation and legitimation in antidiscrimination law. In K. W. Crenshaw, N. Gotanda, G. Peller, & K. Thomas (Eds.), *Critical race theory: The key writings that formed the movement*. New Press.

Dabashi, H. (2006). Native informers and the making of the American Empire. *Campus Watch*. https://www.meforum.org/campus-watch/10542/native-informers-and-the-making-of-the-american

Dabashi, H. (2015). *Can non-Europeans think?* Zed Books.

Dagbladet. (2011). Derfor mener de denne mannen er sinnsyk. *Dagbladet*. https://www.dagbladet.no/nyheter/derfor-mener-de-denne-mannen-er-sinnsyk/63436677

Dagbladet. (2019). Nekter å dø på grunn av en hvit nasjonalist. https://www.dagbladet.no/kultur/nekter-a-do-pa-grunn-av-en-hvit-nasjonalist/71558504

Dagsavisen. (2022). Bernt Hulsker dømt til 18 dagers betinget fengsel – anker ikke. https://www.dagsavisen.no/oslo/2022/10/13/bernt-hulsker-domt-til-18-dagers-betinget-fengsel/

Danielson, R. (1969). To whom it may concern; keep this nigger – Boy. *Minnesota English Journal*, *5*(1), 53–59.

Davis, A. (1981). *Women, race & class*. Penguin Books.

Dawidowicz, L. (1987). *The war against the Jews*. Penguin Books.

Dehghan, S. K., & Norton-Taylor, R. (2017, December 1). CIA admits role in 1953 Iranian coup. *The Guardian*. https://www.theguardian.com/world/2013/aug/19/cia-admits-role-1953-iranian-coup

Delgado, R., & Stefancic, J. (1998). Critical race theory: Past, present. *Current Legal Problems*, *51*(1), 467.

Delgado, R., & Stefancic, J. (2012). *Critical race theory: An introduction*. New York University Press.

DiAngelo, R. (2021). *Nice racism: How progressive white people perpetuate racial harm*. Beacon Press.

Dodds, P. (2015). The parallels between international adoption and slavery. *Sociology Between the Gaps: Forgotten and Neglected Topics*, *1*(1), 76–81. https://digitalcommons.providence.edu/cgi/viewcontent.cgi?article=1010&context=sbg

Dodds, P. F. (1997). *Outer search inner journey: An orphan and adoptee's quest*. Aphrodite Publishing Company.

Dostoevsky, F. (2007). *Karamazov brothers*. Wordsworth Classics of World Literature.

Douglass, F. (2014). *My bondage and my freedom*. Yale University Press.

Du Bois, W. (1903). The souls of Black folk. https://www.gutenberg.org/files/408/408-h/408-h.htm

Du Bois, W. (1970). *W.E.B Du Bois speaks: Sppeches and adresses 1920-1963*. Pathfinder.

Du Bois, W. (1990). *The souls of Black folk*. Vintage.

Du Bois, W. (2021). *Darkwater: Voices from within the veil*. Verso.

Ducey, K., & Feagin, J. R. (2021). *Revealing Britain's systemic racism: The case of Meghan Markle and the royal family*. Routledge.

Durkheim, E. (1982). *The rules of sociological method and selected texts on sociology and its method* (L. Steven, Red., & W. Halls, Overs.). Free Press.

Durkheim, E. (2001). *The elementary forms of religious life*. Oxford University Press.

Eddo-Lodge, R. (2020). *Why I'm no longer talking to white people about race*. Bloomsbury Publishing.

Ellison, R. (1980). *Invisible man*. Penguin Random House.

Emberland, T., & Kott, M. (2012). *Himmlers Norge*. Aschehoug.

Esposito, J. L., & Mogahed, D. (2007). *Who speaks for Islam? What a billion Muslims really think*. Avenue Press.

Evaristo, B. (2021). *Manifesto on never giving up*. Penguin.

Ezema, V. S., Areji, A. C., & Ohubuenyi, A. G. (2017). Implications of Friedrich Nietzsche's master-slave morality in inter-personal relationship. *European Journal of Social Sciences, 55*(3), 262–274.

Faktisk. (2021). 22. juli: Massakren på Utøya. *Faktisk*. https://www.faktisk.no/artikler/je9qx/22-juli-massakren-pa-utoya

Fanon, F. (1986). *Black skin, white masks*. Pluto.

Feagin, J. (2013). *The white racial frame: Centuries of racial framing and counter-framing*. Routledge.

Feagin, J. R., & O'Brien, E. (2003). *White men on race: Power, privilege, and the shaping of cultural consciousness*. Beacon Press.

Filler, E., McGrath, E., & McKenzie, S. L. (2021). Moses' cushite wife. *Encyclopedia of the Bible and Its Reception, 19*, 1154–1162. https://www.degruyter.com/database/EBR/entry/rkey_9536787/html

Fischer, C. (2002). *The rise of the Nazis*. Manchester University Press.

Foucault, M. (1977). *Discipline and punish* (A. Sheridan, Trans.). Vintage Books.

Foucault, M. (1980). *Power/knowledge*. Harvester.

Fraser, A. (1973). *Cromwell: Our chief of men*. Phoenix.

Fredrickson, G. (2002). *Racism: A short history*. Princeton Unviersity Press.

Freire, P. (1996). *Pedagogy of the oppressed*. Penguin.

Fukuyama. (1992). *The end of history and the last man*. The Free Press.

Garvey, M. (2004). *Selected writings and speeches of Marcus Garvey*. Dover Publications.

Gebrial, D. (2018). Rhodes must fall. In G. K. Bhambra, D. Gebrial, & K. Nişancıoğlu (Eds.), *Decolonizing the university* (pp. 19–37). Pluto Press.

Gilroy, P. (2013). *There ain't no Black in the Union Jack*. Routledge.

Gilroy, P. (2019). *The Holberg lecture: "Never Again: Refusing Race and Salvaging the Human"* [Lecture]. https://holbergprize.org/events-and-productions/holberguken-2019/holbergforelesningen-never-again-refusing-race-and-salvaging-the-human/

Global Times. (2023). Iraq war a scandal, fraud pushed by US media as part of military-industrial complex: Former CIA analyst. https://www.globaltimes.cn/page/202303/1287606.shtml

Gordon, L. (2022). *Fear of Black consciousness*. Allen Lane.

Griech-Polelle, B. (2018). Jesuits, Jews, Christianity, and Bolshevism: An existential threat to Germany? *Journal of Jesuit Studies, 5*, 33–53.

Grinder, S. T., & Martinsen, J. (2014). Bunads and folk costumes as wearable knowledge and cultural expression. *Norges Husflidslag*. https://www.ichng oforum.org/heritage-alive-news/bunads-folk-costumes-wearable-knowledge-cultural-expression/

Gudbrandsdalen. (2022). Kvinnelig samfunnsdebattant har anmeldt Atle Antonsen - hevder hun ble verbalt og fysisk trakassert. https://www.gd.no/kvinnelig-samfunnsdebattant-har-anmeldt-atle-antonsen-hevder-hun-ble-verbalt-og-fysisk-trakassert/s/5-18-1656053?key=2024-04-22T10:22:05.000Z/retriever/0acb522fbe96 408f416f5b55d23933dee4c352d5

Gule, L. (2022). Nedtoningens og bortforklaringens tid bør være over nå. *Aftenposten*. https://www.aftenposten.no/article/ap-dw4MVz.html?mon_ref=retriever-info.com

Gullestad, M. (2005). Normalising racial boundaries. The Norwegian dispute about the term neger. *Social Anthropology*, *13*(1), 27–46.

Hacker, A. (2010). *Two nations: Black and White, separate, hostile, unequal*. Simon and Schuster.

Hall, S. (2017a). *The fateful triangle: Race, ethnicity, nation*. Harvard University Press.

Hall, S. (2017b). *Familiar stranger: A life between two islands*. Penguin Random House.

Hamad, R. (2020). *White tears, brown scars*. Trapeze.

Harris, C. (1995). Whiteness as property. In K. Crenshaw, N. Gotanda, G. Peller, & K. Thomas (Eds.). *Critical race theory: The key writings that formed the movement*. The New York Press.

Hauser, T. (1991). *Muhammad Ali: With the cooperation of Muhammad Ali*. Pan Books.

Hedstrøm, Ø (2023). Forslag fra stortingsrepresentant Øystein. *Stortinget*. https://www.stortinget.no/nn/Saker-og-publikasjonar/publikasjonar/Innstillingar/Stortinget/1994-1995/inns-199495-185/1/

Herf, J. (2006). *The Jewish enemy: Nazi propaganda during world war II and the holcaust*. First Harvard University Press.

Hitler, A. (1939). *Mein Kampf* (J. Murphy, Overs.). Hurst & Blackett. https://mk.christogenea.org/_files/Adolf%20Hitler%20-%20Mein%20Kampf%20english%20translation%20unexpurgated%201939.pdf

Holen, Ø (2023). Johan Golden. *Stor Norske Leksikon*. https://snl.no/Johan_Golden

Hopkins, D. (2013). *Peter Thonning and Denmark's Guinea commission*. Brill.

Huntington, S. (1996). *The clash of civilizations and the remaking of world order*. Simon & Schuster.

Huntington, S. (2004). *Who are we? The great American debate*. The Free Press.

Ignatiev, N. (2022). *Treason to whiteness is loyalty to humanity* (G. Dhondt, Z. Kurti, & J. Shanahan, Red.). Verso.

Johnson, J. (1995). *The autobiography of an ex-colored man*. Dover Publications.

Karlsen, O. (2014). Den norske terroristen gir opp sin tro. *ABCNyheter*. https://www.abcnyheter.no/nyheter/2014/11/12/211703/den-norske-terroristen-gir-opp-sin-tro

Kaufmann, E. (2018). *Whiteshift: Populism, immigration and the future of white majorities*. Penguin.

Kennedy, R. (2008). *Sellout: The politics of racial betrayal*. Random House.

Khaldun, I. (1967). *The Muqaddimah*. Princeton University Press.

Kibar, O. (2024). PST advarer om høyreekstreme mindreårige i Norge. *DN*. https://www.dn.no/magasinet/dokumentar/hoyreekstremisme/hoyreradikalisme/nazisme/pst-advarer-om-hoyreekstreme-mindrearige-i-norge-vi-opplever-na-at-det-er-mange-derfor-er-vi-bekymret/2-1-1611299

King, A. (2004). The prisoner of gender: Foucault and the disciplining of the female body. *Journal of International Women's Studies*, *5*(2), 29–39. https://vc.brid gew.edu/jiws/vol5/iss2/4

Kuflu, N., & Libanos, S. (2022). Rasisme er et stort problem. Men frykten for å bli utsatt for det er kanskje et enda større. *Aftenposten*. https://www.aftenposten.no/article/ap-0QpXL2.html?mon_ref=retriever-info.com

Kuruvilla, C. (2021). 'The most segregated hour': One woman's quest to promote dialogue between Black and white Christians. *The Guardian*. https://www.the guardian.com/world/2021/aug/15/be-the-bridge-dialogue-black-white-christians

Laclau, E. (2005). Populism: What's in a name. In F. Panizza (Ed.), *Populism and the mirror of democracy*. Verso.

Lawton, L. (2021). *Raceless*. Sphere.

Levi, P. (2017). *The drowned and the saved*. Simon & Schuster.

Lewis, B. (1990). The roots of Muslim rage. *The Atlantic Online*. http://tony-silva.com/download/muslimrage-atlantic.pdf

Lewy, J. (2006). A sober reich? Alcohol and tobacco use in Nazi Germany. *Substance Use & Misuse*, *41*(8), 1179–1195.

Lie, K. (2020). Drabantby. *Store Norske Leksikon*. https://snl.no/drabantby#:~:text=Drabantby%20betyr%20i%20byplanlegging%20et,periferien%20av%20en%20st%C3%B8rre%20by

Lorde, A. (2003). The master's tools will never dismantle the master's house. In R. Lewis & S. Mills (Eds.), *Feminist postcolonial theory: A reader* (pp. 25–28). JSTOR.

Maalouf, A. (2001). *In the name of identity: Violence and the need to belong*. Arcade Publishing.

Macaulay, T. B. (2018). A minute to acknowledge the day when India was 'educated' by Macaulay. *India Today Web Desk*. https://www.indiatoday.in/education-today/gk-current-affairs/story/a-minute-to-acknowledge-the-day-when-india-was-educated-by-macaulay-1160140-2018-02-02

Magubane, Z., Back, L., & Solomes, J. (2022). American sociology's racial ontology. In L. Black & J. Solomos (Eds.), *Theories of race and racism* (pp. 100–115). Routledge.

Maslow, A. (1968). Some educational implications of the humanistic psychologies. *Harvard Educational Review*, *38*(4), 685–696.

Mæhlum, A. (2019). Jeg følte meg mindre norsk i bunad. *NrK*. https://www.nrk.no/ytring/jeg-folte-meg-mindre-norsk-i-bunad-1.14544685

McGhee, H. (2022). *The sum of us: What racism costs everyone and how we can propser together*. Profile Books.

McIntosh, P. (1989). White privilege: Unpacking the invisible Knapsack. *Wellesley Centers for Women*. https://nationalseedproject.org/images/documents/Knap sack_plus_Notes-Peggy_McIntosh.pdf

Mesman, J., Janssen, S., & Van Rosmalen, L. (2016). Black Pete through the eyes of Dutch children. *PLoS One*, *11*(6), e0157511.

Mills, C. (1997). *The racial contract*. Cornell University Press.

Møllersen, J. (2017). FrPs opphavsmann Anders Lange advarte mot «jødeinvasjonen og de farvede raser». *Radikal Portal*. https://radikalportal.no/2017/09/08/frps-opphavsmann-anders-lange-advarte-mot-jodeinvasjonen-og-de-farvede-raser/

Morris, N. (2021). *Mixed/other: Explorations of multiraciality in modern Britain.* Trapeze.

Mühlberger, D. (1980). The sociology of the NSDAP: The question of working-class membership. *Journal of Contemporary History*, *15*(3), 493–511.

Mulroy, C. (2020). Elections 2020. *USA Today*. https://eu.usatoday.com/story/news/politics/elections/2023/12/21/how-many-people-voted-trump-2020/71754812007/

Myrdahl, E. (2014). Recuperating whiteness in the injured nation: Norwegian identity in the response to 22 July. *Social Identities*, *20*(6), 486–500.

Nerbøvik, J. (1998). Nasjonalismen innanfor og til venstre for Venstre. In Øystein Sørensen (red.), *Jakten på det norske. Perspektiver på utviklingen av en norsk nasjonal identitet på.*

Nettavisen. (2008). Ta medaljene fra Gjems-Onstad! https://www.nettavisen.no/nyheter/ta-medaljene-fra-gjems-onstad/s/12-95-3422869542

Neumann, I. B. (2000). State and nation in the nineteenth century: Recent research on the Norwegian case. *Scandinavian Journal of History*, *25*(3), 239–260.

Noah, T. (2016). *Born a crime*. One World.

Nettavisen. (2020). *Ukjente meldinger fra avdød stesøster: «Philip er rasistisk og hatefull. Jeg føler meg ikke trygg».* https://www.nettavisen.no/nyheter/ukjente-meldinger-fra-avdod-stesoster-philip-er-rasistisk-og-hatefull-jeg-foler-meg-ikke-trygg/s/12-95-3423964136

Nietzsche, F. (1973). *Beyond good and evil*. Penguin Classics.

Nilssen, D. (2012). Lærer fikk sparken etter voldsfilmer og Breivik-uttalelser. *VG*. https://www.vg.no/nyheter/innenriks/i/4yAJE/laerer-fikk-sparken-etter-voldsfilmer-og-breivik-uttalelser

Nome, P. (2011). Til dere som fostret en drapsmann. *Dagsavisen*. https://www.dagsavisen.no/kultur/2011/07/26/til-dere-som-fostret-en-drapsmann/

Norgeshistorie. (2024). Norgeshistorie. *Oslo får drabantbyer*. https://www.norgeshistorie.no/velferdsstat-og-vestvending/1840-oslo-far-drabantbyer.html

Norsk-Colombianos Forening. (2015). Norsk-Colombianos Forening – et samlingspunkt for adopterte. https://www.mynewsdesk.com/no/adopsjonsforum/news/norsk-colombianos-forening-et-samlingspunkt-for-adopterte-142630

NrK. (2021, July 20). Støre: – En ekstrem handling og det må vi ta klart avstand fra. *NrK*. https://www.nrk.no/stor-oslo/minnesmerket-til-benjamin-hermansen-utsatt-for-haerverk-1.15581471

NrK. (2010). Avviser SAS-bytte til bare halal. *NrK*. https://www.nrk.no/norge/avviser-sas-bytte-til-bare-halal-1.7291736

NrK. (2011). Breivik forberedte terror i ni år. *NrK*. https://www.nrk.no/norge/breivik-forberedte-terror-i-ni-ar-1.7724894

NrK. (2012). Beskriver Breivik som en «eksemplarisk» fange. *NrK*. https://www.nrk.no/227/artikler/beskrives-som-en-eksemplarisk-fange-1.8193381

NrK. (2015). Mer radikal enn noen gang. *NrK*. https://www.nrk.no/norge/xl/nekter-a-snakke-med-psykiater-_-mer-radikal-enn-noen-gang-1.12678021

NrK. (2018). Drapet på Benjamin Hermansen [Registrert av NrK]. *Oslo, Norway*. https://radio.nrk.no/podkast/hele_historien/sesong/drapet-paa-benjamin-herm

ansen/nrkno-poddkast-26578-129665-23012018050000. Accessed on April 03, 2024.

Nrk. (2021). Benjamin er 100 prosent ikke glemt. https://www.nrk.no/stor-oslo/20-ar-siden-benjamin-hermansen-ble-drept-av-nynazister-pa-holmlia-1.15345504

NrK. (2021). Støre: – En ekstrem handling og det må vi ta klart avstand fra. *NrK*.https://www.nrk.no/stor-oslo/minnesmerket-til-benjamin-hermansen-utsatt-for-haerverk-1.15581471#:~:text=Oslo%2Dpolitiet%20mener%20det%20er,kan%20ha%20skjedd%20tirsdag%20formiddag.&text=Dvorak%20Lagos%20%2F%20Privat-,Minnesmerket%20til%20Benjamin%20Hermans

NrK (a). (2022). Politianmelder Atle Antonsen for rasisme: – Sa jeg var for mørkhudet til å være der. *NrK*. https://www.nrk.no/nordland/sumaya-jirde-ali-politianmelder-atle-antonsen-for-rasisme-1.16180349

NrK (b). (2012). Derfor mener dommerne at Breivik er tilregnelig. *NrK*. https://www.nrk.no/227/artikler/–derfor-er-breivik-tilregnelig-1.8293402

OECD. (2021). Trust in Government. *OECD*. https://data.oecd.org/gga/trust-in-government.htm

Olsen, I. A. (2001, February 03). *De sier det er første gang*. Aftenposten/Retreiver.

Olusoga, D. (2021). *Black and British: A forgotten history*. Picador.

Online Etymology Dictionary. (2024). Denigration. https://www.etymonline.com/search?q=denigration

Øverland, A. (1936). Du må ikke sove. I Worm-Muller. *Samtiden*, *47*, 318–320.

Oxford Learner's Dictionaries. (2024). Qusiling. https://www.oxfordlearners dictionaries.com/definition/english/quisling?q=quisling

Painter, N. (2010). *The history of White people*. Norton.

Pierce, C. (1970). Offensive mechanisms. In C. Pierce & F. B. Barbour (Eds.), *The Black seventies: An extending horizon book* (pp. 265–282). Porter Sargent Publisher.

Pierce, C. (1974). Psychiatric problems of the black minority. In I. Arieti (Ed.), *American handbook of psychiatry*. Basic Books.

Pierce, C. (1995). Stress analogs of racism and sexism: Terrorism, torture, and disaster. In V. Charles, P. Perri Rieker, B. Kramer, & B. S. Brown (Eds.), *Mental health racism and sexism* (pp. 227–293). University of Pittsburgh Press.

PM News. (2019, September 17). Norway mosque shooting suspect's stepsister shot 4 times. https://pmnewsnigeria.com/2019/09/17/norway-mosque-shooting-suspects-stepsister-shot-4-times/

Poynting, S., & Morgan, G. (2012). Introduction: The transnational fok devil. In S. Poynting & G. Morgan (Eds.), *Global islamophobia: Muslims and moral panic in the west* (pp. 1–14). Routledge.

Priest, J. (1845). *Slavery, as it relates to the Negro, or African race: Examined in the light of circumstances, history and the holy scriptures; with an account of the origin of the Black man's color, causes of his state of servitude and traces of his character as well*. C. van Benthuysen and Company.

Ramadan, T. (2009). *Radical reform: Islamic ethics and liberation*. Oxford University Press.

Ray, M. (2019). Were the Nazis socialists? *Encyclopedia Britannica*. https://www.britannica.com/story/were-the-nazis-socialists

Rbnett.no. (2022). Molde-kvinne i ny dokumentar: – Adopsjonen min var ulovlig. https://www.rbnett.no/nyheter/i/x8vpQX/molde-kvinne-i-ny-dokumentar-adopsjonen-min-var-ulovlig

Reid, S. A. (2023, October 17) How the U.S. Issued its first ever order to assassinate a foreign leader. *Politico*. https://www.politico.com/news/magazine/2023/10/17/patrice-lumumba-congo-washington-00121755

Riis, O., & Woodhead, L. (2010). *A sociology of religious emotion*. Oxford University Press.

Ringen, S. (2023). *The story of Scandinavia: From the Vikings to social democracy*. Weidenfeld & Nicolson.

Robinson, C. (1983). *Black Marxism: The making of the Black radical tradition*. Zen.

Rodney, W. (1972). *How Europe underdeveloped Africa*. Bogle-L'Ouverture Publications.

Roediger, D. (1994). *Towards the abolition of whiteness: Essays in race, politics, and working class history*. Verso.

Roland, P. (2012). *Nazis and the occult: The dark forces unleashed by the third reich*. Arcturus Publishing Limited.

Said, E. (1978). *Orientalism*. Pantheon Books.

Said, E. (2003). *Orientalism*. Penguin.

Sartre, J. (1948). *Anti-semite and Jew*. Shocken Books.

Sartre, J. (1958). *Being and nothingness: An essay on phenomenological ontology*. Metheun.

Schwartzstein, P. (2012). 90 percent of Europeans would vote for Obama: Poll. *Reuters*. https://www.reuters.com/article/idUSBRE89U19C/

Seierstad, Å. (2016). *One of us: The story of a massacre in Norway—And its aftermath*. Farrar, Straus and Giroux.

Seneca, L. (2020). *Letters from a stoic*. Collins Classics.

Shirky, C. (2008). *Here comes everybody: How change happens when people come together*. Penguin UK.

SIAN. (2011, November 21). Kjempet for frihetens sak til det siste. https://www.sian.no/artikkel/kjempet-for-frihetens-sak-til-det-siste

Skoglund, A. (2013). *Sinte Hvite Menn: De Ensomme Ulvenes Terror*. Humanistforlag.

Smith, J., & Tromp, B. (2009). *Hani: A life too short*. Jonathan Ball Publishers.

Smooth, J. (2014). How I learned to stop worrying and love discussing race. *Youtube*. https://www.youtube.com/watch?v=MbdxeFcQtaU

South China Morning Post. (2020, June 11). Far-right Norwegian gunman jailed for 21 years after killing Chinese stepsister and attacking mosque. *South China Morning Post*. https://www.scmp.com/news/world/europe/article/3088651/far-right-norwegian-gunman-jailed-21-years-after-killing-chinese

Soyinka, W. (2012). *Of Africa*. Yale University Press.

Stanfield, J. (1985). *Philantropy and Jim Crow in American social science*. Greenwood Press.

Stawski, S. (2018). Denmark's veiled role in slavery in the Americas: The impact of the Danish West Indies on the transatlantic slave trade. *Harvard Library*. https://dash.harvard.edu/bitstream/handle/1/37365426/STAWSKI-DOCUMENT-2018.pdf?sequence=1&isAllowed=y

Strandberg, L., & Thomas, P. (2024). Decolonising teacher education. *Education in the North*, *31*(1), 19–38.

Sue, D. (2017). Microaggressions and "Evidence": Empirical or experiential reality? *Perspectives on Psychological Science*, *12*(1), 170–172.

Svendsen, N. (2020). Helt greit å fjerne Holberg-statuen, mener vinner av Holbergprisen. *Khrono*. https://www.khrono.no/helt-greit-a-fjerne-holberg-statuen-mener-vinner-av-holbergprisen/496200

Tambo. (2014). *Oliver Tambo speaks*. Kwela Books.

Tatum, B. (1997). *Why are all the Black kids sitting together in the cafeteria?: And other conversations about race*. Penguin Random House.

The Hill. (2024, November 28). Trump, MAGA and the insidious underbelly of white supremacy in America. https://thehill.com/opinion/campaign/4330735-trump-maga-and-the-insidious-underbelly-of-white-supremacy-in-america/

Thomas, P. (2016). "Papa, am I a Negro?" The vexed history of the racial epithet in Norwegian print media (1970–2014). *Race and Social Problems, 8*, 231–243.

Thomas, P. (2017). The portrayal of non-westerners in EFL textbooks in Norway. *Cogent Education, 4*(1), 1275411. https://www.tandfonline.com/doi/full/10.1080/2331186X.2016.1275411

Thomas, P., & Alhassan, A. (2022). Challenging antisemitism: A pedagogical approach in a Norwegian school. In A. Lange, D. Porat, K. Mayerhofer, & L. H. Schiffman (Eds.), *Confronting antisemitism from perspectives of philosophy and social sciences* (pp. 345–367). De Gruyter.

Thomas, P., Alhassan, A. R., & Kaarstad Lie, L. A. (2022). Bunad, minorities and belonging in Norway. National Identities. *National Identities, 24*(2), 165–186.

Thomas, P., Alhassn, A. R., & Ali, A. (2023). 'Seeing Whiteness' in Norwegian education challenging a discourse of silence. *Whiteness and Education*, 1–26. https://doi.org/10.1080/23793406.2023.2222126

Thomas, P., Changezi, S. F., & Enstad, M. (2016). Third space epistemologies: Ethnicity and belonging in an 'immigrant'-dominated upper secondary school in Norway. *Improving Schools, 19*(3), 212–228.

Thomas, P., & Hof, J. V. (2024). Norway's involvement in the transatlantic slave trade: A discourse analysis of media coverage and implications for education. https://www.tandfonline.com/doi/full/10.1080/23311886.2024.2331418

Thomas, P., & Selimovic, A. (2015). "Sharia on a Plate?" A critical discourse analysis of halal food in two Norwegian newspapers. *Journal of Islamic Marketing, 3*, 331–353.

Thomas, P., & von Hof, J. (2024). Norway's involvement in the transatlantic slave trade: A discourse analysis of media coverage and implications for education. *Cogent Social Sciences, 10*(1), 1–13. https://doi.org/10.1080/23311886.2024.2331418

TV2. (2023). https://www.tv2.no/nyheter/innenriks/norske-myndigheter-uenige-om-gransking-av-adopsjon/15399560/

TvedtenBergen, S. A. (2001, January 31). Frp og drapet på Holmlia. Bergenstidende. https://www.bt.no/btmeninger/i/9pLP9/frp-og-drapet-paa-holmlia

Ulvund, F. (2021). Jødeparagrafen. *Store Norske Leksikon*. https://snl.no/J%C3%B8deparagrafen?gclid=Cj0KCQjwn7mwBhCiARIsAGoxjaJ6L1mmrQcZk1TxQWZJRJum_ZM4ZhBH2ft-LFwUWU-ueRoRL36jHP4aAmItEALw_wcB

United States Holocaust Memorial Museum. (2023). Dietrich Bonhoeffer. https://encyclopedia.ushmm.org/content/en/article/dietrich-bonhoeffer

Vetsreng, T. (2014). Klassedelt lenge før innvandrerne kom. *Dagsavisen*. https://www.dagsavisen.no/nyheter/innenriks/2014/11/24/klassedelt-lenge-for-innvandrerne-kom/

VG. (1979). Erik Gjemstad.-Onstad innrømmer: E-agent for Rhodesia. *VG*. https://
print-pdf.prod.retriever.cloud/?id=055016197904192Rqt9t1MkZ7J3Ymhf63VY08
O100201010i14&x=fde60be18e8875d6ee99c0dc55662f0f

VG. (2001). Tatt 27 ganger. https://www.vg.no/nyheter/innenriks/i/RxxAwa/tatt-27-
ganger

VG. (2011). Breivik var ukjent for PST. *VG*. https://www.vg.no/nyheter/innenriks/i/
QGM4q/breivik-var-ukjent-for-pst

VG. (2022). Johan Golden om Antonsen. https://direkte.vg.no/nyhetsdognet/news/nrk-
johan-golden-om-antonsen-det-han-gjorde-var-100-prosent-rasistisk.ZPGMkL6on

VG. (2024). Flertall for å kun ta imot ukrainere i Drammen. *VG*. https://www.vg.no/
nyheter/innenriks/i/4oMnW6/betent-ukraina-konflikt-i-drammen-skal-avgjoeres-i-
kveld

Volker, U. (2017). *Hitler: Ascent: 1889–1939* (J. Chase, Overs.) Vintage.

Wallis, J. (2016). *America's original sin: Racism, white privilege, and the bridge to a new
America*. Brazos Press.

Wikipedia. (2024a). Ibn Nafis. https://en.wikipedia.org/wiki/Ibn_al-Nafis

Wikipedia. (2024b). William Harvey. https://en.wikipedia.org/wiki/William_Harvey

Wimmer, A. (2013). *Ethnic boundary making*. Oxford University Press.

Winant, H. (1998). Racism today: Continuity and change in the post-civil rights era.
Ethnic and Racial Studies, 21(4), 755–766.

Woodson, C. (2023). *The mis-education of the Negro*. Penguin.

X, M. (1964). *The autobiography of Malcolm X*. One World.

Zondag. (2011). Muslimer ble hetset etter terroren. *NrK*. https://www.nrk.no/norge/
meldinger-om-muslim-hets-i-oslo-1.7723535

www.ingramcontent.com/pod-product-compliance
Lightning Source LLC
Chambersburg PA
CBHW070327270326
41926CB00017B/3799